AQA Citizenship Studies

GCSE

Joan Campbell
Sue Patrick

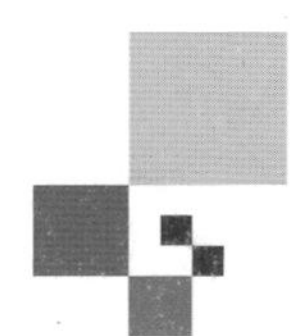

Nelson Thornes

Published in 2009 by:
Nelson Thornes Ltd
Delta Place
27 Bath Road
CHELTENHAM
GL53 7TH
United Kingdom

09 10 11 12 13 / 10 9 8 7 6 5 4 3 2

A catalogue record for this book is available from the British Library

ISBN 978 1 4085 0332 4

Cover photograph/illustration by Getty Images

Illustrations by Wearset Publishing Services, Boldon, Tyne and Wear and Oxford Design Illustrators

Page make-up by Wearset Publishing Services, Boldon, Tyne and Wear

Printed in China by 1010 Printing International Ltd

Contents

Nelson Thornes and AQA

Nelson Thornes has worked in partnership with AQA to make sure that this book offers you the best possible support for your GCSE course. All the content has been approved by the senior examining team at AQA, so you can be sure that it gives you just what you need when you are preparing for your exams.

How to use this book

This book covers everything you need for your course.

Learning Objectives

At the beginning of each section or topic you'll find a list of Learning Objectives based on the requirements of the specification, so you can make sure you are covering everything you need to know for the exam.

Objectives

Objectives

Objectives

Objectives

First objective.

Second objective.

AQA Examiner's Tips

Don't forget to look at the AQA Examiner's Tips throughout the book to help you with your study and prepare for your exam.

AQA Examiner's tip

Don't forget to look at the AQA Examiner's Tips throughout the book to help you with your study and prepare for your exam.

AQA Examination-style Questions

These offer opportunities to practise doing questions in the style that you can expect in your exam so that you can be fully prepared on the day.

AQA examination questions are reproduced by permission of the Assessment and Qualifications Alliance.

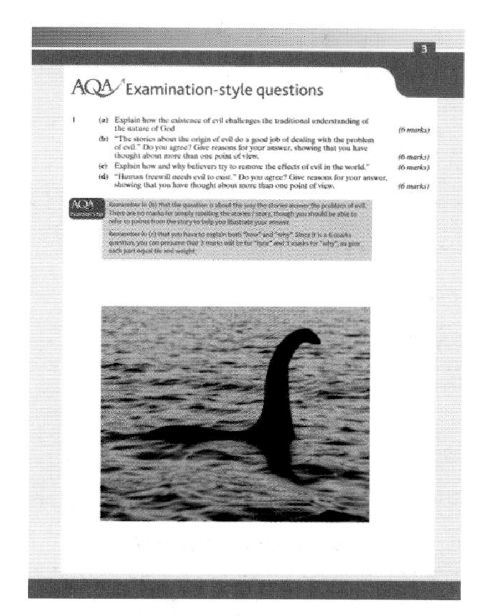

Visit **www.nelsonthornes.com/aqagcse** for more information.

AQA GCSE Introduction to Citizenship Studies

You will have been studying citizenship for a while. Perhaps you did not realise this, it may have been as part of another course. This GCSE Citizenship Studies is a totally new course which will be examined for the first time in 2010 for the short course and 2011 for the full course. It replaces the current short course with more emphasis on you taking part in citizenship activities using a range of skills as well as learning about a variety of citizenship concepts.

This book is to help you gain the knowledge, understanding and skills that you need.

We hope it will guide you through the Controlled Assessment and help to prepare you for the exam at the end of the course all with extra advice from your teacher. All the details about the assessment are in chapter 17. See what this chapter has to say about each unit as you work through it.

You may be entered for the short or full course. The full course is designed to explore the citizenship concepts and skills in different areas from the short course to extend your knowledge and understanding of the issues involved. For both courses you are required to complete one active participative citizenship task, known as the Controlled Assessment, formerly known as coursework and one exam paper which lasts an hour.

Throughout the course you will be expected to take an active part in finding out about a variety of topics that are in the news at the time. The issues may be local, national or international. It is suggested that you find out about the problems involved from a range of media, including the internet. Gather a number of opposing views on the issues and then you will be able to form your own opinion because you will be well informed and will have considered many aspects of the case. Some of these issues may come up in exam questions so be prepared to state your view and argue the case for it.

The Controlled Assessment cannot be done by simply sitting in a classroom or in front of a computer. You have to be involved and participate in taking reasoned, responsible action. It will require you to work in a small group to research information and opinions, plan a course of action, assess the impact your actions have had and then review how the activity went. You are asked to advocate a cause and do something to advance that cause, to make a change for the better by the responsible action you have followed, making a positive contribution to your community by being an active citizen. You will be asked to complete a Skills Profile which will ask you questions about the activity to lead you through all the stages.

Why study citizenship?

The purpose of the course is to:

- equip young people with the skills, knowledge, understanding and confidence
- learn how we are governed
- understand and participate in the democratic processes
- encourage young people to use their vote wisely
- value our rights and freedoms
- accept responsibility for our actions
- understand fairness and justice
- value and respect cultural diversity
- challenge racism and discrimination
- take responsible action
- stand up for what you believe in and voice your opinions
- take part in informed discussions and debates
- know how to make your voice heard
- understand the effects of national and global issues on communities
- develop a critical awareness of media reporting
- experience working collaboratively to meet set targets
- become well-informed active citizens willing to participate in decision making
- give young people the confidence to make a difference and make a positive contribution to society.

By the end of the course it is hoped that you will have found inspiration to become lifelong well-informed, critical, active participants in contributing to the life of the community you live and work in.

The structure of the courses

The short course consists of Units 1 and 2. The full course consists of Units 1, 2, 3 and 4. Diagram A shows the structure of both the short and full courses and some details about the exam papers. It is an easy way to begin to understand the courses.

Both the short and full courses involve the study of the Themes 1, 2, 3 and 4.

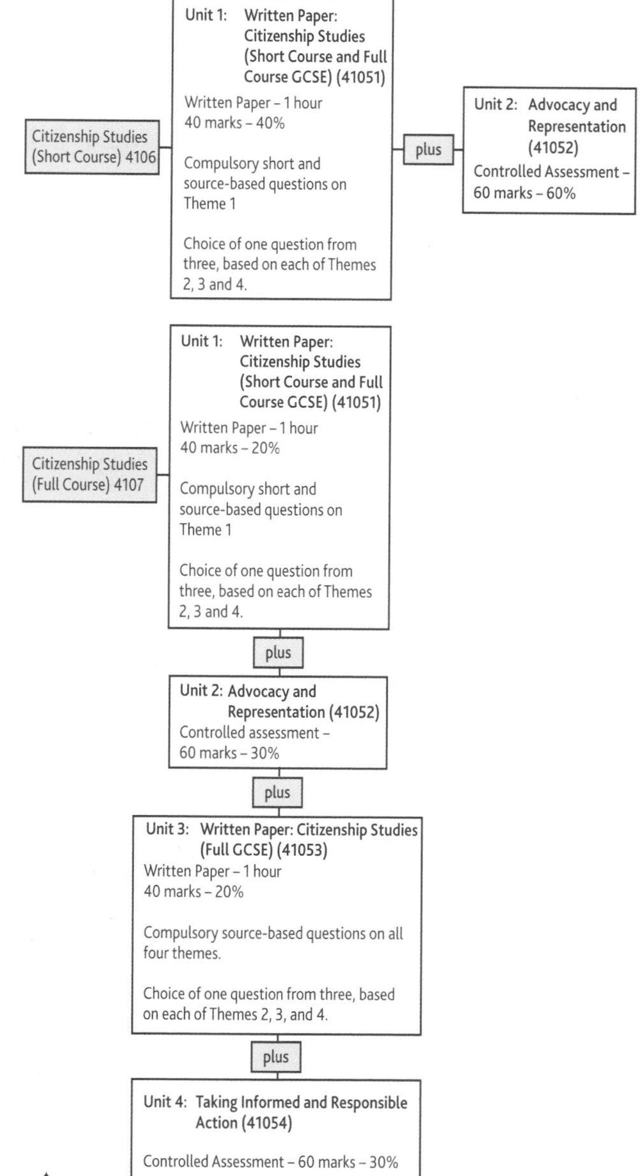

A *The structure of the course*

Theme 1. Community action and active citizenship

Community action and active citizenship is about how citizens can participate in activities to make a difference, raise awareness, and take action to bring about a change. It is also concerned with how local government is organised throughout Britain and how citizenship issues are relevant in the workplace.

Theme 2. Democracy and identity

Democracy and identity is about how we are governed, how Parliament works and makes laws. It looks at the different voting systems and devolution of powers and how we can participate in the democratic process. It explores our national identity and the cultural diversity within the UK.

Theme 3. Fairness and justice

Fairness and justice involves the rights and responsibilities of citizens in their different roles, what our human rights are and how laws affect us. You will learn about the legal framework and how the criminal justice system works. We will examine the influence of the media and investigate what is meant by the information society.

Theme 4. Global issues and making a difference

Global issues and making a difference looks at different international organisations, as well as international conflicts and how they may be resolved. You will learn about international interdependence and cooperation and how global challenges may be tackled. We shall also discover how individuals and groups can influence human rights and make a difference to global situations.

Unit 1 and Unit 3

These units cover all themes.

These are the units that the questions on the exam paper will be based on.

Unit 3 of the full course has extra topics to cover which increase the knowledge and understanding gained in Unit 1 during the short course.

Unit 2 and Unit 4

These are the units that deal with the Controlled Assessment – the tasks you participate in. The tasks are different for the short course Unit 2 and the full course Unit 4.

The task in Unit 2 is about '**Advocacy** and representation', while the task in Unit 4 is about 'Taking informed and responsible action'.

Marks for the quality of written communication are included in each stage of the assessment for both Units.

Key terms

Advocacy: the representation or support of a person or an organisation by writing, speaking or taking action on behalf of that person or organisation.

Citizenship concepts and skills

During the course you are expected to demonstrate knowledge and understanding of a number of different citizenship concepts.

The main ones are:

- democracy
- identity
- fairness
- multiple identity
- justice
- diversity/culture/ethnicity
- rights
- community cohesion
- responsibilities
- discrimination
- freedoms
- stereotyping
- sustainable development
- conflict
- global interdependence
- extremism
- global challenges
- racism
- equal opportunity
- the role of the media
- making a difference
- debate
- political literacy
- raising awareness.

During the tasks you will participate in you are expected to use and develop a range of citizenship skills.

The main ones are:

- critical thinking
- decision making
- critical enquiry
- informing opinions
- advocacy
- making judgements
- representation
- negotiation
- active participation
- tolerance
- responsible action
- assess impact of actions
- campaigning
- collaborative working.

B *Active participation*

AQA GCSE Advice for teachers

Introduction

The aim of this section of the book is to support teachers in the delivery of AQA GCSE Citizenship Studies. The chapters in this book meet the requirements of the AQA Specification and the Key Stage 4 Programme of Study for Citizenship. The book can be used to fulfil the requirements of the AQA short and full courses. It can be used to fulfil the requirements of the National Curriculum where schools choose not to examine citizenship.

Because Citizenship involves a broad range of topical issues and concepts, its content will cross over into other areas of the school curriculum. As the course aims to encourage young people to play an active part in the community, it is advisable to involve key personnel from relevant local agencies and organisations to support pupil learning and experience.

Teachers should ensure that they have access to:

- National Curriculum Key Stage 4 Programme of Study for Citizenship
- AQA Specification for GCSE Citizenship, and
- Specimen Assessment Materials (SAMS) for Citizenship.

At the end of the book in Appendix 1 you will find four case studies, one for each theme. These studies give additional/alternative material for classroom activities.

What are the essential elements of citizenship teaching?

Citizenship education involves a wide range of different elements of learning including:

Knowledge and understanding:

This includes the topics:

- laws and rules
- the democratic process
- the media
- human rights
- diversity
- the world economy
- sustainable development and
- the world as a global community

and the concepts:

- democracy
- justice
- equality
- freedom, and
- authority and the rule of law.

Skills and aptitudes:

This includes:

- critical thinking
- analysing information
- expressing opinions
- taking part in discussions and debates
- negotiating
- the ability to argue effectively
- the ability to challenge injustice and inequalities
- respect for people and things, and
- participating in community action.

Values and attitudes:

This includes:

- respect for justice, democracy and the rule of law
- openness
- tolerance
- sense of identity and self-esteem
- commitment to social justice and equity
- value and respect for diversity
- concern for the environment
- belief that people can make a difference
- courage to defend a point of view, and
- a willingness to listen to, work with and stand up for others.

Citizenship is a practical study of the world, its people, its processes, its resources, its strengths and weaknesses and their interdependence. Pupils should acquire the skills required to be effective citizens. These include:

- acquiring knowledge from a variety of sources and media
- working alone and with others
- taking the lead and working as part of a team
- informed and responsible action

- critical thinking and enquiry
- advocacy and representation
- reflection, planning, research and evaluation
- reporting in both spoken and written forms
- empathy, understanding and tolerance, and
- support and respect for other people and their opinions.

The role of the teacher in the learning process

The teaching of citizenship requires teachers to adopt a flexible, well-organised and supportive approach to teaching and learning. The teacher's role will change depending on the different activities and experiences offered to the pupils. Teachers will:

- teach using traditional methods using speech, books and worksheets as the means of learning
- act as a facilitator in situations involving role play, debates and discussions to encourage meaningful and structured inputs
- use skilful questioning to bring out the best in pupils
- handle sensitive issues with skill and understanding making sure that individual pupil's cultural, political and religious beliefs are respected
- help pupils to understand that sometimes there are no clear-cut answers to problems and that there are times when a consensus is the only answer, and
- act as assessor for the Controlled Assessment task and exam questions given to the pupils for practice throughout the book.

Learning in citizenship education should be:

- **active**: emphasises learning by doing
- **interactive**: uses discussion and debate
- **relevant**: focuses on real-life issues facing young people and society
- **critical**: encourages young people to think for themselves
- **collaborative**: employs group work and cooperative learning; and
- **participative**: gives young people a say in their own learning.

This type of learning requires the teacher to develop a climate for learning by creating an environment that is non-threatening, in which young people can:

- express their opinions freely
- experiment socially without embarrassment, and
- use their initiative without undue fear of failure.

Such a climate takes time to develop and is built up gradually.

Pupil experiences and activities will need to reflect the fact that citizenship issues are:

- **real**: actually affect people's lives
- **topical**: current today
- **sometimes sensitive**: can affect people at a personal level, especially when family or friends are involved
- **often controversial**: people disagree and hold strong opinions about them
- **ultimately moral**: relate to what people think is right or wrong, good or bad, important or unimportant in society.

In the modern world, developed democracies depend upon citizens who are:

- aware of their rights and responsibilities as citizens
- informed about the social and political world
- concerned about the welfare of others
- articulate in their opinions and arguments
- capable of having an influence on the world
- active in their communities
- responsible in how they act as citizens.

The activities presented to the pupil in the book have been designed to develop and extend pupil awareness, understanding and participation. From time to time, it will be necessary for the teacher to select an activity to suit a pupil's ability. There is a range of activities for further study at the end of each chapter. It is not intended that all of the pupils will attempt all of the activities. The reference section provides information about conventions, charters and processes to allow detailed investigation.

Global citizenship is about understanding that our decisions may have an impact on someone in another part of the world. Global citizenship is about the responsibility we take for the choices we make.

Oxfam describes the Global Citizen as someone who:

- is aware of the wider world and has a sense of their own role as a world citizen
- respects and values diversity
- has an understanding of how the world works
- is outraged by social injustice
- participates in the community at a range of levels, from the local to the global
- is willing to act to make the world a more equitable and sustainable place
- takes responsibility for their actions.

AQA Citizenship Studies aims to involve the pupil in participatory activities that will deliver the required elements of local, national and global citizenship.

The role of the teacher in the assessment of the course

The new AQA specification changes the weightings for the examination and the Controlled Assessment. The weightings are now:

Short course (Units 1 and 2)

Examination	Controlled Assessment
Unit 1 40%	Unit 2 60%

Full Course (Units 3 and 4)

Examination	Controlled Assessment
Unit 1 + Unit 3 20% + 20% = 40%	Unit 2 + Unit 4 30% + 30% = 60%

Teachers will note that the emphasis of the course has moved from the examination to the Controlled Assessment task and the active involvement of pupils in the process.

Preparing pupils for the examination

The written examinations are both one hour in duration. However, the content of the examinations is different.

Unit 1 (Short course)

Section A:

A number of questions requiring short answers. The questions will be based on Theme 1. The questions are worth a total of 20 marks. This type of question can be found at the end of each chapter in the book.

Section B:

There will be a choice of question. The topics for these questions will be sent to you before the examination. Pupils will need to select one to answer. The question is in three sections. The question is worth 20 marks.

Unit 3 (Full course)

Section A:

The pupils will be given information in one or two sources. They will need to answer questions from the sources and add details from their knowledge of the course they have studied. There are four questions and they are worth 20 marks.

Section B:

Pupils will choose one question from three set questions. The topics for these questions will be sent to you before the examination. The question is in three parts. The last part requires an extended piece of writing. The section is worth 20 marks.

Full details of the examination requirements are given in chapter 17.

The role of the teacher in the Controlled Assessment

The teacher plays a major role in the Controlled Assessments of both the short and full courses (Units 2 and 4). It is important that the teacher reads the AQA set assignment carefully. It may be necessary to modify the material or to adapt it to meet the specific learning and community environment in which the pupil will work. This must be done without alteration of the content to an extent that would affect a pupil's level of achievement.

It is important that the teacher maximises pupil involvement and encourages pupil activity. To enable this the teacher will need to:

- fit the resources available to the pupils to the set task
- check the community can meet each pupil's chosen task
- ensure that pupils work independently or in small groups
- give appropriate supervision to the tasks
- ensure that pupils complete the skills profile individually. (We would advise that this is done under supervision at the end of each stage of the task.)

Teachers should note that Stage 3 in both tasks involves teacher assessment. The assessment is based on the *action* the pupil has taken.

At Stage 4, candidates need to assess the *impact* of the task. This section is assessed using the same criteria in both units, but the task it is applied to is different, so the outcomes will be different.

Pupils need to collect evidence throughout the tasks they undertake for the assessment. This can take a variety of forms. For example:

- Photos (digital or printed)
- PowerPoint presentation printout
- Written and signed report from an organisation
- Cd/dvd/video.

Teachers will record their assessment of the evidence in the skills profile. The school needs to retain pupil evidence. AQA may require the evidence in certain circumstances.

THEME 1 Community action and active

In this Theme you will learn how to become an active well-informed citizen and how community action has brought about change in our society.

The three chapters are:

1. Effective active citizenship
2. Making a difference
3. Citizenship issues in the workplace

Key terms

political groups local national change community historical struggle media indirect action direct action campaign decision making influence petition propaganda participation suffrage target group

1 Effective active citizenship

In this chapter we will look at the factors that make for effective active citizenship.

This includes learning about pressure groups, campaigning and how this influences political decision making as well as finding out about some historical campaigns. You will learn about how you can become a well-informed active citizen, making a contribution to your community.

Concepts

change being an active citizen campaigning pressure groups political literacy

A Campaigning now and then

B Campaigning now and then

2 Making a difference

In this chapter we will look at taking part in the democratic process, both at a local and national level and who holds power in Britain. You will learn about voluntary groups, charities, trade unions and the influence of the media.

Concepts

- power in Britain
- local government
- participating in the democratic process
- voluntary groups and charities
- trade unions
- democracy

1	JONES Jane Mary Jones 10 Acacia Avenue Nowhere Town, NO10 1AB Conservative and Unionist Party	
2	SMITH Bob Smith 15 Hill View Nowhere Town, NO11 2CD Labour Party	
3	WILLIAMS James Anthony Williams 32 High Street Nowhere Town, NO12 1EF Liberal Democrats	

C *Use your vote*

Key terms

influence government political power opinion volunteers collective action boycotts petitions involvement local authority cabinet metropolitan unitary borough

3 Citizenship issues in the workplace

In this chapter we will look at a number of issues that could occur in the workplace and some of the laws which apply to the rights and responsibilities of employers and employees, equal opportunities, discrimination, health and safety and sustainability systems in workplaces.

Concepts

- rights and responsibilities
- equal opportunities
- health and safety
- sustainability
- consumer rights

D *Sustainability*

Key terms

responsibilities employer employee discrimination policies disability ethnicity organization contracts business companies complaints economy grievance

1 Effective active citizenship

1.1 What factors make for effective 'active citizenship'?

Individuals can bring about change within their **community** if they become active citizens by joining one or more local groups. When several individuals cooperate to achieve a common aim they have a greater chance of success; the more people involved the better. There are a variety of groups in all communities, including voluntary groups, charitable organisations, and interest groups for music, drama, and sport. Other groups may have a particular political or religious connection. Your local Civic Centre will have a list of all the groups within your area.

Pressure groups try to influence the policy of local or national government, try to influence those in power to make changes to laws, or influence businesses, or bring about changes on a global scale. This is best understood by looking at some examples.

People join a group because of their interest in something or a strong feeling that something needs to change within their community. A local group of people who want to make a change or who object to something that is being proposed such as a new road, a new supermarket, the closure of a school, or the closure of a local post office often form a 'focus group'. The focus group arranges meetings and organises a campaign of action to achieve their goal. They disband (cease to exist) when that target is reached. This is one form of small pressure group.

A national pressure group will campaign about a single issue: the National Society for the Prevention of Cruelty to Children (NSPCC) campaign for children's rights, the CND (Campaign for Nuclear Disarmament) is against nuclear weapons and nuclear power stations. Some pressure groups are involved on a wider scale. Greenpeace and Friends of the Earth, for example, who both campaign on environmental issues, campaign in Britain as well as in many places around the world. Amnesty International campaign to stop abuses of human rights such as imprisonment without charge or a fair trial, and the torture of prisoners, worldwide.

Have you heard of any of these groups? How did you hear about them?

The pressure groups mentioned above have different ways of **campaigning** and attracting people's attention to gain support for their cause. The support offered could be financial (contributing money) or could be people joining the group and taking an active part in the campaign.

The tactics or strategies different groups employ vary considerably. The actions taken are all intended to bring about a change in some way, to make a difference and to achieve the aim of the group. The types of actions taken are described as direct or indirect action.

Objectives

To understand the meaning of pressure groups and the different types of campaigning.

Key terms

Community: the people living in an area, or place, or the people who work in a particular place, for example, the school community.

Pressure group: a group of people who take action to try to influence the government (local or national) about a specific issue.

Campaigning: actions or events organised by an individual or a group of people to achieve an aim.

Political literacy: knowledge of politics and how democracy works.

Information

If you would like to know more about different types of pressure groups look at pages 20–21 in Unit 3.

Direct action is a form of protest used to bring an issue to the attention of the **target group** and the general public. It could involve a strike, a sit-in, a march, a demonstration, a large public meeting addressed by famous people (speech making), or one of a variety of publicity stunts including disruptive demonstrations – such as slow-moving vehicles, disturbing the flow of traffic, to protest about the cost of fuel. A boycott is when people stop buying a certain product or refuse to use a particular service until the company makes the change the pressure group wants. The company will lose money and incur bad publicity, and therefore may make the change.

Indirect action is campaigning by letter writing, making and distributing leaflets (to raise awareness), petitioning, lobbying Members of Parliament (MPs), and E-campaigning (the use of the internet to send emails and to create E-petitions).

Voting in elections is an indirect action because by casting your vote you are choosing the party whose policies you consider to be the most effective; the aims may be achieved at a later date if that party is elected.

Key terms

Target group: a target group is the organisation that the action is aimed at.

Activities

Try some of these on your own or in a small group

1. Make a list of pressure groups you have heard of. What do they campaign for?
2. What celebrities do you know of who have actively campaigned about an issue?
3. How many recent campaigns can you list? Write a paragraph about how successful each one was.
4. Find out what 'propaganda' is and how it is used.
5. Make a chart of all the direct and indirect actions mentioned, and which pressure groups have used which actions.

AQA Examiner's tip

Be able to explain the key terms and give examples of charities, pressure groups and types of action.

A *Direct action*

1.2 Key factors in successful campaigning

Consider the variety of groups, the types of action, and what factors are involved in different campaigns. In small groups or pairs, discuss and then complete the following chart. Can you add any local examples of a protest or petition? Some parts have already been done.

Objectives

To understand what makes a successful campaign.

A

Pressure Group/ organisation	Aim	Target group	Type of action	Factors involved	Achieved
Fire-fighters	More pay Better conditions	Government	Indefinite strike, media publicity	Ballot – majority in favour, indefinite strike, negotiation	Yes
	Reduce petrol prices				
Political parties		General public		Finance	
Fathers 4 Justice					
	Save the Whale				
Live 8	Make poverty history				
			Internet petition		
	Don't attack Iraq	Government			No
Amnesty International			Letter writing		

From the discussion you should now realise that there are a variety of different ways to campaign and make a difference, to bring about change or at least to make your voice heard (have your say). Everyone is entitled to have their opinion; this is part of our entitlement to 'freedom of expression'. Being an active citizen and participating in your community is to allow others their right to voice their opinion, be able to listen to them respectfully and learn from them, as you would expect them to listen to you and consider your view.

There are many factors which can help a campaign to be successful, these include gaining multimedia attention and keeping the issue alive; involving a large number of people; finance; being persistent. Some campaigns may not appear to have been very successful, but they will have had an impact on people, the government, businesses, etc. and may have an influence on future decisions that are made or policies that are developed.

There are other forms of action which are sometimes used but are against the law. If a march or demonstration gets out of hand then a riot can take place. Some militant groups have deliberately provoked disturbances in otherwise peaceful protests. These do not usually achieve the aims and often deter supporters who may have joined a peaceful movement. Riots are illegal, as is civil disobedience and criminal damage. Over the last few years we have all become aware of terrorism which some see as a form of protest; it is illegal and many people have been killed or maimed and much property has been destroyed.

Peaceful protests are much more likely to be successful.

Activities

1. From Source A choose one campaign and explain why you were pleased it succeeded.
2. Which pressure group would you choose to join and why?
3. What type of action do you think is the most effective – why?
4. Discuss the differences between 'Freedom Fighters' and 'Terrorists'.
5. Research and write a short case study of your own on the Jarrow March,

   or the Campaign for Nuclear Disarmament (CND),

   or the campaign against the Poll tax,

   or Stop the War campaign.

Information

The campaign for women's suffrage lasted many years.

- One of the first supporters of women's suffrage was John Mill who raised the issue in the election of 1865.
- Emily Davison was killed when she stepped in front of the King's horse in the Epsom Derby in 1913.
- The Representation of the People Act 1918 gave women over 30 the vote if they met the property or education qualifications.
- New Zealand was the first country to give all women the vote in 1893.
- USA gave votes to women in 1920.
- British women were given the same voting rights as men in 1928.

Key terms

Suffrage: the right to vote.

Case study

The following case study shows how a struggle has achieved a right and some of the campaigning strategies used.

The Suffragettes. Votes For Women.

The term 'suffragette' was first used by a newspaper, in a derogatory way, to describe members of the Women's Social and Political Union (WSPU) which was led by Emmeline Pankhurst.

Many thousands of women all over the country were involved in the movement.

The concept of allowing women to vote caused much debate, controversy and newspaper coverage. (The range of media was far less then than it is today.) The direct actions included some suffragettes chaining themselves to the railings of prominent buildings, smashing windows, many marches/ demonstrations, and there were also frequent large meetings in towns and cities to advocate women's **suffrage**. A number of important men supported the cause too.

B *Votes for women*

Many suffragettes were arrested and imprisoned, where some went on hunger strike. This led to them being force fed, which was a terrible ordeal. This would not be allowed today as it contravenes human rights. Many women became ill; they were allowed out to recover and then imprisoned again. All this took its toll and many women had their lives shortened because of this treatment.

During World War I (1914–18) women took on traditional male roles because so many men were serving or killed in the war. This was a major factor in changing views. Eventually the struggle was successful. Every woman should appreciate what the suffragettes went through to achieve their aim – to give them, and all women in future generations, our right to vote.

1.3 Types of pressure groups

Promotional/causal groups

These groups want to exert their influence for a particular cause, to influence policy and change public opinion. The membership of such groups is open to everyone who believes in, and wants to campaign for that cause. They try to gain popular support to give strength of numbers to their campaigns. The majority of promotional groups campaign for environmental or welfare issues, for example, Greenpeace, Friends of the Earth, Campaign for Nuclear Disarmament (CND), Shelter, Fair Trade, Age Concern, National Society for the Prevention of Cruelty to Children (NSPCC), Amnesty International, Royal Society for the Prevention of Cruelty to Animals (RSPCA), Countryside Alliance, Liberty, and Oxfam.

Sectional/interest groups

These groups represent a particular section of our society, for example, teachers. They exist to further the interests of their members and influence the general public by raising their awareness of the campaign. Members of these groups usually stand to benefit as a result of their campaign, for example, all members of a trade union will benefit financially if the union wins a campaign for more pay. Many sectional groups are trade unions. To be a member of these groups you have to work in a particular trade/occupation or have a professional qualification. Examples of sectional groups include all trade unions, the Law Society, the Confederation of British Industry (CBI), the British Medical Association, the Royal British Legion, and the Federation of Small Businesses.

Insider pressure groups

These **insider groups** are ones that the government (local and national) choose to consult on a regular basis because of their expert knowledge on specific issues. They are independent groups, and usually, but not always, sectional groups. They are therefore very influential in the decision-making process and may meet with Councillors, civil servants, and ministers – this is known as being part of the consultative process. All other groups are therefore outsider pressure groups. The status of insider and outsider groups can change as different governments are elected to power.

Objectives

To discover more about the different types of pressure groups.

To understand how pressure groups and the media make representatives accountable.

Information

The next pages in this chapter deal with Unit 3 for the full course. They are written to help you to extend your knowledge and understanding.

In Unit 1 (short course) the term 'pressure group' was used as a generic term to include all campaigning groups. In general there are two distinct categories of pressure groups, promotional or causal groups and sectional or interest groups.

Key terms

Insider group: this is a pressure group that the government recognises and consults when forming policies associated with their cause or interest.

Activities

1. Write a short case study of a pressure group you are interested in.
   You should consider the following – type of group; aims/mission; how funds are raised; who is in charge; how is it run; who can join the group; how does the group attract new members; what recent action has the group been involved in – was it successful – why.

2. Complete this chart adding as many rows as you can.

Promotional/causal groups	Sectional/interest groups	Insider groups

A *Whose logo is this?*

Accountability

This section briefly looks at how pressure groups and the media ensure that our representatives are accountable.

Being accountable means that they are held to account. They may be called to justify their decisions and take responsibility for their actions.

Our representatives are people we have elected to represent us either locally as Councillors, nationally as Members of Parliament (MP) or internationally as Members of the European Parliament (MEP). When these people are campaigning for votes they make promises about what they will do if they are elected. It is the responsibility of the opposition on a Council or in parliament to keep watch over what goes on and make challenges as necessary. All forms of the media are willing to find out about what is going on for the general public and publish many news stories about the information they discover. This is done through researching documentation, talking to people and asking questions. Since the Freedom of Information Act came into force in 2005 it has been much easier to discover information by requesting what you want to know. A reply has to be given within a month or the reason for the refusal explained. This has meant that there is far more public scrutiny. In this way political parties and businesses are far more accountable. Pressure groups are part of ensuring this accountability as they will watch for their own particular interest/cause and will bring attention to what goes on as far as it affects them. Our representatives are well aware of this because now information can be discovered and published that was previously unavailable. This means the pressure groups as well as the media combine to ensure that our democracy is more open and transparent to the people of the country.

Activities

3 List three recent events where a politician or a business has been held accountable for an action.

4 Discuss these events in a small group – discover other people's opinions.

5 Discuss how local councillors may be held to account.

6 Look through your local newspaper and find out how many voluntary groups, charities, pressure groups or community groups are mentioned or have placed adverts in the paper.

Information

The Freedom of Information Act came into force on 1 January 2005.

In May 2007 the Ministry of Justice took over responsibility for the freedom of information from the Department of Constitutional Affairs.

To make a request all you have to do is give your name and a contact address with a clear, concise description of what you want. You can ask for any information about any public authority. Most information is supplied free, but some charges can apply depending on the amount of work involved. The reply should be given within a month. If the information cannot be supplied or it will take longer to find, you must be informed of the reasons.

1.4 Factors in a successful campaign

There are several factors which will have an impact upon the success or failure of any campaign.

Finance

Finance is vital to any initiative; without money a pressure group is unlikely to succeed. Fund raising is very important and is done in a great variety of ways. Money is needed to attract more members, make and distribute leaflets to raise awareness, make posters, advertise, and organise events, for example, rallies.

Membership

The more members the more powerful the group will be. The government or target group will take notice of a well-supported group who are active on a national scale. At a local level a small but very vocal, active, well-funded group of people with influence, can have a major effect in bringing about change and influencing political decisions. At national level legal forms of direct action get the group noticed and will attract more activists. If the general public perceives a group to have the 'wrong type of membership' it will not gain momentum and will ultimately fail.

The nature of the cause and methods used

If the nature of the cause is not a popular one, or the methods used by the group are not approved of by the general public, again failure is likely. For example, animal rights activists who intimidate workers or break into property are very unlikely to gain more members or achieve their aims. The cause may be popular but their methods are not. People may oppose the building of a new road, but not many would be willing to live in trees or chain themselves to trees to stop its development as one group did.

Status

If the group is recognised as an insider group by the government it will be more effective and influential.

Media

The role of the media is very important to all pressure groups. The media can have a tremendous effect on the success of any campaign. Most pressure groups will want to attract the attention of the media. Legal direct actions are a good way of doing this, so that events are reported in news bulletins on television, radio and online as well as in the press. Video clips and photographs will attract people's attention. This raises awareness and gathers support and often generates more publicity. Follow-up interviews with the media keep the issue in the public eye and help to gain more influence. The more media hype the better for the pressure group. This will influence the target group to take notice. Conversely, if a pressure group attracts the wrong sort of media attention and receives negative reporting the campaign will fail.

Objectives

- To discover more about the factors in successful campaigning.
- To discover how information is used in discussions and policy making.

Activities

1. Choose one recent local and one national pressure group campaign and use the headings above to help you to give reasons why the campaign was successful or not.
2. Discuss examples of the information a pressure group has used to advocate their cause. Why did it stimulate public debate or concern?
3. Why are campaign logos important? Find six different logos, draw them and write a paragraph about each.
4. If your council was considering the closure of a school which 'groups' could they consult?
5. The government has made many changes to the NHS. Discuss which groups they could have involved in the consultation process.

Public debate and policy formation

All pressure groups will research and present reputable, reliable, up-to-date information to advocate their cause in an eloquent and persuasive dialogue to achieve their aims. If misleading information was used they would be found out, losing support and credibility.

Much detailed information is published, especially on their website, with more targeted information presented in campaigning leaflets to get the message across. A public debate can be started by advertising campaigns, eye-catching stunts or peaceful demonstrations. The media will become involved and the publicity is self-perpetuating once the public interest is captured.

When a Council or government department are forming policies or drafting new laws they will consult widely with people who are experts. An active pressure group is most likely to have current research available to them and may be part of the consultation process. Pressure groups are an important part of democracy. The information they provide is used to stimulate debate, inform opinion and given consideration when policies are formed.

AQA Examiner's tip

Exam questions on the factors involved in campaigning appear quite often. You should be able to give examples of types of campaigns and be able to justify an opinion on why they were successful or not.

> *"Not one, not two, but at least three climate change-related happenings popped up around the country yesterday, many of them carried out by Climate Camp attendees. Although the camp is primarily focused on coal and the proposed new power station at Kingsnorth, today's activities also highlighted other climate threats such as aviation and biofuels. Here is just a taste of what's been happening:*
>
> *Campers made their way this morning to a biofuel depot in Essex to take part in a blockade. According to news reports, people created a barrier in the road to prevent lorries gaining access to the depot, while others were chained to a fuel storage tanker. And this on the day that a government report finds that supposedly sustainable biofuels might not be so sustainable after all.*
>
> *Meanwhile campers of the Plane Stupid variety headed to Gatwick Airport, where they occupied the roof above the train station and the arrivals lounge with banners unfurled with aplomb. Others provided leaflets about the climate impacts of aviation to passengers and staff."*
>
> *www.greenpeace.org.uk*

A *Climate action at Legoland. © Hans Bricks*

Look at the press cutting and answer these questions:

- What type of pressure group is Greenpeace?
- What type of actions are described?
- List the three protests.
- Where did the actions take place?
- What is the common theme of these protests?
- Do you think these protests were successful? Why?

Go to **www.greenpeace.org.uk** if you would like to find out more.

1.5 National and local campaigns

Case study

A *Conflict*

The Miners' Strike 1984/5

A national campaign

This was the longest and most fierce and bitter struggle in the second half of the last century. It was the last campaign of the Nation Union of Mineworkers (NUM). This strike had a major effect on industrial relations in Britain.

Background

The NUM was formed in 1945 from the Miners Federation of Great Britain (1888). In the NUM each area had its own degree of control through a District Association. They had the power to call their own strikes. Then a national strike required a ballot with a two-thirds majority in favour. This was difficult to achieve so it was reduced to 55 per cent in 1970 and 50 per cent in 1984. The Miners Union was extremely powerful throughout the last century in politics as well as in The Trade Union movement; this was lost by the failure of the 1984/5 strike.

In 1984 Mrs Thatcher was the Conservative Prime Minister. The National Coal Board (NCB) controlled all coal mining and Arthur Scargill led the NUM. During the 1970s and early 1980s there had been several confrontations. In 1984 the NCB announced the closure of 20 pits that were 'uneconomic' causing the loss of 20,000 jobs. Five pits were to close within five weeks.

The areas most affected were the North of England and Wales. Scargill called a strike. It was to last for a whole year, as did the media frenzy that ensued.

There has been controversy ever since about the legality of the strike and the lack of a formal ballot.

In August 1984 there was a court case and the decision was that the strike was not 'official', which meant that striking miners and their families would not receive any state benefits. Poverty and hunger quickly became apparent in the areas where the strike was strongly supported. Many groups were set up to support the miners. Some branches of the NUM fully supported the strike; some were against, setting miner against miner. '**Flying pickets**' were organised to try to prevent working miners crossing **picket** lines; there were many instances of violence. The government sent in police to try to stop pickets travelling, a cause of much protest and many confrontations with the police. The miners and the country were divided on the issue. The strike held in many areas, in others there was a slow return to work. The strike did not produce the blackouts and three-day working week that had been seen in the 1970s. In March 1985 the strike ended and the miners returned to work – defeated by the government.

Activities

1. How many working mines were there in 1980?
2. Talk to your family, friends, and neighbours and ask them what they remember about the miners' strike. In small groups exchange the anecdotes/evidence and form your own views on the last major strike in Britain.
3. What were the new laws introduced after the miners' strike in reference to flying pickets, calling a strike and the power of the unions?

Key terms

Flying pickets: pickets transported from one region to another.

Pickets: people who stand outside a place of work trying to persuade workers not to enter.

AQA Examiner's tip

Research other campaigns – national and local, successful and unsuccessful – that you could quote in an exam question.

Information

In many areas the NCB was the only employer. If the pit closed there would be no jobs at all.

Before the pit closures were announced the government had made sure there were stock piles of coal at the coal fired power stations.

Miners who did not join the strike were called scabs or blacklegs, this refers to all workers who continue to work when their colleagues are on strike.

There were arguments put forward against pit closures – the north sea oil and gas would eventually run out and then Britain would not have its own source of power supply apart from nuclear power.

The coal industry was privatised in 1994, now known as UK Coal.

In 2008 UK Coal had four deep mines and six surface/open cast sites.

After the strike the government introduced new laws about strikes and other laws to curb the power of the unions.

Case study

Case Study of a Local Campaign

St. Oswald's Hospice

This is a hospice in Newcastle-upon-Tyne. It was established through the determination of Dorothy Jameson. Dorothy's daughter worked in a hospice in London, and Dorothy thought that terminally ill people of the North East should be able to access the same type of care and support. Dorothy talked to many people about her idea including businesses, legal and medical people and encouraged many people to become involved.

In 1982 she established a committee to find a suitable site to build the hospice, registered it as a charity and set about fund raising. £2 million was the target. Different methods of campaigning were used, publicity was a key factor, successful media campaigns raised awareness and attracted donations. The local press were involved and the people of the region supported such a necessary campaign.

The philosophy –

> *"St. Oswald's Hospice is a charity that values the life of each person and is committed to excellence in Specialist Palliative Care."*

The hospice opened in 1986, it provides care for terminally ill people of all ages, helping the families of these people is important work too. There is no charge for the services they provide. Since 1986 St. Oswald's has continued to develop the services it offers. This has included the opening of a Day Services Wing in 1997 and a special Children's Service opened in 2003. In 2007 the latest project was launched to build a centre for adult day care services to provide a range of specialist treatment/therapy rooms to satisfy an ever increasing demand.

Local Health Authorities provide some funding. The running costs exceed £7m per year and £5m has to be raised from donations. Many people in the region donate and volunteer their services to keep St. Oswald's running. Fund raising includes a weekly lottery, sponsorship from companies, bequests, shops in a number of towns, a Christmas Fair etc.

Dorothy's original concern for the terminally ill, her initiative and determination, has made a difference for so many people in the region.

Adapted from St. Oswald's Hospice website. www.stoswaldsuk.org

Chapter summary

1

What you should know:

From this chapter your knowledge should now cover:

Short course

- ✔ what pressure groups do
- ✔ different types of action used in campaigning
- ✔ factors in successful campaigning
- ✔ at least one historical campaign

Full course

- ✔ what pressure groups do
- ✔ different types of action used in campaigning
- ✔ factors in successful campaigning in detail
- ✔ two historical campaigns
- ✔ different types of pressure groups
- ✔ accountability of representatives
- ✔ how information from pressure groups is used to inform debate and influence policy

Check your knowledge

You should be able to answer the following questions without looking back over the text. If you cannot answer all of the questions you need to learn the material more thoroughly. These types of questions will appear in the Unit 1 exam paper as Section A.

1. Name one national and one international pressure group.
2. Name two different forms of direct action.
3. Identify two factors involved in a successful campaign.
4. When did British women obtain the same voting rights as men?
5. Name a recent national campaign.
6. How can the internet be used in campaigning?
7. What is a focus group?
8. What did Live 8 campaign for?
9. What does 'advocate' mean?
10. Define a section or interest group.

Further study

Investigate and write a report on Rosa Parks and the Montgomery bus boycott of 1955/6 and Dr Martin Luther King and the Civil Rights Movement in USA.

Your report should include:

- what the campaign was about
- when and where the campaign took place
- how long the campaign lasted
- the people involved
- the strategies used in the campaign
- was the campaign successful or not and why.

Fair trade

The Fairtrade Foundation

The Fairtrade Foundation works with businesses, community groups and individuals to improve the trading position of producers in developing countries and to deliver sustainability for farmers, workers and communities. It does this through licensing products that meet internationally agreed standards to carry the Fairtrade mark. The Fairtrade mark on a product guarantees a fair price for producers in developing countries and an additional amount to invest in projects that benefit their communities and the environment.

A *Fairtrade shopping basket*

Tasks

Is Fairtrade a pressure group?

Visit the Fairtrade Foundation website and find out:

- at least eight products that carry the Fairtrade mark
- four countries where Fairtrade products are farmed
- when the Fairtrade Foundation started
- what methods they use to campaign
- what Fairtrade Fortnight is
- how much UK shoppers spent on Fairtrade products last year.

Activities

Choose and complete one of these:

- Make a poster to advertise a Fairtrade product.
- Prepare a PowerPoint presentation on Fairtrade.
- Participate in a small group discussion about Fairtrade.
- Write (and present) a short speech to advocate Fairtrade products.

2 Making a difference

2.1 Local government

Wales, Northern Ireland and Scotland all have the same system of local government. Each area has a single local authority in place, known as a unitary or single tier authority. This body is responsible for all the local government functions within that particular area.

Objectives

To understand the structure of local government, who holds power, and how it is exercised.

The structure of local government in England

The structure of local authorities in England is quite complex. Over the last 30 years there have been a number of re-organisations which have resulted in the present system. The easiest way to explain this is in a diagram.

The Government
↓
Government Office Region (9)
↓

Greater London Authority	Unitary Authorities (56)	County Councils (27)	Metropolitan Counties (6)
↓ London Borough District Councils		↓ Metropolitan Councils	↓ Borough Councils
↓ Parish Council		↓ Parish Council	↓ Parish Council

A *The structure of local government in England*

AQA Examiner's tip

It is important that you know the names and types of councils and what they are responsible for.

It is important that you are able to name and describe what your local Council does.

It is important that you are able to explain how power is exercised locally, regionally and nationally.

There are now nine English regions, they are:

North East North West
Yorkshire and Humberside East Midlands
West Midlands East of England South East
South West London

There is a government office in each region; this network is the means of carrying out government policies within the regions. Each regional office has its own Regional Development Agency.

Regional assemblies

Regional assemblies were set up in 1998; they correspond to the nine regions. The only region to have an elected assembly is London where the Greater London Authority (GLA) came into being in 2000. All other regional assemblies are appointed, not elected. Representatives on Regional Assemblies are nominated by the Councils within their region.

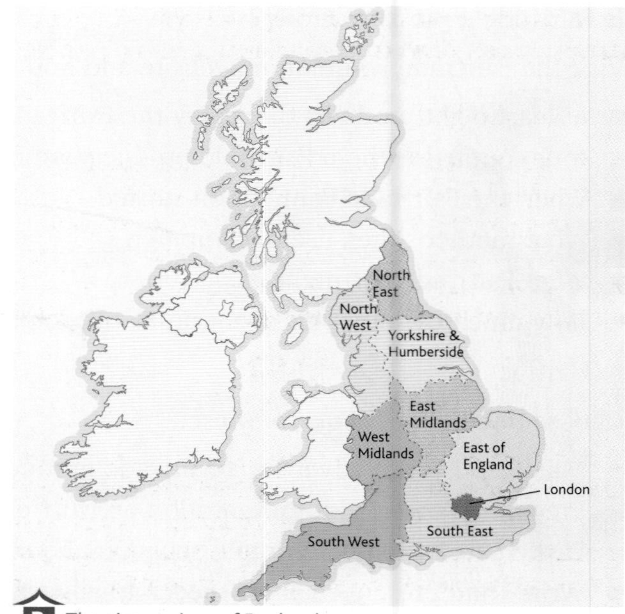

B *The nine regions of England*

In November 2004 the North East region voted in a referendum and rejected the proposal to create an elected Regional Assembly. It was decided that no other referenda would be called. In 2007 the government published proposals to abolish the regional assemblies by 2010.

Unitary authorities

These are often known as the 'shire counties'. These are single tier authorities (one level) it is this Council that takes responsibility for everything in their area. These services include finance, education, planning, social services, emergency services, transport, housing, leisure and recreation, waste disposal and recycling, trading standards and environmental health.

County Councils and District Councils

These are the two tier authorities where most of the services are governed by the County Council.

The County Council is responsible for education, transport, social services, trading standards, and waste disposal. The District Council is responsible for leisure and recreation, planning permission, housing, waste collection and recycling, and environmental health.

The Metropolitan counties

The Metropolitan counties are Tyne and Wear, South Yorkshire, West Yorkshire, Greater Manchester, Merseyside and West Midlands. These authorities are responsible for transport, civil defence and the emergency services, whilst the **Metropolitan Borough Councils** are responsible for all of the other services.

The Greater London Authority (GLA)

This is composed of the Mayor and the London Assembly (25 members). They are responsible for the city wide planning of developments, transport, emergency services, and economic development. There are 32 London boroughs which are responsible for education, housing, social services, waste disposal, local planning, leisure and recreation.

Parish Councils

There are very few Parish Councils. Where they exist they are responsible for a very small area and oversee such services as leisure and recreation. They have very limited powers and usually have a larger District Council which provides other services. There may be a Parish Council as part of a Metropolitan borough or London borough, but they are very rare. Are there any Parish Councils in your area?

Discussion activity

Who holds power?

The government holds the power in this context and they exercise this power through the network of regional offices and the grants which are given to local authorities to pay for services. Power is passed to each local authority to make decisions appropriate for the area. The people of that area hold the power to elect the Councillors that they choose to represent them. Who elected the government – we, the people did.

Information

- The nine English regions have been the basis of the European Parliamentary Constituencies since 1999.
- In 2006 the 10 National Health Service (NHS) Strategic Health Authorities were established, these cover the same areas as the 9 regions except for the South East region which was divided into eastern and western areas.
- Over 2 million people are employed by local authorities.
- Council Tax is paid to the local Council and in general accounts for about 25 per cent of the money spent by the Council on the provision of services to the community. The other 75 per cent comes from central government from the taxes all citizens pay.

Activities

1. Find out the name of your local Council.
2. How many Councillors serve on your Council?
3. What type of authority is it? Metropolitan borough/District/London borough?
4. Look at your local authority's website to find more information about the services they provide. Create a chart to show this.
5. Find out what changes are proposed for some local authorities in 2009.

2.2 Taking part in the democratic process

Information

All local authorities now have a written constitution which gives all the details about how the authority works and the ways in which the electorate can ensure that Councillors are accountable.

Every Council must have an Overview and Scrutiny Committee which is made up of Councillors who are not in the cabinet (non-executive) and members of the public. These committees will have members of all the political parties that have been elected to the Council. This committee ensures that the cabinet is accountable.

Political structure

Each Council will be made up of elected Councillors from different political parties. The party with the most councillors is known as the majority party. This party will therefore elect the leader and probably the cabinet. The other parties will form the Opposition. Where there is an elected mayor, they may not belong to the same political party as the ruling (majority) party in the Council.

A ***Democracy*** *in action*

The Local Government Act 2000 created changes to the way local authorities in England and Wales are structured. Generally it meant that the committee structure of the decision-making process was altered to create an executive style. Each local authority had to make a choice between four options. One authority chose an elected mayor and a council manager structure. A very small number chose an elected mayor and cabinet. The vast majority chose to have a leader of the Council with a cabinet.

This means that the leader and cabinet form the executive and are the ones with the decision-making powers.

All the Councillors in the executive will be from the majority party on the Council because they are appointed directly by the leader or by the full Council. Each Councillor in the cabinet (executive) will have a special responsibility for one of the services, for example, education.

Objectives

To understand the structure of a local authority.

To know how to participate in the democratic process.

Key terms

Democracy: rule by the majority of the people.

Democratic process: the actual process of electing the people's representatives.

Electorate: the people eligible to vote in an area.

Research activities

1. Find a map of your area showing each ward of the council.
2. Mark on the map your home, your school, the council offices.
3. Draw a chart to show the structure of your council and name the Mayor, Leader of the Council, Cabinet members and which services each Cabinet member is responsible for.
4. Discuss what is good about your community.
5. Discuss what you think could be improved in your community.

This Act ensured that each authority had an ethical (moral) framework giving codes of conduct for Councillors and establishing Standards Committees to make sure the codes are followed. This is one way Councillors can be held accountable.

The democratic process

The **democratic process** is the actual process of electing the people's representatives to either local or national government, or to the European Parliament. Local elections usually take place every year at the beginning of May; a fixed number of Councillors will stand every year, on a rolling programme. A Councillor usually serves a term of three years. The whole Council area is divided into wards and a ward will elect one or more Councillors. In Parliamentary elections a much larger area is known as a constituency and elects one Member of Parliament (MP) to represent that area for the length of that Parliament. If a Councillor or MP dies or resigns their seat, then a by-election must be held. A General Election is when all Members of Parliament are elected at the same time. There must be a general election every five years. Each ward will have approximately the same number of electors. This applies to constituencies, but they are far greater in size.

Political parties will campaign for votes before an election. They do this in a number of ways. Most parties will send out election addresses, send out leaflets telling people about their policies and the person standing for election, engage in canvassing – from door to door, meet the **electorate** in busy shopping centres, hold public meetings, engage in debates on TV or radio, write in newspapers, and create a website. The people make their choice and cast their vote. The person who wins the most number of votes is elected to represent that ward or constituency. This is known as the first past the post system. Other systems will be discussed in a later chapter. Casting your vote or participation in the democratic process is very important and is one means of being involved in decision making within communities. It is often called a civic duty.

If you want to influence decisions made at a local level or to make a change you have to persuade others, especially Councillors, to support your view. You can talk to your Councillor(s) at their local surgery or contact them by letter, email or telephone; visit the council offices to gather information or use the website, write or phone; talk to a council official; set up a focus or **community group** to attract like-minded people; write a letter to the local press, etc.

These are all ways that people can be involved. Participation is important; knowing who to contact and how makes getting involved much easier.

Activities

1. Which political party controls your local authority? What is their majority?
2. Who are your local representatives? When are they due to stand for re-election? Which party do they belong to?
3. Who is your MP? Which party do they belong to?
4. Invite a Councillor to your school to talk to you about their work.

Information

You can vote in the first election after your 18th birthday. There are some arguments to support lowering this age to 16 – do some research and thinking and then discuss this issue.

Just because you are not quite old enough to vote, it does not mean that you cannot have your say on issues you feel strongly about. How can you make your voice heard? You can also get out into your community and join a group and make a difference. **It's never too early to get involved.**

Key terms

Community group: a group of people who meet together to follow a shared interest (for example, a craft group, a sports team) or to influence a decision or campaign for a change.

B *The democratic process*

AQA Examiner's tip

Know how the democratic process works. Make sure you can explain it clearly.

2.3 Community involvement

Information

This website gives information on community groups which may be useful:

www.directgov.uk select 'getting a community group started'.

Your local authority will have a list of all community and voluntary groups in your area.

Community groups

In most areas there are a large number of community groups. A community group may be a focus group trying to influence a decision (chapter 1). It may be a group of people who meet to share a common interest such as a sport or hobby or a youth group. You may be a member of one of these already. Young adults and people in these groups get to know each other and increase their knowledge of a wider range of people, often meeting others from different backgrounds and cultures which creates better understanding and makes for a greater awareness within the community. This helps to make the community a happier and safer place because of the better understanding and tolerance of other people's culture and their views.

Voluntary groups

Voluntary groups exist to provide a service for others which is not provided by the state or a private organisation. They do not have any funding from the government and therefore can also be called Non-Governmental Organisations (NGOs). Voluntary groups are also non-profit making; their funds come from donations and are used to benefit the people the group was set up to help. The volunteers receive no payment for their work, hence the name voluntary groups. Could you be a volunteer?

Charities are governed by The Charity Commission under the new Charities Act of 2006. This Act is being implemented in stages and sets out new definitions and purposes. For more information about charities go to **www.charitycommission.gov.uk**.

The Act has clarified and simplified many aspects of the law. Most charities rely on donations and grants, some have government funding. Charities are usually non-profit making organisations, but many do have to pay staff, cover rent, insurance and other running costs which must be taken from the monies received. Charities always welcome new people who want to get involved and help to make a difference to the lives of others who are less fortunate than themselves.

Objectives

- To understand what community involvement is.
- To discover more about community groups, voluntary groups and charities.
- To look at how the media forms and reflects public opinion.

Key terms

Voluntary group: a group of people who work without pay to provide a service for others, for example, St John's Ambulance.

Charities: local, national or international organisations to help others in need, for example, Children In Need.

Media: referring to the mass media – television or radio broadcasts or printed media as in newspapers and magazines or mass communication via the internet.

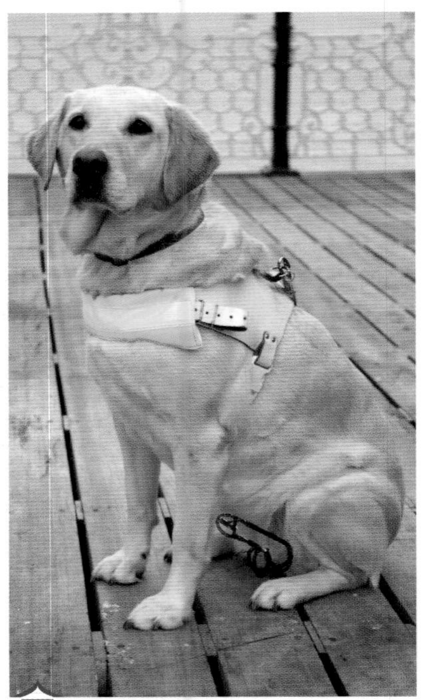

A *Name the charity*

Media influence

There has been a rapid increase in the number and type of mass **media** available during the last twenty years. The most rapid explosion in mass communication has been due to the internet, where there is a constant global availability of news and events 24/7/52. The media pervades our lives without us realising it. We are all influenced by various forms of media and advertising. In many respects the media influences and can change public opinion by the style and content of information presented about people and events. Media reporting is often biased to influence the public in one direction or another especially at election times. The internet has encouraged more participation in the exchange of opinions through interactive websites.

The media can reflect public opinion as well as influencing it. When an opinion poll is conducted the results are widely reported with much comment. This is making known to the wider population a snapshot of the general public's view on an issue. How influenced are we by this? Does this make us think again? If it does, then taking time to reconsider where you stand is a good thing. It is a bad thing, however, if you simply change your mind because you hear of some survey results. Media reporting of campaigns is a reflection of public opinion – can you give some recent examples?

To have a truly well-informed view it is best to gather information from a number of sources, then make up your own mind. **Who influences you?**

B *Who influences you?*

AQA Examiner's tip

Know the key terms.
Have a justifiable opinion on media influences.

Activities

1. Gather a selection of newspaper reports about the same event and compare how the reporting differs.

   Discuss your findings in small groups – which report is most likely to influence people?

2. Conduct a short questionnaire to find out which form of the mass media people prefer for
   - a news
   - b fashion
   - c music
   - d sport.

   Produce some graphs on the results.

3. Choose a current topic or issue that you are interested in and write a biased news report about it.

2.4 Trade unions

Activity

1 Look at these union logos and find out which union they belong to, and who each union represents.

Trade unions first began as far back as the 18th century, when they were isolated groups of workers in different industries. Now unions are well organised and are recognised in all industries. There have been many workers' disputes and many cases where industrial action has been a key feature. Today there are not as many struggles which lead to industrial action as there were 30 years ago. Industrial action causes disruption to services or the manufacturing of goods. It does damage to both sides involved.

Most workers join a **trade union** so that they can benefit from the services a union provides. You cannot be forced to be a member of a union; it is matter of personal choice. You cannot legally be discriminated against by other workers or your employers because you are a member of a union or because you choose not to become a member. To belong to a union you must work in that particular trade or profession; for some unions a qualification is necessary.

People join a union because:

- the union negotiates pay deals – **collective bargaining**
- the union negotiates terms and conditions for workers
- the union can provide legal help in disputes
- the union can provide advice and support in personal disputes with employers
- the union can negotiate with employers in general disputes
- unions can organise official industrial action
- some unions provide training courses for members.

When a dispute with an employer arises there are opportunities to resolve the issue without recourse to industrial action. ACAS (Advisory, Conciliation and Arbitration Service) will work with both sides to try to negotiate an agreement.

Objectives

To understand what trade unions do and the possible effects of various types of industrial actions.

Information

Types of Industrial Action

A Strike: employees refuse to go to work as normal. The rules for calling a strike must be followed. Strikes may last for a stipulated time of one or two days or may be an indefinite strike where there is no date set for a return to work.

A Wildcat Strike: this is unplanned, unexpected and unofficial. This is where workers decide to stop working without notice or an official ballot. These types of strikes are rare now. There were some in January 2009 – what were these about?

Overtime ban: employees refuse to work beyond the hours stipulated in their contract of employment. If overtime working is normal practice within the company the workers will lose money and the company will lose some production.

Work to rule: employees will only undertake official specified work, this could reduce production. An overtime ban could be part of a work to rule.

Key terms

Trade union: a trade union is a group of workers in the same trade or profession who join together to protect their rights and pursue common interests.

Collective bargaining: an agreement negotiated by a union on behalf of its members about an issue, for example, salaries.

If the two sides cannot settle a dispute then the union may decide to take industrial action. This could be a strike, a walk out, a work to rule, an overtime ban, or a boycott.

For any industrial action to be 'official' it must be backed by the union. A secret postal ballot must have been held (within the four weeks before a strike), with a majority voting in favour of the action. The employer must be given details of the action before it takes place.

If there are more than 50 employees then an independent person known as a Scrutineer is needed to ensure the correct procedures are followed.

All types of industrial action will have an impact on the employers, the workers, their families, the local community and economy. If it is a national strike the whole country will be affected.

Effect on communities

If a strike is local involving a major employer in the area, it can cause many problems for the people living in that community. Employers do not pay people for being on strike. Sometimes the union will give strike pay, but this will not be as much as normal earnings. There is less to spend on essentials – food, heat, etc. and there is nothing for the extras usually taken for granted. Industrial action means hardship for all concerned. The employer will lose money as there is no production of goods or no service being provided. This could lead to loss of profits and contracts and a reduction in the number of jobs. If contracts are lost permanently it could lead to closure of the business and the loss of all jobs. This would send the local economy into decline and people would begin to look at other towns/cities for jobs and move out of the area altogether. This would have a knock on effect on the business that remained, as there would be fewer people to support trade in what remained in that local economy.

A *Find out what happened to this company*

Activities

2. Write an informative newspaper article about the TUC – when was it formed – what does it do – what is Worksmart – how many affiliated unions are there – how many people are members of a union? **www.tuc.org.uk** may be useful.
3. Invite a speaker from the TUC to address your group.
4. Find out more about collective bargaining rules.
5. In small groups discuss the different forms of industrial action and decide which may be the most effective.

Information

ACAS was set up in 1975. It is now funded by the Department for Business, Enterprise and Regulatory Reform (BERR). ACAS works to improve employment relations.

The Employment Relations Act 2004 – This is the latest legislation concerning employment. It was 'mainly concerned with collective labour law and trade union rights' – BERR.

For more information on specific unions see their individual websites.

AQA *Examiner's tip*

Be able to explain what a trade union is, who may belong to it, the role of trade unions, the different types of industrial action and how successful they may be – know some recent examples of successful and unsuccessful industrial actions.

2.5 The Impact of government actions on citizens

The government is responsible for every aspect of running the country, so all decisions and laws passed will affect us all, some in more major ways than others. This is easier to understand by looking at some examples. Every year the Chancellor of the Exchequer delivers financial plans for the coming year; this is known as The Budget. In 2007 when Gordon Brown was the Chancellor he gave notice that the 10 per cent tax rate would be abolished in 2008. Some MPs and others raised objections to this and gave details of how many people this could affect. Nothing more was done until this came into effect in 2008 when there was a public outcry. At the same time the standard rate of tax was reduced from 22 per cent to 20 per cent. The effect of this was that everyone who had paid part or all of their tax at 10 per cent was now paying 20 per cent; this was about 5 million people, in several different categories. There was so much news and comment and political capital made out of the situation. Eventually the Chancellor, Alistair Darling, announced some amendments to alleviate the problem. In other words a compromise was reached, and various changes were made.

Another area to consider is transport and fuel costs. When the price of petrol and diesel goes up we are all affected. Companies involved in the transportation of people and goods pass on the extra fuel cost to the travelling public and consumers. In 2008 there was a huge increase in the price of petrol and diesel. This is not the fault of the government – it is due to international trading prices for a barrel of oil. Most people know this but still think the government could help to alleviate the situation. How?

There are many other ways government actions affect us all. Complete the task in the activity box to learn more.

For every litre bought at the pumps the
the government receives almost 70% of the cost of petrol

A

Objectives

To learn about the impact of a government's actions on citizens.

To discover what happens when large numbers of people choose not to be active citizens.

Information

The government charges two taxes on fuel at the pumps: one is a Fuel Duty the other is VAT. This means that for every litre bought at the pumps the government receives just under 70 per cent of the cost of petrol and about 67 per cent for diesel.

Activity

1. In small groups choose an area and discover an action the government has taken that has had an impact on us, then share the information with the rest of the group. Choose from social services, education, health services, or law enforcement.

Information

Direct tax is taken from all employed citizens' wages and is calculated on how much they earn. People who earn more pay more. Income tax and National Health Insurance are examples.

Indirect tax, like VAT or tax on alcohol and cigarettes, is paid as part of the price of the product being bought.

Government decisions on how much tax to collect directly affects how much money people have, and how much things cost. How much money the government collects directly affects how it is spent on things like schools, hospitals, power stations, roads, railways, the Armed Forces and benefits.

Consequences of people not participating as active citizens

In this chapter we have looked at many ways people can be active citizens within their communities. This includes becoming a member of a community group for a sport or hobby, being a volunteer to help provide a service to help others, becoming active within a charity, being a member of a union, being actively involved with a political party, voicing your opinion on community or national issues in the local media or online, and, as explored in chapter 1, various opportunities to be an activist in a pressure group and participate in a campaign. We have seen how important it is to take part in the democratic process.

If all of these opportunities were not taken up by a vast number of people what would happen?

If everyone lost interest there would be very few community activities, there would be no sports clubs to join, there wouldn't be many of the extra services currently run by volunteers, there would be very few special events, and there would not be many charities because there would be few supporters. Think of all those who benefit from all of these activities – our communities would not be lively places at all.

Many young people often say 'there is nothing to do around here'. So do something about it. Find out what other people would like to see, start to ask people in power, for example your Councillors, what they could do to help, get some support, be active, see what could be achieved. Don't just sit and whinge – do something.

Many people believe in being active in some way in their community, usually for the benefit of others; it would be a very dull place if suddenly they all became inactive.

Activity

2 One important part of being an active citizen is participating in the democratic process – use your right to influence the people in charge of local and national government. From previous activities you should know the website of your Council. Look at the results of the last elections for Councillors – find out:

a who was elected in your ward

b the percentage turnout – was this more or less than the previous year?

c if there was any overall change of control in the Council

d the number of votes – did the person elected have more than 50 per cent of the vote?

In a group discuss what you have found out.

Chapter summary

What you should know:

From this chapter your knowledge should now cover:

Short course

- ✔ the structure of local government within Britain
- ✔ who holds power
- ✔ how power is exercised
- ✔ the structure of local authorities
- ✔ how to participate in the democratic process
- ✔ community groups, voluntary groups and charities
- ✔ influence of the media

Full course

- ✔ the structure of local government within Britain
- ✔ who holds power
- ✔ how power is exercised
- ✔ the structure of local authorities
- ✔ how to participate in the democratic process
- ✔ community groups, voluntary groups and charities
- ✔ influence of the media
- ✔ trade unions and their role
- ✔ the effect of industrial action on communities

Check your knowledge

You should be able to answer the following questions without looking back over the text. If you cannot answer all of the questions you need to learn the material more thoroughly. These types of questions will appear in the Unit 1 exam paper as Section A.

1. Describe the type of local councils in Wales.
2. What are Unitary Authorities in Scotland responsible for?
3. How many government office regions are there in England?
4. Name three Metropolitan counties.
5. How do local authorities obtain finance?
6. Describe local government in London.
7. What did the Local Government Act of 2000 do?
8. Define a voluntary group.
9. What is a trade union?
10. What do political parties campaign for?

Further study

Discuss a range of people who may have power in a community besides the ones mentioned in this chapter. Visit the website **www.Number10.gov.uk** and click communicate, then e-Petitions, and then write a short report for your local newspaper concerning what the public have been petitioning the Prime Minister about recently. Discuss this in a small group to find out what other people think. (There are other links on this site that you may find interesting to browse.)

The Housing Strategy in context

The Housing Strategy illustrated below was developed in relation to relevant national, regional and local policies and other related strategic documents. The main policies and strategies linked to the Housing Strategy are summarised as follows:

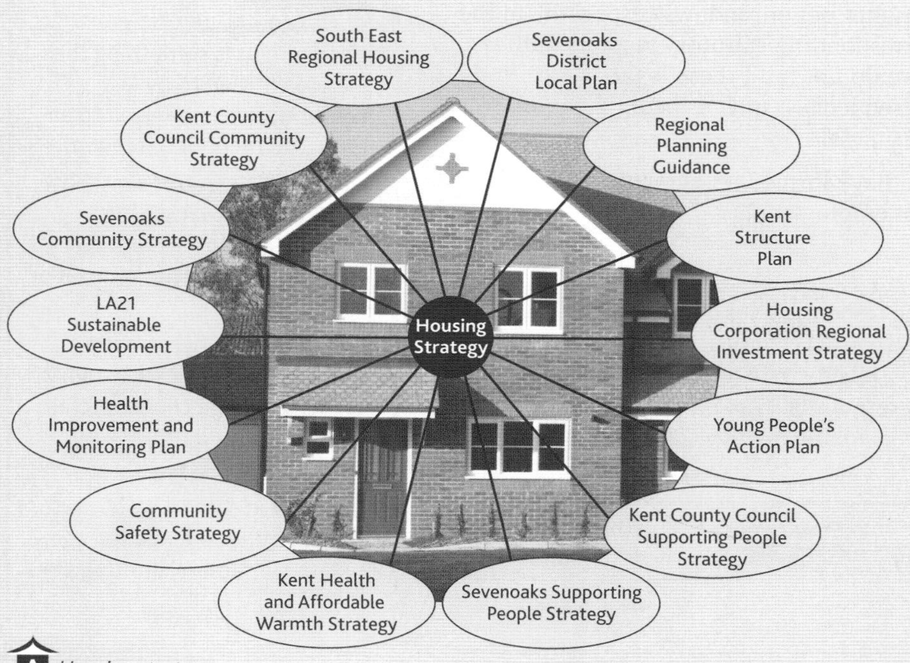

A *Housing strategy*

- Look at the diagram above and read all the different considerations that are applied to build up (formulate) a policy.
- Discuss and decide which of these strategies have come from the government via the regional office and which have been developed by Sevenoaks. This should help your understanding of how government actions impact on citizens.
- Kent County Council is mentioned; what does this indicate about the structure of local government in this area?

3 Citizenship issues in the workplace

3.1 Rights and responsibilities

We are going to examine a variety of citizenship issues that apply to the workplace, including **rights** and **responsibilities**, health and safety, and **equal opportunities**. Most people will have a job at sometime during their lives, and work is frequently the place where **discrimination**, harassment and breaches of our rights occur. If this does happen there are procedures to deal with it. As long as you follow the procedures properly you should be dealt with fairly and your rights should be restored. If you belong to a trade union they will help you. Compensation may be sought; this would mean taking the employer to an Employment Tribunal.

We have statutory rights (legal rights, set out in laws) especially in the workplace, but we also have corresponding statutory responsibilities that we are accountable for. If we do not fulfil these legal responsibilities there will be consequences, such as being given written warnings which could lead to dismissal.

When you accept a job offer you have formed an agreement with an employer known as a contract of employment.

Activity

Here is a jumbled list of rights and responsibilities of employers and employees. Sort them out into the correct columns, copy the headings, use one line for each right or responsibility. Where you have a right or responsibility is there a matching responsibility or right for another column along the same row? Complete the rows by colour coding. An example has been done for you.

Employers' right	Employers' responsibility	Employees' right	Employees' responsibility
Expect staff to arrive on time			Be punctual

Be punctual,
pay salaries on time,
follow the dress code,
issue a contract,
expect loyalty,
provide training in health and safety,
do the job properly,
provide a safe place to work,
attend training courses,
fair treatment,
follow the rules and company policies,
provide adequate heat,
light and ventilation,
to abide by the terms of the employment contract,
not to cause risk to anyone,
provide protective clothing when necessary,
report concerns about safety,
allow correct amount of time for breaks,
illness should be genuine,
comply with statutory holiday entitlements,
follow grievance procedures,
pay the minimum wage,
expect responsible behaviour.

Objectives

To learn about the rights and responsibilities of employers and employees.

To learn how health and safety laws apply to working situations.

Key terms

Rights: a right is something that we are entitled to by law, sometimes also referred to as an entitlement or a freedom.

Responsibilities: a responsibility is something that we are expected to do – a duty. Responsibilities may be legal or moral.

Equal opportunities: treating everyone with the same rights, giving the same chances to all.

Discrimination: treating someone unfairly because they are different in some way because of their gender, sexuality, age, religion, disability, or ethnicity.

A written statement should be given to you within eight weeks. This written document sets out the terms of your employment and should include the following:

- the title of the position (job title)
- a description of the job
- the address of the employer
- address or location of the place of work or each location if there is more than one
- the normal working hours and the days when the hours will be worked
- clear details of any overtime working
- arrangements for sick pay
- details of holiday entitlement
- the number of days or weeks required for notice to be given, on both sides
- information on grievance and disciplinary matters.

As well as the details in the contract all your statutory rights apply.

A *Production worker, bank teller and market trader*

Information

Information for employees

The legislation introduced during the past decade has set out a framework of rights and entitlements during employment. These include:

- Pay: Everyone is entitled to the National Minimum Wage, and men and women must be paid the same amount for the same work.
- Working hours: The Working Time Regulations limit the number of hours you can work in a week, unless you choose to, and have introduced minimum standards for work breaks and the amount of paid annual leave you are entitled to.
- Family life: Working parents have rights which include: maternity, paternity and parental leave, the right to apply for flexible working hours and the right for time off to look after dependants.
- Unfair dismissal: Once you have been employed for more than 12 months you get the right to claim unfair dismissal.
- Discrimination: You have the right not to be discriminated against at work because of your gender, age, religion or belief or because of a disability.
- Part-time or fixed-term work: Workers on fixed-term or part-time contracts are protected by law and must not be discriminated against or treated differently to other workers.

Taken directly from www.employmentlaws.co.uk

Case study

Steve is 17. He works on a Saturday in a shop selling computers. He has been working for three months and has not had any written statement of his terms of employment.

One Saturday the manager asks Steve if he can work extra hours the next day.

Steve has a lot of homework to catch up on and says that he can't manage it. The manager is annoyed at this and tells Steve that he is no longer required on Saturdays.

What can Steve do?

Consider – no contract, age related laws on working, Sunday working, statutory rights.

links

The work on discrimination and equal opportunities in the workplace together with the laws relating to equal pay, age, disability, ethnicity, religion, gender, and sexuality are all found in chapter 9 pages 114–115. You must look at chapter 9 in conjunction with this chapter to gain the best information about citizenship issues in the workplace.

AQA *Examiner's tip*

Be able to explain employers' and employees' rights and responsibilities.

3.2 Health and safety

Objectives

To learn about the rights and responsibilities of employers and employees in making workplaces safe.

Information

The Health and Safety Executive (HSE) website (**www.hse.gov.uk**) says

" *Our mission is to protect people's health and safety by ensuring risks in the changing workplace are properly controlled.*

We do this through research, information and advice, promoting training, new or revised regulations and codes of practice, inspection, investigation and enforcement.

HSE's job is to protect people against risks to health or safety arising out of work activities. "

The Health and Safety at Work Act 1974

This is the main Act that deals with all Health and Safety laws. It has been amended and further regulations have been added, but it is still the primary piece of legislation on Health and Safety at Work. It is enforced by the HSE.

There is a European Agency for Safety and Health at Work; they work from Bilbao, Spain. They try to make workplaces across the European Union (EU) safer by gathering and sharing information. They also help in explaining EU legislation on Health and Safety.

There used to be two organisations that were responsible for Health and Safety at work, the Health and Safety Executive and the Health and Safety Commission. On 1 April 2008 these two merged together and are now known as the Health and Safety Executive. This body assumed the powers of both previous organisations in setting policy, giving advice to companies and working with local authorities to enforce the law.

There are well over 2,000 pieces of legislation about health and safety practices in all types of industries and businesses. We saw on the last pages how rights and responsibilities play an important part of working life; this applies to matters of Health and Safety too. Employers and employees have to work together to make working practices safe.

Some of the major responsibilities of an employer are to:

- carry out a risk assessment by a special Health and Safety person and produce a report of the assessment
- devise plans to deal with the risks identified
- formulate a Health and Safety policy
- make all employees aware of the policy.

This should ensure that all working practices are safe, and that machinery is regularly checked. Training must be given on the use of machinery and substances used in manufacturing processes; safety clothing and equipment must be provided by the employer where necessary. Accidents and injuries must be recorded and reported.

AQA Examiner's tip

Be able to explain the importance of Health and Safety legislation.

As an employee you have the right to:

- work in conditions where risks are minimised and controlled
- tell your employer if you consider there are any health and safety risks involved in your work
- contact the HSE (Health and Safety Executive) if your employer will not take action
- stop working if you think you are in danger.

An employee must be responsible for their own Health and Safety and must ensure that their actions do not put anyone else at risk.

A *Hard hat area*

Most workplaces will have a Health and Safety Representative. These people have had special training on Health and Safety matters and should be allowed time during working hours to carry out their responsibilities and attend further training courses as necessary. In larger companies the Health and Safety person may be a full time company employee who makes sure that all the correct procedures are being followed and that all the documentation is up to date. Many companies will have their premises inspected by independent trained inspectors who ensure that the company is complying with the appropriate industry standards.

Case study

This case could easily arise; look at the laws about discrimination in chapter 10 and visit the Trades Union Congress (TUC) website to find the answers.

Jade has worked in a local supermarket for 18 months. She is hard working and has been told that she is in line for promotion to Assistant Manager. She raises concerns that a fire door is regularly blocked by stock when large deliveries of goods arrive. The Manager is also the Health and Safety Rep. There is a lot of fuss, but nothing really changes. Over the next few weeks Jade is not asked to work overtime and someone else becomes the Assistant Manager. Jade is really upset by this, she thought she was contributing to her own and others safety at work. What should she do?

Activities

John works in a factory. Some new machines have been placed in the assembly line. The workers have been given training and provided with suitable protective clothing. Several accidents, involving the new machines, have been narrowly avoided. John talks to the company Heath and Safety person about the problems, raising his concerns about the safety of the new machines.

1. What should happen next?
2. What should John do if nothing happens?
3. Can John get into trouble or lose his job for raising his concerns?
4. What could be the consequences if nothing was done and a serious accident did happen?

links

Useful websites for finding out more information:

www.osha.europa.eu
www.direct.gov.uk
www.hse.gov.uk
www.tuc.org.uk

3.3 Consumer rights

Most people involved in the sale of goods and services to consumers are decent, honest workers trying to make a profit and earn a living. However there are some who are not very honest and have become known as 'cowboys' or rogue traders; their goods and services are sub-standard and sometimes unsafe. There are Trading Standards Offices in all local authorities who are there to help you. They will give free advice and investigate complaints. These are usually the people who enforce the laws on consumer affairs.

The Office of Fair Trading (the OFT) is a government department that deals with consumer issues; it was set up in 1973. The Enterprise Act 2003 established the OFT as a statutory corporation (governed by a Board, a chairperson and directors). They produce posters and information leaflets as well as the Consumer Direct service. This is a website and a telephone line that everyone can contact with a consumer problem.

The OFT can work with agencies for the benefit of consumers. It studies all aspects of the supply of goods and services and recommends what action should be taken when necessary. The OFT provides guidance for businesses and ensures that they follow the consumer laws (compliance); it can also act to stop people who constantly disregard such laws.

Most of the legislation concerning consumers has been put in place during the last 20 to 30 years. There are two major pieces of legislation that everyone should know about.

A *An issue of* Which *magazine*

Objectives

- To learn about the laws on consumer rights.
- To learn about the organisations involved with consumer affairs.
- To know your basic rights when buying goods.

links

Useful websites:

Office of Fair Trading www.oft.gov.uk

Consumer Direct www.consumerdirect.gov.uk

Which www.which.co.uk

Trading Standards can be contacted through your local authority. You should know how to contact your local authority from chapter 2.

AQA Examiner's tip

Learn about the legislation and how it is applied. Be able to explain what to do when goods are faulty.

Information

You may have heard of *Which* magazine and the reports it publishes on the testing of products. It also investigates services.

Which is a completely independent organisation that started in 1957. It has grown considerably since then to become the 'largest consumer body in the UK with over 650,000 members'. It is 'a registered charity and plough everything back into consumer interests and services for our members'. **www.which.co.uk** – Who we are – Overview.

1. The Sale of Goods Act 1979 and its amendments

This refers to all goods sold and states that they should be: as described (either a written or verbal description) of satisfactory quality, and fit for purpose.

If the goods are not of merchantable quality or very quickly become faulty and have not been misused then you could be entitled to a full refund of your money. Do not delay in returning the goods to the place where they were purchased. Explain politely and clearly the nature of the problem. This way you are far more likely to get what you want. If you experience difficulties ask to see the manager. If you still achieve nothing take the faulty goods away with you and contact your local Trading Standards Office or Consumer Direct. If goods become faulty after a short time of correct use you may still be entitled to a refund with a deduction from the full price for the use you have had from the goods (this is known as wear and tear). You should be offered a repair or a replacement of the goods. Most companies want your custom and will do their best to resolve problems.

2. The Sale of Goods and Services Act 1982

This deals with services that you pay for from hairdressing to building and decorating.

The same laws apply to services, they must be of reasonable standard of workmanship and should be carried out within a reasonable length of time. The cost, details of the work and the time it will take should be agreed before any work begins. It is best to put the details in writing as you make this contract which can then be referred to if things go wrong.

Most laws dealing with consumer affairs are based on what is reasonable, using sensible judgements.

The European Union (EU) has a Commissioner for Consumer Protection. Directives are produced which member countries have to implement. The Sale of Goods to Consumers Regulations 2002 was a result of an EU directive. This does not change the principles of the existing law.

Discussion activity

In small groups discuss the following scenarios and decide what you would do. See if other groups agree with you.

Sarah buys a new pair of trainers. After she has worn them once she notices a split between the sole and the upper part of the shoe. Sarah still has the receipt for the purchase. Is she entitled to her money back? How should she approach her request for this? What is the key phrase to remember?

Matt buys a new iPod. After two months it stops playing. He does not have the receipt, but he does have the guarantee with the shop's date stamp on it. Is he entitled to a full refund? Why or why not? What can he do?

3.4 The economy, citizenship and community cohesion

Information

In the last chapter we saw how central government implements policies through the regional government offices. The **economy** of each region is important because collectively it forms the national economy. The Government Office provides the link between central government and the regions; it is a two-way dialogue. It is important that business and industry develop around the regions so that the local economy supports the communities in these areas and maintains the prosperity of the area and contributes to the national economy. There are various government departments involved in economic development. The main ones are Communities and Local Government, the Department for Business Enterprise and Regulatory Reform (BERR), previously the Department of Trade and Industry (DTI), and the Treasury.

Key terms

Economy: this term describes the financial and production levels of a country or region in relation to the manufacture and use of food, products and services.

Community cohesion: enabling people within an area to have shared values and understanding and a sense of belonging, by providing good facilities and the same opportunities for all.

All the policies and government initiatives on **community cohesion** really started after the summer of 2001.

During this summer there were a number of major riots in some northern towns and cities. Most of these were due to tension between different sections of people from different ethnic backgrounds. There were riots in Bradford and Oldham and to a lesser extent in Leeds and Burnley.

A number of strategies were introduced to improve the local economies. Many areas in the country have seen the more traditional industries of mining, manufacturing and ship building decline or disappear altogether. This led to fewer jobs, high levels of unemployment, few prospects of career development, less money available within the community, a decline in the health of the people, the poor maintenance of property, and greater stress on social services as more and more people were using them. Different ethnic groups did not integrate with each other; they did not understand each other's culture, and sections of the community felt that they were treated differently, that others were better off, had more facilities and access to services and had greater opportunities. This led to resentment between a variety of sections within communities.

In 2001 the National Strategy for Neighbourhood Renewal was established to try to improve (regenerate) deprived areas and create community cohesion. The focus of the Neighbourhood Renewal was to improve the community as a whole including better services, better housing, education and health care (more doctors, clinics, and dentists in the community) creating opportunities for ethnic groups to meet and develop understanding of each other's culture and appreciate the diversity of their community, bringing increased trust and tolerance within the community as well as encouraging economic development. New industries had to be attracted to these areas and given time to establish, thereby creating new job opportunities, increasing the flow of money within communities so that trade and commerce prospered again, and generally improving the quality of life within the neighbourhood in every respect.

Part of neighbourhood renewal was the development of Local Strategic Partnerships (LSPs). The funds for this were carefully targeted to the 86 (some reports say 88) most deprived local authorities. Working through the government office for each of the regions, the government encouraged the establishment of LSPs within these targeted local authorities. The LSP was to be a mixture of local groups and organisations cooperating and working together with local people in their communities to identify their needs and bring about changes to reduce crime, improve conditions, and generate the economy. This was thought to have better chances of success and increase participation in local democracy, by asking local people to be active in improving their own community, and by working with children and young people as well as adults in making their community safer, healthier and more prosperous.

It was envisaged that to create an improved and sustainable community and local economy many people from a variety of voluntary organisations, public services and business would need to work together in partnership to create lasting means of communication between all groups, so they could meet together to increase understanding and tolerance, so that values are shared and community cohesion created to replace community tension. The involvement of young people was important. The opinion and concerns of young people on their own issues and those of the wider community were valued and taken into account. As the local economy improved there would be more jobs and careers for young people, giving more opportunities for them to associate with others from different ethnic groups, an important aspect of developing community cohesion.

A *Tension*

B *Cohesion*

Activity

Find out about the different sectors and what industries are involved in each. Use primary, secondary and tertiary sectors as headings and list the companies/businesses in your region that fall into these categories.

Look at different websites to find out more about the background to the riots in 2001.

Discuss the following topics as a class or in small groups:

- How far has Neighbourhood Renewal and the Local Strategic Partnership succeeded in creating community cohesion?
- What is a divided community? What are some of the causes of divisions within a community?
- Why is a thriving local economy important in reducing tension between ethnic groups in a community?
- Why are equal opportunities important in communities?

AQA *Examiner's tip*

Be able to explain the different initiatives connected to community cohesion and what they were designed to do. Have an opinion on how successful they have been.

3.5 Case studies

Objectives

To look at two different companies and discover how they have voluntarily contributed to local, national and international policies on sustainability.

Key terms

Sustainability: a system where natural resources are used and replaced so that they are not depleted.

Case study

Cadbury

What does the name mean to you? Most people would say 'chocolate' and start to name a number of their products. John Cadbury first opened a shop in Birmingham in 1824 selling mainly tea and coffee and soon after cocoa and drinking chocolate were added, products that he made himself. Since then the company has expanded and has introduced many innovations in making chocolate and today Cadbury is a worldwide company.

The Cadbury brothers built the company on the principle that business should be 'a force for good in a troubled world'. Today, the challenges are more complex but this legacy of responsible business lives on more than 100 years later. Cadbury has always had concern for its employees and those farmers and workers within its supply chain. The company's concern for the environment has been shown particularly through two initiatives: Purple Goes Green and the Cadbury Cocoa Partnership.

In July 2007 Cadbury launched **Purple Goes Green**, an industry-leading environmental strategy designed to transform the company's manufacturing processes and assets in response to the challenge of climate change. Cadbury set out industry leading targets, namely reducing energy use by cutting carbon emissions by 50 per cent, reducing packaging by 10 per cent for products with a 25 per cent reduction in packaging of seasonal ranges. They also aim for 60 per cent of packaging to be biodegradable and have a policy to reduce the use of water.

In addition to Cadbury's environmental strategy, the company is also committed to ethical and sustainable sourcing. In January 2008, the **Cadbury Cocoa Partnership** was launched to support the communities that produce one of their most crucial raw ingredients – cocoa. This ground-breaking partnership aims to secure the economic, social and environmental **sustainability** of around a million cocoa farmers and their communities in Ghana, India, Indonesia and the Caribbean.

Alongside the farmers and local groups within the partnership are a number of organisations, including the United Nations Development Programme (UNDP), the Government of Ghana, trade unions and non-governmental organisations including CARE, VSO and World Vision. The aim is to increase productivity and the yield in cocoa farming, therefore increasing the cocoa farmer's income, to introduce new funding so that rural businesses can start up and expand, and improve cocoa communities through education and building wells for clean water.

Cadbury has an Ethical Trading policy which encompasses all of its commercial activity throughout the supply chain. The policy covers core labour rights and dignity at work, health and safety in the workplace, fair remuneration, diversity and respect for differences and opportunity for development.

Cadbury is a member of the International Cocoa Initiative. This organisation works with the governments in cocoa producing countries to remove child labour and abuses of human rights in cocoa production to support cocoa growing communities and ensure long-term sustainability.

Cadbury

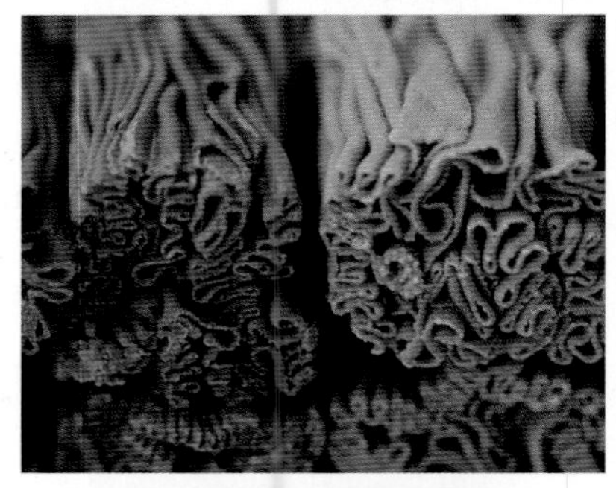

A

Case study

Nissan

Nissan UK have been producing cars in Sunderland since 1986. They have contributed to regeneration within the North East region. They have always had environmentally friendly policies and have supported local initiatives. Their latest contribution to Tyne and Wear (the local authority) was the installation of a wind farm in 2005 to provide a renewable energy resource, contributing to sustainability and reducing carbon dioxide emissions by 3,300 tonnes a year. Tyne and Wear has a renewable energy target and this wind farm meets 18 per cent of it.

Nissan UK have a policy to reuse, recycle and recover as much as they can in the design, production and dismantling of vehicles. They have achieved more than a 90 per cent recycling rate. In the design stage materials are selected for ease of recycling. Waste has been reduced as much as possible in manufacturing and when vehicles are dismantled all fluids are drained and recycled wherever possible, metals, tyres and batteries are removed and dealt with by specialist recycling companies. Parts of some vehicles are suitable to be shredded and reused. Improvements in recycled plastics have meant that Nissan has developed more than 50 different car parts from recycled plastics.

Nissan have demonstrated how manufacturing and dismantling processes can be environmentally friendly.

B

Cadbury and Nissan are two very different companies. They both contribute to the local and national economy and have policies which encourage sustainability.

Activity

Choose a company in your area and look at its contribution to local or national targets. It could be a manufacturer, retailer or from a service industry.

Some clothing companies do not care about ethical trading. Find out about this and discuss what you find out with your friends. Write a short newspaper report about it.

Information

The Kyoto Protocol of 1997 set targets to reduce carbon emissions by 12.5 per cent of 1990 levels by 2012.

The UK has set a target of a 60 per cent reduction of the 1990 levels by 2050.

In 2007 the Committee on Climate Change was established to monitor progress in achieving targets.

Research activity

The credit crunch and recession began in 2008. Find out the effect of this on car manufacturing in Britain.

Chapter summary

What you should know:

From this chapter your knowledge should now cover:

Short course

- ✔ the rights and responsibilities of employers and employees
- ✔ how health and safety law is applied in the workplace
- ✔ laws relating to consumer rights
- ✔ organisations involved with consumer affairs

Full course

- ✔ the rights and responsibilities of employers and employees
- ✔ how health and safety law is applied in the workplace
- ✔ laws relating to consumer rights
- ✔ organisations involved with consumer affairs
- ✔ what is meant by the local and national economy
- ✔ factors which influence community cohesion

Check your knowledge

You should be able to answer the following questions without looking back over the text. If you cannot answer all of the questions you need to learn the material more thoroughly. These types of questions will appear in the Unit 1 exam paper as Section A.

1. Define the terms 'right', 'responsibility', 'equal opportunity', and 'discrimination'.
2. List six points of information that should be in a contract of employment.
3. What is the HSE?
4. Identify three responsibilities of an employer in relation to health and safety.
5. Describe three rights of an employee in relation to health and safety.
6. What is the role of a Health and Safety representative?
7. Outline the function of the OFT.
8. Name two important Acts of Parliament relating to consumer law.
9. Explain the sectors of industry.
10. What do we mean by 'sustainability' – give an example.

Picture stimulus

Which sectors would you put these different industries in?

Why?

Further study

- When you go to your work experience placement you could ask if you could look at a standard contract of employment. If the details were completed would it give all the necessary information?
- Ask if you could look at a copy of their Health and Safety policy. What information should it contain?
- Find out about the Reporting of Injuries Diseases and Dangerous Occurrences Regulations (RIDDOR) 1995.
- What does this mean in the workplace?
- Who is responsible for making sure the regulations are met?
- Find out what the Control of Substances Hazardous to Health (COSHH) is and the implications for employers and employees.
- Who is responsible for enforcement?

Remember

Part of the work about rights and responsibilities is covered within chapter 9. You need to look at the relevant pages to complete your knowledge on discrimination and equal opportunities in the workplace, especially in regard to equal pay, age, ethnicity, religion, gender, and sexuality.

THEME 2 Being a citizen in the UK:

In this Theme you will learn about our parliamentary democracy, different types of voting systems, and diversity within society.

The four chapters are:

4 The role of parliament and government

5 Electoral systems

6 Understanding diversity

7 Effects on community life

4 The role of parliament and government

In this chapter you will learn how our parliamentary democracy functions by discovering how laws are made and the roles of political parties, the government and the opposition.

Key terms

parliament representation legislation cabinet opposition devolution referendum public services scrutiny executive legislature manifesto constitutional monarchy disposable income inflation interest rates anarchy dictatorship communism oligarchy

Concepts

Political literacy Government Parliament Devolution

A *Democracy*

B *Our constitutional Monarch*

5 Electoral systems

In this chapter you will learn how to register to be able to vote and how to vote. We will look at the different types of voting systems used within Britain. We will examine the possibility of making voting compulsory and reducing the voting age to 16.

Key terms

electoral process lobbying voting compulsory general election voter apathy fairness proportional representation involvement democratic

Concepts

Citizens and the electoral process

Democracy Lobbying

C *Lobbying*

6 Understanding diversity

In this chapter we will investigate the origins of diversity, religious and ethnic identities, both regionally and nationally. We will examine the importance of identity and tolerance.

Concepts

Perceptions of being British

Identity Discrimination

Inclusion Tolerance

Key terms

diversity religious ethnic respect discrimination inclusion tolerance prejudice stereotypes labelling barriers identity

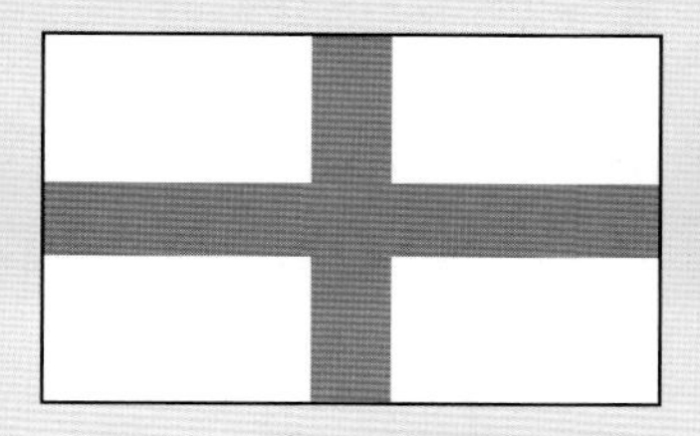

D *National identity*

7 Effects on community life

In this chapter we will take a closer look at how schools and communities can promote equal opportunities. We will examine how migration can affect communities and issues relating to a multicultural society and community cohesion.

Concepts

Multiculturalism

Equal opportunities

Community cohesion

Key terms

culture multiculturalism migration perspectives values integration pluralism host nation perspective community cohesion commission

E *Community cohesion*

4 Parliament and government

4.1 The role of parliament and government

What is parliament?

Parliament is housed in the Palace of Westminster in London. Parliament consists of the House of Commons and the House of Lords. These are two separate chambers (very large halls) within the palace. The seating in the Commons is green and in the Lords it is red. The Queen opens a new session of parliament every year in October at the State Opening of Parliament. This ceremony takes place in the House of Lords; the Members of Parliament walk across the lobby from the House of Commons into the House of Lords to listen to the Queen's speech. In this speech the Queen outlines the bills the government will bring before parliament in the coming session. The speech is written by the Prime Minister. This is the only time when the Queen, the Lords and the Members of Parliament are all together. The Monarch never goes into the House of Commons; it is a custom which goes back centuries.

A *Parliament*

Objectives

- To understand how parliament works.
- To learn how laws are made.
- To be able to explain the role of government, the cabinet, the opposition, and political parties.

Information

The role of parliament

The role of parliament is to represent the people of the country when new laws are being made, by debating the **bill** before parliament. Parliament debates issues of the day and scrutinises the work of government through the Select Committees and by constant questioning of ministers. Every government department has a select committee which will investigate its work.

Parliament is sometimes called the legislature – responsible for making the laws of the land.

The role of political parties

The role of political parties is to formulate policies which they present to the electorate in a **manifesto** at the general election. To select candidates to stand for election. The party campaigns for votes in local and national elections to try to win power and put their policies into practice.

The role of the cabinet

The cabinet is the most important committee within the government structure. The cabinet decides on the priorities for the nation. The cabinet meets in Downing Street every Tuesday morning except when parliament is in recess. There may be up to 22 paid members of cabinet. They are the Secretaries of State, the most senior appointment in the government.

The cabinet has a collective responsibility to parliament, and therefore all members support cabinet decisions.

Key terms

Bill: draft of a law.

Constitutional monarchy: a democracy where a monarch is the head of State but the government is responsible for running the country.

Manifesto: a list of policies that a political party would introduce if elected.

How parliament works

The House of Commons

The House of Commons is made up of 646 Members of Parliament, who are elected by the people of the country in a general election. The party that wins the most seats (has the most MPs) forms the government. The leader of the winning party is asked by the Queen to form a government. The leader becomes Prime Minister and appoints people to run the Departments of State – the Secretaries of State. Others may be appointed as junior ministers to work in the departments. The senior ministers have a place in the cabinet. The positions and the names of the departments may change with each new government.

The Prime Minister and the cabinet are often referred to as the Executive, because they are responsible for deciding on the priorities of the government, and responding to issues as they arise.

Debating

When debates take place the Speaker will sit in the Speaker's chair, the government sit on the Speaker's right and the opposition on the left. Ministers and shadow ministers sit on the front benches nearest to the large tables in the chamber. Other MPs belonging to these parties sit behind the front bench and are often called backbench MPs. Debates can take place on any topic, they usually involve issues of national and international importance.

A debate will begin by the Speaker asking an MP to address the House. All speeches are addressed to the Speaker. In the House MPs are called the Honorable Member for '*name of their constituency*'. Ministers are addressed by the name of their department. The house always debates a motion, for example, 'To consider that the Health and Safety Regulations ... be passed.' After discussion the Speaker will repeat the motion and call for a division (a vote). Each MP then walks through the 'Aye' or 'No' division lobby and the numbers for and against are recorded. The result is announced to the Speaker.

Committees

Most of the work is done in committees. A committee is made up of a number of MPs belonging to different political parties. Committees usually conduct their business in the mornings.

There are different types of committees. They are:

- General Committees
- Public Bill Committees
- Joint Committees
- Grand Committees
- Select Committees.

Find out what each type of committee does.

AQA *Examiner's tip*

Be able to explain the role of parliament, political parties, the government, the cabinet, and the opposition.

Know what parliament does.

Activities

1. Find a map of your region which shows the different parliamentary constituencies. Highlight the one you live in.
2. Which party has the most constituencies in your region?
3. Find out about your MP:
   Name?
   Party?
   Years as an MP?
   How can you contact them?
4. Participate in a role play of a parliamentary debate. The topic for debate should be a current national or international issue.

4.2 How parliament works

Information

The role of the government

The role of the government is to govern the country; they decide how the country will be managed. The government do this by making new laws, amending existing laws and removing old laws (repealing laws). They set the rate of all forms of taxation to ensure that there is enough money to provide for essential public services (health, education, defence, policing, etc.). The government pursue the policies they were elected on.

The role of the Opposition

The role of the Opposition is to form a shadow government, to debate issues of the day and oppose the government. By asking questions they continually hold the government to account for its decisions and actions. The constant questioning of policy and proposals ensures that every issue is thoroughly discussed.

The House of Lords

There are over 700 Lords. They are not elected and do not receive payment for their work, except expenses. Each member decides when they want to attend the House. The House of Lords is composed of people from different political parties, and some do not belong to any party. The House of Lords Act 1999 reformed the House; before this date the Lords were hereditary peers. There are four types of Lord – life peers, hereditary peers, Law Lords and Bishops. Now there are 92 hereditary peers, 26 clergy (Archbishops and Bishops) and about 500 Lords who have been appointed (life peers). The House of Lords debates and scrutinises Bills from the Commons, suggests amendments, debates issue, scrutinises European legislation and introduces new Bills.

Most of their work is done in committees. Many Lords are well-known experts in certain fields and contribute their knowledge and experience in committees to advise on, amend and scrutinise legislation.

The Appellate Committee is the Court of Appeal, the highest court in Britain. There are 12 very experienced judges who are appointed as Law Lords. They work full time for the House and do receive a salary. In 2009 when the Constitutional Reform Act 2005 takes effect, this function will cease and there will be a separate 'Supreme Court'. This means that the judicial functions will be separated from parliament and the government.

Information

Deciding on a bill

The Executive (Prime Minister and cabinet) decide on the priorities for making new laws. The minister and civil servants in that department begin to draft the bill. If major pieces of legislation are being considered a consultation paper known as a White Paper or Green Paper is published and a date set for the end of the consultation time. (See chapter 1 about consultation.) After consultation all opinions are considered and the details of the Bill are written.

How are Laws made?

The First Reading is when the bill is first presented to the House – there is no discussion.

At the Second Reading there is a general debate. Under normal circumstances there is no time limit for the length of debate at this stage. It is usually the minister responsible for the Bill that the Speaker asks to open the debate, then the Shadow spokesperson from the opposition responds, and any backbenchers wanting to contribute have their turn to represent the views of their constituents (the people who elected them). If the proposals in the bill are strongly opposed then the Speaker may call for a division at the end of the debate.

The committee stage of the bill is where the Public Bill Committee (normally 18–25 members) goes through each part or clause of the bill in very fine detail. They can recommend changes.

The report stage is where changes made by the committee are looked at carefully. New clauses may be introduced at this stage. All MPs can discuss the changes.

The third reading is the final debate in the House often held immediately after the report stage. The bill then goes to the House of Lords.

The House of Lords follow much the same procedure as the Commons. However some things are different, such as that the committee stage involves debate by the whole House so any Lord can contribute.

If there are no changes to the bill then it passes onto the next stage. If the Lords want amendments the bill goes back to the Commons. Here the changes may be accepted or rejected and the bill goes back to the Lords. Generally at this stage it is accepted. If not there are procedures which assert the authority of the elected House of Commons who will achieve success in the end. The Lords can delay legislation they cannot stop a bill.

The Royal Assent is the final stage. The Queen gives her assent (agreement) and the bill becomes law.

The law is then implemented. This can be immediately or a date may be fixed when the new law will come into force.

Activities

1. Draw a flow chart to show the stages of how a bill becomes law.
2. Choose a bill now at the second reading. During your course track what happens to the bill and how long it takes to become law.
3. Make a list of all current Cabinet members – name and position held.
4. Identify the different types of bill.
5. Find out more about the reform of the House of Lords. Discuss different opinions about whether it should become an elected chamber.

AQA Examiner's tip

- Know the stages of how a bill becomes law.
- Know about the House of Lords Reform, the types of Lords and the work it does.

A *The House of Commons*

B *The House of Lords*

4.3 Devolution

Devolution

This is when the central government of Britain gave some powers to the other national bodies in Wales, Scotland and Northern Ireland. Acts of Parliament were necessary to do this; there is a separate Act for each country. The result was the formation of the National Assembly for Wales, the Northern Ireland Assembly and the Scottish Parliament. There are no devolved powers for England except for the London Assembly and the Greater London Authority (see chapter 2).

Power was devolved in 1999 with the first elections and meetings of the new bodies. Elections now take place every four years.

The powers that were devolved were not the same for all three bodies. The method of electing representatives is different too. An explanation of voting systems can be found in the next chapter.

Objectives

To learn about the recent changes to the operation of democracy in Britain.

Key terms

Referendum: a vote on a single issue.

National Assembly for Wales

In 1979 there was a **referendum** in Wales about setting up a national assembly; the result was a very decisive 'No'. The referendum in 1997 gave a small majority in favour, the result a 'Yes'. The National Assembly for Wales was established by the Government of Wales Act 1998. There are 60 Assembly Members (AMs). The first elections, using the additional member system, took place in May 1999. The Assembly meets at the Senedd in Cardiff. The Government of Wales Act 2006 has replaced the 1998 Act. The new Act set up a division between the law making, legislative, National Assembly and the Welsh Assembly Government which is the Executive. This gives powers to make laws known as 'Measures' in a number of areas.

A *The Senedd in Cardiff*

The Scottish Parliament

In 1997 the electorate voted in favour of a Scottish Parliament. The Scotland Act 1998 established the Scottish Parliament. There are 129 Members of the Scottish Parliament (SMPs). They are elected by the additional member system. The first elections were held in May 1999. The Scottish Parliament meets at Holyrood in Edinburgh. This Parliament has different powers. It is able to set the level of income tax at +/– 3 per cent of that in England. It has powers over education, health services, housing, planning, economic development, police and fire services, most aspects of transport, social services, most criminal and civil law. Currently the Scottish National Party (SNP) are in power and they want Scotland to be a completely independent country.

B *The Scottish Parliament in Edinburgh*

Northern Ireland Assembly

This Assembly is different again from the other two devolved powers.

The Belfast agreement of 1998 established this Assembly. The agreement was signed after much consultation between all the political parties in Northern Ireland and the governments of Ireland and Britain. The Northern Ireland Act 1998 is the statute.

The Assembly was suspended in October 2002, and power reverted back to Westminster. The Northern Ireland Assembly was reinstated in May 2007. The Assembly meets at Stormont in Belfast. There are 108 Members of the Legislative Assembly (MLAs). They are elected by the single transferable vote system. The devolved powers include health, education, employment, social services, leisure and culture.

C *Stormont Castle, home of the Northern Ireland Assembly*

In Cornwall there is a campaign by the party Mebyon Kernow and the Liberal Democrats who aim to set up a Cornish Assembly. There are other groups who support this aim. A petition with 50,000 signatures was delivered to Downing Street in December 2007.

Discussion activity

1 What about England?

Let's look at the opportunities for the electorate to participate in the democratic process and the changes **devolution** has made, that is, who can we vote for?

In all four countries citizens can vote for Councillors in their local authority, Members of Parliament in Westminster, and Members of the European Parliament in Brussels (MEP).

Citizens in Wales, Scotland and Northern Ireland also have another tier of government in their own assembly or parliament.

England is the only country of the United Kingdom that does not have its own devolved representative body where English people can make their own decisions.

Members of Parliament in Westminster from constituencies in Wales, Scotland and Northern Ireland vote on matters that affect England only. This has caused difficulties in Westminster when controversial bills are put to the vote. This has become known as the West Lothian question because it was the MP for West Lothian, Tam Dalyell, who raised a very similar question a long time ago.

What do you think?

a Should England have an English Parliament?

b What would be the arguments for and against it?

Discuss this within a small group, and then as a whole class group.

Key terms

Devolution: this is the transfer of some powers from the Government to the Welsh Assembly, the Northern Ireland Assembly and the Scottish Parliament.

AQA Examiner's tip

Be able to explain devolution, the names of the three devolved powers and what the elected members are known as, how they are elected and some differences between them.

4.4 The effect of government decisions on citizens

Think back to what you have learned so far about the structure of national and local government in Britain. There is constant moving of information up and down the lines of communication.

A diagram may help to clarify this. This is the structure in England; for Wales, Scotland and Northern Ireland the process is slightly different because of the devolved powers.

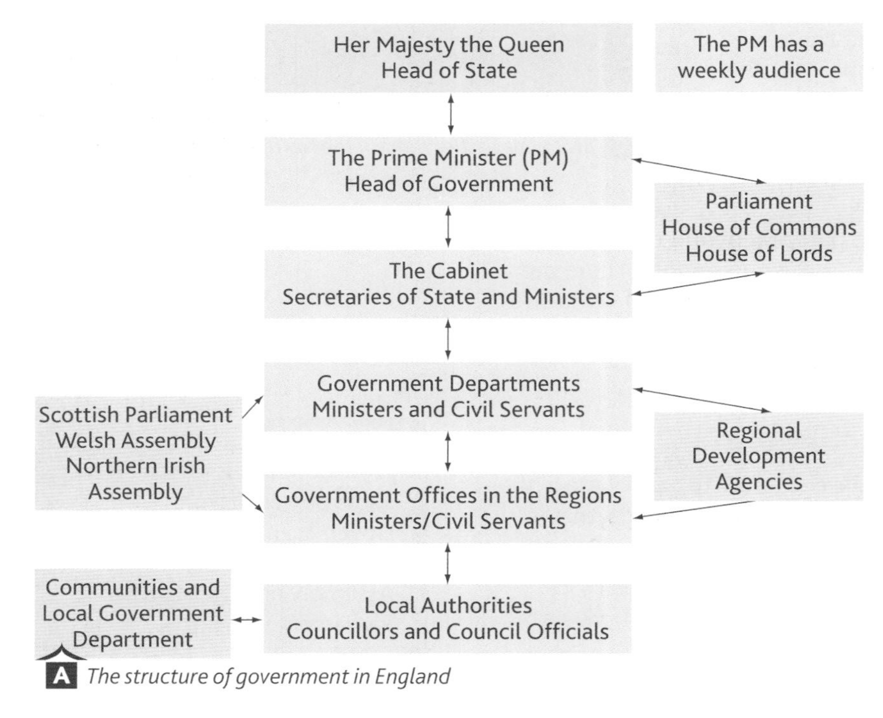

A *The structure of government in England*

How does all this affect the everyday lives of citizens? Our local community and the facilities and services it provides for us together with the amount of money we have to spend are the major influences on our wellbeing.

The local authority has the day-to-day control over the facilities and services within communities. Local authorities are funded from three sources:

- grants from central government
- the council tax
- the business rate.

The amount of the government grant changes annually. It is based on a standard calculation applied to every authority. This is a direct influence of government on local situations. The council sets the level of council tax annually depending on what they decided was the priority for spending and the amount of the government grant. The business rate (or national non-domestic rate) is the tax charged to business, based on their business premises.

Objectives

To understand and learn how government decisions affect people in their everyday life.

Information

Interest rates

These affect the money supply. The Bank of England sets a base rate, which is the lowest rate of interest charged on loans. All other banks, building societies and loan companies charge above this rate, so they can make a profit. When the base rate is increased, cost of mortgages, credit cards, and loans all rise, leaving us with less money to spend.

Inflation

Inflation is a measure of the cost of goods. It is a comparison done annually and quarterly.

In 2007 and 2008 the price of a barrel of oil increased dramatically, causing a higher rate of inflation than had been anticipated. During the same time the price of basic foods increased on world markets. There is little the government can do about this, but it has affected the rate of inflation, pushing up prices on most of the foods we buy.

Key terms

Inflation: a measure of the amount of increase in prices.

The national economy affects us all; when it is going well and expanding, there are more jobs available, interest rates and income tax are moderate, and inflation is low, so we all feel better because we generally have more **disposable income**. However when the economy slows down or ceases to expand or even contracts (a recession) the reverse happens, fewer jobs, sometimes higher interest rates and higher inflation – people do not have as much money and the 'feel good' factor is reduced.

Inflation is another factor which determines how much money we have. One way of trying to control inflation is through changes to the base rate of interest. The Bank of England review the base rate once a month.

There are two forms of direct tax; these are amounts of money taken directly from earnings.

One is income tax (used to pay for public services and benefits), the other is National Health Insurance which is used to pay for the National Health Service (NHS). Both of these taxes are variable and may be changed annually in the Budget, a speech given by the Chancellor of the Exchequer outlining the government's financial plans for the coming year. The higher the rate of income tax the less disposable income we have.

As we have seen before, the government sets out policies and they are delivered at a local level.

Over the last 15 to 20 years there have been many changes in the type and level of public services. Public services are things such as education, health (hospitals, doctors, dentists), policing, and transport. How these services are organised and how much funding (money) they receive is a matter of government policy; how the services are delivered is left to the regional and local authorities. Opinion is divided on how beneficial some of the changes have been.

B *What is the difference between a credit card and a debit card?*

Information

Value Added Tax (VAT)

This is charged on all goods and services except for most items of food, children's clothing, books, newspapers and magazines. All European Union (EU) countries charge VAT. The rate is 17.5 per cent, temporarily 15 per cent in 2009, and a reduced rate of 5 per cent is applied to domestic fuel.

Key terms

Disposable income: money we have left to spend when all direct taxes have been taken from earnings.

Activity

The National Institute for Clinical Excellence (NICE) is frequently in the news for its recommendations on the use about the cost-effectiveness of new drugs within the NHS.

In some areas of the country some drugs will be prescribed and in others they will not. This has led to the term 'a post code lottery'. This directly affects people when they are ill and less able to cope with finding solutions to such problems.

Find out more about NICE in newspaper articles and discuss the reports in your group.

4.5 Forms of government

Case study

The Republic of Cuba

- Cuba is the largest island in the Caribbean. It lies about 90 miles south of Florida USA.
- Language spoken: Spanish. Currency: Cuban peso. Population: 11.3 million.
- Capital city: Habana (Havana). First claimed for Spain by Columbus in 1492.
- Major exports: sugar, tobacco and nickel.
- Major trading partners: exports to Netherlands, Canada, China and Spain. Imports from Venezuela, China, Spain, Germany, Canada and Italy. Tourism now plays an important part in the economy.
- Type of government: Communist since 1965.
- President: Raul Castro since February 2008.
- Previous President: Fidel Castro 1959–2008 (brother of Raul).

A *The Cuban flag*

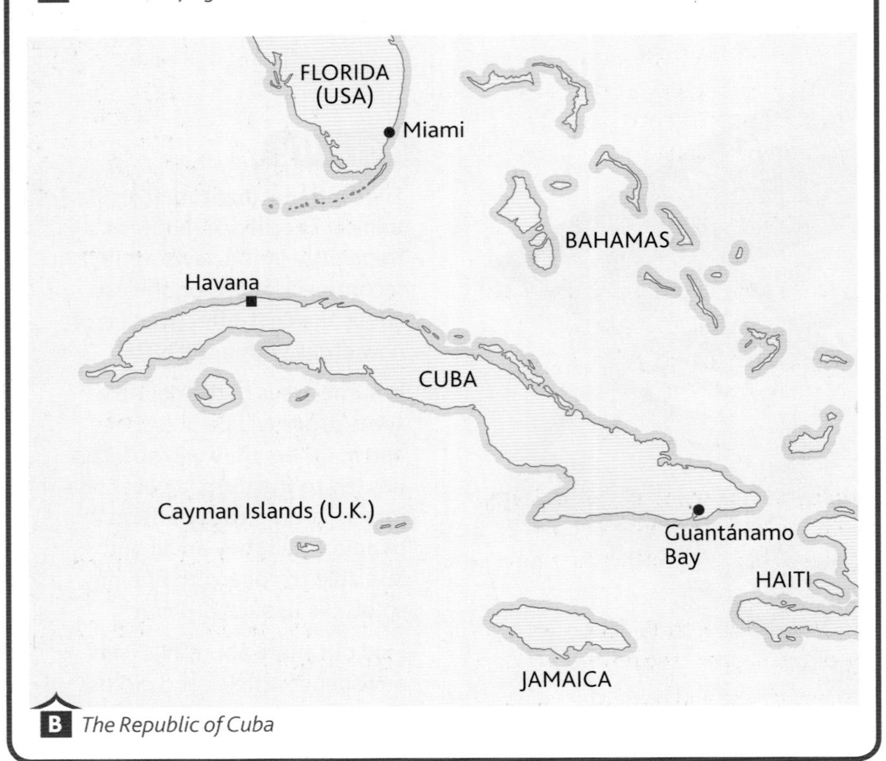

B *The Republic of Cuba*

Objectives

To discover how a non-democratic form of government works.

Key terms

The types of government may be defined by looking at who rules that country, for example:

Anarchy: a state of lawlessness and disorder where there is no government and no laws.

Democracy: rule by the majority of the people.

Oligarchy: rule by a small group of people.

Dictatorship: ruled by one leader.

Totalitarianism: the State rules every aspect of life, the economy, media, values in society.

Communism: State controls the economy, media, police, ownership of property and businesses.

History

Cuba was a Spanish colony for centuries, gaining independence in 1898. The USA took over for four years until 1902 when they left, but continued to lease Guantanamo Bay as a naval base.

There followed a number of violent uprisings, with notable Soviet influences. Eventually Fulgenico Batista was ousted from power by an all-out rebellion led by Fidel Castro. The rebels entered Havana in January and Castro became Prime Minister in February 1959.

The new government took over all public services, took over property and businesses, placed many controls on private businesses, and shut down the gambling industry. Many American nationals left because their businesses had been nationalised by the new government. There were many trials and executions of alleged Batista supporters. Not all Cubans supported Castro and many left for the USA.

Castro made an alliance with Soviet Russia, and received huge amounts of aid. Castro involved Cuba in developing countries; he frequently offered them military help. Castro's Cuba became a heavily dominated military State; this has been very much reduced since the fall of the Soviets in 1991.

In 1963 President Kennedy (USA) imposed diplomatic and trade sanctions on Cuba. Cuba developed more links with the Soviets and became a Communist State in 1965.

Communist Cuba

Cuba's geographical position, so close to the USA, was extremely important to the Soviets during the 'Cold War' years, so they supported Castro with huge aid programmes. The collapse of the Soviet Union in 1991 was disastrous for Cuba; the economy went into decline as exports to the Soviet Union at inflated prices ceased and so did the aid programme. There was a sharp decline in living standards, most things were rationed. Trade has developed with different trading partners since and things have gradually improved.

The Communist Party of Cuba is the only political party allowed; opposition parties are illegal. Citizens are not allowed to criticise the government; those who have, at least lost their jobs, many have been imprisoned. The number of political prisoners is not known.

There have been complaints of human rights abuse, torture, and unjust imprisonment.

When elections take place there is one candidate from the Cuban Communist Party.

The press lost its freedom of expression in 1959; there are no independent newspapers in Cuba.

Employment

The economy is controlled by the State, production is organised by the State, and the State employs the workers. Prices are set by the government and there is rationing. Almost all workers belong to the trade union, which is Communist controlled.

The State runs all education, which is compulsory from 5 to 15. There are opportunities for higher education, as long as you support the government.

The state runs a good health service, with many clinics and hospitals and has especially good care for children.

Information

Cuban missile crisis 1962

Castro made an alliance with Soviet Russia. This led to the Cuban missile crisis of 1962 when the world stood on the brink of nuclear war between USA and Soviet Russia. (Kennedy against Khrushchev.) The Soviets believed the presence of USA missiles in Turkey was a nuclear threat to them, so placed their missiles in Cuba. The USA blockaded Cuba and the real crisis began. Soviet ships carrying more missiles for Cuba stopped just short of the blockade. Kennedy agreed to take missiles out of Turkey and not to invade Cuba.

C *President Fidel Castro*

Activity

There are different forms of government throughout the world. Many of these are not democratic.

Look at the key words and terms and make a list of countries where these forms of government exist.

Keep a note in your file, it may come in useful.

Chapter summary

What you should know:

From this chapter your knowledge should now cover:

Short course

- ✔ the role of government, the cabinet, the Opposition, parliament, and political parties
- ✔ how parliament works
- ✔ how laws are made

Full course

- ✔ the role of government, the cabinet, the Opposition, parliament, and political parties
- ✔ how parliament works
- ✔ how laws are made
- ✔ devolution – the Assemblies in Northern Ireland and Wales and the Scottish Parliament
- ✔ how citizens' lives are affected by government decisions
- ✔ different forms of government – a look at a Communist State

Check your knowledge

You should be able to answer the following questions without looking back over the text. If you cannot answer all of the questions you need to learn the material more thoroughly. These types of questions will appear in the Unit 1 exam paper as Section A.

1. What is the main role of the government?
2. What is the cabinet?
3. Name the two Houses in parliament.
4. Where does parliament meet?
5. Who is in charge of debates in the House of Commons?
6. What is the main aim of political parties?
7. Where does the Welsh Assembly meet?
8. How many Members of Parliament are there?
9. Describe a Bill.
10. What is the final stage of a Bill?

Further study

Divide the class into small groups of three or four. Each group is to choose a political party and find out what that party's policy is on education, the health service, and the European Union. As a whole class share and discuss the information you have found, noting the similarities and differences.

Visit the website **www.parliament.uk** and find out how many different political parties there are in the House of Commons and the House of Lords. How many MPs and Lords belong to the different parties?

- Draw a diagram to show the layout of the House of Commons and where the government and opposition sit.
- Try to find out why the seats are green in the House of Commons.

Do you know about the UK Youth Parliament and what it does?

Interested?

- Find out more: **www.ukyouthparliament.org.uk**
- It is worth a look – information – discussions – online petitions …

> ### About UK Youth Parliament
>
> *The UK Youth Parliament (UKYP) enables young people to use their energy and passion to change the world for the better. Run by young people for young people, UKYP gives the young people of the UK, between the age of 11 and 18, a voice, which is heard and listened to by local and national government, providers of services for young people and other agencies who have an interest in the views and needs of young people.*

A

Debatable

B

Manifesto

C

5 Electoral systems

5.1 The different electoral systems

Proportional representation has been discussed for many years in politics. Before the Liberal Democrat party was formed, the Liberals were advocating proportional representation in their manifestos.

In the **general election** of 1997 the Labour Party manifesto said that a referendum would be held on how the House of Commons was elected. Has this happened? The Labour Party won that election with a landslide majority. They set up the Jenkins Commission to look at a proportional representation system for Britain. The report was published in 1998; it recommended a mixture of two systems called the AV plus the Alternative Vote system with a top up. Not a lot has happened since, except for the systems used to elect the devolved powers and Members of the European Parliament (MEP).

The different proportional representation (PR) systems in use now are:

- First Past The Post (FPTP)
- Single Transferable Vote (STV)
- Additional Member System (AMS)
- Supplementary Vote (SV)
- Closed Party List System (CPL).

First Past The Post

This is the system used in general elections and in many council elections in England and Wales. It works by a simple majority: the one that wins the most votes is elected. In a general election each constituency elects one Member of Parliament. The party who has the most number of MPs is the majority party; they win the election and form the government. Every elector has one vote.

Single Transferable Vote

This system is used for all elections in Northern Ireland except for a general election. It is also used in Scotland for local elections. Electors put their preferences on the ballot paper by putting '1' next to their first choice '2' next to their second choice etc. The number of votes a candidate would need in order to be elected is calculated from the total number of people on the electoral register. If a candidate wins more votes than required to be elected these extra votes are transferred to the next most popular candidate and so on.

Objectives

To learn about the different voting systems used in Britain.

Key terms

Proportional representation: a system of electing people that reflects the wishes of the voters.

General election: an election where the country elects a new government.

1	JONES Jane Mary Jones 10 Acacia Avenue Nowhere Town, NO10 1AB Conservative and Unionist Party	
2	SMITH Bob Smith 15 Hill View Nowhere Town, NO11 2CD Labour Party	
3	WILLIAMS James Anthony Williams 32 High Street Nowhere Town, NO12 1EF Liberal Democrats	X

A *First Past The Post ballot*

1	JONES Jane Mary Jones 10 Acacia Avenue Nowhere Town, NO10 1AB Conservative and Unionist Party	2
2	SMITH Bob Smith 15 Hill View Nowhere Town, NO11 2CD Labour Party	3
3	WILLIAMS James Anthony Williams 32 High Street Nowhere Town, NO12 1EF Liberal Democrats	1

B *Single Transferable Vote ballot*

Additional Member System

This system is used for the Scottish Parliament and the Welsh Assembly. Each elector has two votes – one for a person, the other for a party. Half the members are elected by a first past the post system and the others by the number of votes cast for each party.

Supplementary Vote

This system is used to elect the Mayor of London. Each elector has two votes. There are two columns on the ballot paper. The voter has one vote for each column or just marks their favourite candidate in the first column. All the first choices are added up and if there is a candidate with a majority of votes then that candidate is elected. If there is not a winner the top two candidates remain, all the others are eliminated. In the second round the second preference votes of the candidates eliminated are counted. If there are votes for the two remaining candidates, these are added to the first round totals. The candidate who now has the most votes wins.

		First choice	Second choice
1	JONES Jane Mary Jones 10 Acacia Avenue Nowhere Town, NO10 1AB Conservative and Unionist Party	X	
2	SMITH Bob Smith 15 Hill View Nowhere Town, NO11 2CD Labour Party		X
3	WILLIAMS James Anthony Williams 32 High Street Nowhere Town, NO12 1EF Liberal Democrats		

D *Supplementary Vote ballot*

Closed Party List System

This system is used to elect Members of the European Parliament (MEP) except in Northern Ireland. In this system votes are cast for parties rather than people, so there is less of a connection between the electorate and their representative. Each elector has one vote. Each party receives the number of seats within the constituency according to the proportion of votes cast in their favour. Each party lists their candidates in order of preference.

Activity

So what's wrong with the First Past The Post? Why do we need proportional representation?

To find out, try this:

You have to elect two representatives to the school council. There are four candidates.

Hold elections by using:

- the first past the post
- the single transferable vote
- the supplementary vote.

Discuss the results and which system was the easiest to use and count.

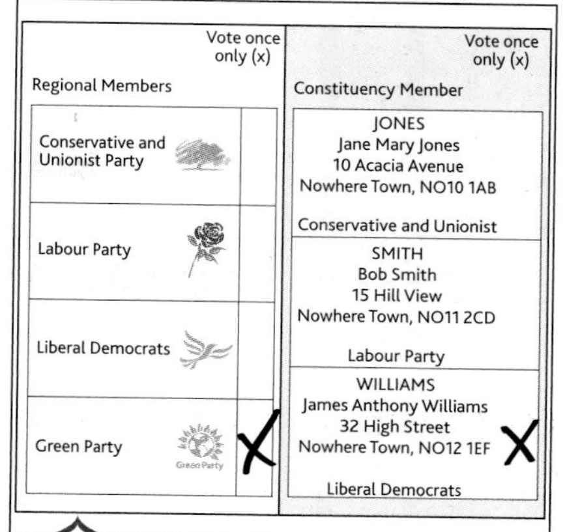

Regional Members	Vote once only (x)
Conservative and Unionist Party	
Labour Party	
Liberal Democrats	
Green Party	X

Constituency Member	Vote once only (x)
JONES Jane Mary Jones 10 Acacia Avenue Nowhere Town, NO10 1AB Conservative and Unionist	
SMITH Bob Smith 15 Hill View Nowhere Town, NO11 2CD Labour Party	
WILLIAMS James Anthony Williams 32 High Street Nowhere Town, NO12 1EF Liberal Democrats	X

C *Additional Member System ballot*

AQA Examiner's tip

Know what each system is and where it is used.

Form an opinion on what you think is the best and be able to explain why.

1	Conservative and Unionist Party	
2	Labour Party	X
3	Liberal Democrats	
4	Green Party	

E *Closed Party List System ballot*

Information

In August 2008 the Electoral Commission published a report entitled 'Electoral Administration in the UK'.

It stated that 'Significant changes are needed now.' They made six different recommendations.

The Joseph Rowntree Foundation have done research into proportional representation and report that the closed list system, the single transferable vote and the additional member system would give fairer results.

5.2 The voting age and compulsory voting

Case study

A UK Youth Parliament report finds that over half of young people do not want the voting age lowered to 16

4 April 2008

In 2007–2008, the UK Youth Parliament surveyed 9,200 young people across the UK to ask them, 'Are you engaged?' We wanted to know how young people felt about lowering the voting age. However, what we found was something very different, bringing into question the value of, and opportunity for, political engagement by young people in the UK.

Of 9,200 young people surveyed across the UK:

- over a third feel that politics doesn't affect them;
- sixty per cent haven't or aren't sure whether they've been taught about government and politics in school;
- seventy per cent of all young people feel that their local council does not value the opinions of young people;
- over half of 16–18 year olds do not believe the voting age should be lowered to 16.

www.ukyouthparliament.org.uk

Objectives

To investigate the opinions on lowering the voting age to 16.

To discover arguments for and against compulsory voting in Britain.

Information

The Liberal Democrats, the Green Party, Plaid Cymru (Welsh National Party) and the Scottish National Party (SNP) are all part of the Votes at 16 coalition.

The UK Youth Parliament and other youth groups are campaigning for the vote at 16. The Electoral Reform Society has produced reports on lowering the voting age.

Consideration was given to lowering the voting age in the Green paper the 'Governance of Britain' 2006.

13% of 18–24 year olds voted in the last general election.

Lowering the voting age to 16

Everyone has an opinion about this, but is it a well-informed opinion, have they really considered what it's all about?

Some of the points for this are that young people between 16 and 18 are allowed to marry with parental consent and to bring up children. They may join the armed forces, with consent. Adult fares are charged on public transport and in many other areas at 16+ you have to pay adult charges, yet you are not considered to be an adult until the age of 18. At 16 you may have a full time job and are therefore paying taxes and contributing to the economy, but do not have a voice in how your taxes are spent. Citizenship studies is part of the school curriculum and teenagers do have an understanding of our democratic system and lowering the voting age would encourage young people to participate in politics and engage the young in participating in society.

Look at the opposing opinions and reasons. Many 16–18 year olds do not want to vote and are not old enough or mature enough to consider all the options that political parties place before them in elections. They may not make informed decisions, rather just voting as their friends and parents do, without considering the alternatives. To counter this you could say that the same argument applies to a number of adults who do not make informed decisions. If we look at voting statistics the age range least likely to vote in elections is the 18–24 year olds, followed by the 25–34 year olds, so statistically there is likely to be little response if the 16–18 group were to be given the vote and it is likely to reduce the overall **turnout**

Key terms

Turnout: this is a percentage figure. It means the number of people who actually cast a vote as a percentage of all those on the electoral register.

Should voting be compulsory?

This is a topic that returns at general elections. As usual there are various shades of opinion and a number of relevant facts.

Over the last 10 to 15 years there has been a decline in participation in the democratic process. The turnout in the last two general elections were 59 per cent in 2001 and 61 per cent in 2005, the lowest figures since the end of World War I. In countries where voting is compulsory the turnout is regularly about 90 per cent.

At present there are 32 countries that operate some form of compulsory voting. The penalties for not voting are varied, they range from fines to **disenfranchisement** to prison (there are no known cases of imprisonment). In some countries there is no real enforcement at all.

By going to a polling station and recording a vote a person could actually spoil their ballot paper and not vote for anyone because the ballot is secret.

The points in favour are that compulsory voting would increase the turnout and thereby increase representation giving a more accurate account of the electorate's wishes. The winning party may actually be elected by a true majority of the people. It is everyone's duty (responsibility) to vote and this would ensure that people did take part, and may engage more of the electorate in becoming involved in their communities.

Against compulsory voting is the fact that it removes a person's choice and is an infringement of the right to make that choice. Some people have no interest and would not make an informed decision. There are some people who just do not want to vote or take part in any political process.

The Electoral Commission believe that a national discussion on compulsory voting would be useful. They are conducting some comparative research in countries where voting is compulsory.

A

AQA Examiner's tip

The voting age and compulsory voting are two topics which are likely exam questions where you may be asked to present a case for or against or argue the case and come to an informed decision.

Key terms

Disenfranchisement: removing a person's right to vote.

Activities

1. Find out more about who is in favour of reducing the voting age.
2. Make a list of organizations who are for and against lowering the age to 16.
3. Form your own opinions about the voting age and be able to justify them. Discuss the issue as a whole class group – you could have a formal debate – 'This house considers that the voting age should be lowered to 16.'
4. Find out which countries use compulsory voting.
5. Which side are you on? Would you like to see compulsory voting or not? Why?
6. You could do a simple survey to see what people think. Choose a varied age range of respondents, collate the results of the whole group to get a wide range of opinion.

links

Useful websites:

www.electoralcommission.org.uk

www.electoral-reform.org.uk

www.ukyouthparliament.org.uk

5.3 Participation and voter apathy

Participation

We have looked at taking part in the democratic process in chapter 2 by casting a vote in local and national elections. There are other ways of taking part in our democracy by communicating with our elected representatives; this can be done by:

- writing a letter or sending an email to a Councillor or MP
- visiting them in person at one of their local surgeries (dates, times and places are published in the local press)
- **lobbying** an MP.

Other methods of participation are:

- joining a political party
- going to meetings and campaigning at election time
- signing petitions
- joining in with e-petitions
- joining a pressure group.

Voter apathy

Over the last 15 years more people have decided not to exercise their right to vote in elections. This is seen in the turnout statistics for local and general elections (**voter apathy**). It means that progressively fewer people are actively involved in electing our representatives.

A lack of interest has arisen for a number of reasons:

- people do not think their vote counts so do not bother to vote
- people have lost their trust in politicians
- people think that politicians are remote and do not listen to voters' opinions
- people do not think there is a great deal of difference between the parties – so it doesn't matter anyway
- confidence in the system has declined, policies not being implemented
- people are dissatisfied with policies
- people perceive that the policies of the main parties are not very different
- people are not as committed to one party.

The effect of fewer people taking part is that elected representatives do not reflect the majority opinions because they are elected by a minority of the electorate. There is a reduced sense of responsibility in the civic duty to cast a vote and people become disillusioned with the system.

Objectives

To review how citizens can participate in democracy.

To examine voter apathy and what is being done to counteract it.

links

- Look back to chapter 2 about taking part in the democratic process.
- Look back to chapter 1 about methods of campaigning.

Key terms

Lobbying: person or group of people meeting and trying to persuade a politician to take up their cause.

Voter apathy: a significant number of the electorate deciding not to vote.

Information

Lobbying – the term originates from lobbyists trying to influence politicians by meeting them in the lobby of Parliament. This is still done. Professional lobbyists can be employed by groups/organisations to influence MPs or Lords. Lobbying can take different forms such as sending detailed information, making a presentation – advocacy, and sometimes mass lobbying.

Solutions?

All political parties are concerned about voter apathy. There have been several strategies discussed to engage more people, and especially younger people, in the democratic process. The government published a white paper in July 2007 entitled 'The Governance of Britain'. It is a lengthy document but sets out ideas for consultation which may result in legislation.

Some of the suggestions for counteracting voter apathy include:

a Make voting more convenient – change the day. A Thursday has been the day when elections have taken place since 1945. Many European countries, however, hold elections at weekends, when people may have more time and inclination to vote.

b Use electronic voting via the internet and mobile phones, even digital television. There would have to be very special controls so that there could be no chance of rigging the results. Some research shows that this would be popular with the 18–24 age group, who are least likely to vote.
Increase postal voting – this has been piloted in some areas and the results were not very good as vote rigging was identified and there have been some successful prosecutions for abuse of the system.

c Consider a form of proportional representation.

d Select more women candidates so that there are more women MPs.

e Increase the number of MPs from ethnic groups.

f Political parties are making far more effort to engage young people in politics – you can join a party at 16.
As we near the next general election there may be more national debate, more interest and an increased turnout, perhaps even a consensus reached about changes to our democratic system.

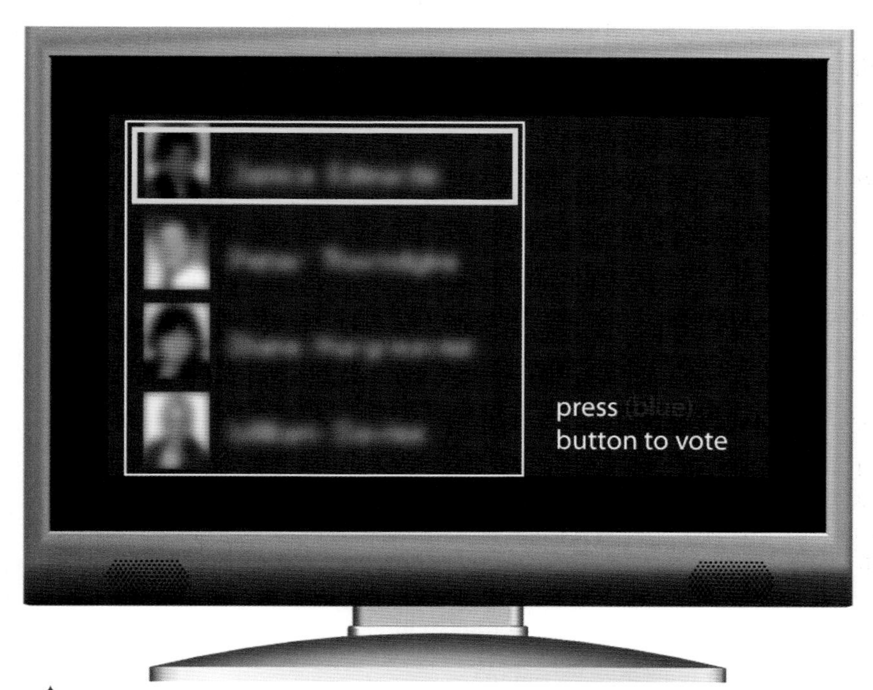

A

AQA Examiner's tip

These topics are possible questions where you will be asked to demonstrate your knowledge and give an opinion.

Activities

1 During your citizenship course watch out for any changes to voting systems and changes to how parliament works.

2 Discuss voter apathy and reach your own informed opinion on how it could be counteracted.

3 Write a newspaper article to voice your opinion on voter apathy.

4 How could the 18–24 year old group be encouraged to vote. Write about your ideas and then participate in a discussion.

5 Carry out a simple survey to find out how many 16 year olds in your school would vote if they could.

Chapter summary

What you should know:

From this chapter your knowledge should now cover:

Short course

- ✔ the types of voting systems used in Britain
- ✔ in which areas and which elections the different systems are used
- ✔ compulsory voting
- ✔ lowering of the voting age to 16

Full course

- ✔ the types of voting systems used in Britain
- ✔ in which areas and which elections the different systems are used
- ✔ compulsory voting
- ✔ lowering of the voting age to 16
- ✔ ways of participating in our democracy
- ✔ voter apathy

Check your knowledge

You should be able to answer the following questions without looking back over the text. If you cannot answer all of the questions you need to learn the material more thoroughly.

1. What is proportional representation?
2. List three methods of proportional representation used in Britain.
3. Which system is used to elect the Welsh Assembly and the Scottish Parliament?
4. Which system is used in Northern Ireland?
5. How old do you have to be to vote?
6. Name two organisations in favour of reducing the voting age.
7. Define the term 'turnout'.
8. List three countries where voting is compulsory.
9. What was the Jenkins Commission?
10. What is a general election?

Further study

Find out:

- how a person can register to vote
- about your local Register of Electors
- how you cast a vote at a polling station
- what a Returning Officer does.

- Write a letter to your MP about compulsory voting or proportional representation.
- Write a convincing newspaper article about lowering the voting age to 16.
- Design a poster for reducing the voting age.

Confused?

- Why do we need all these voting systems?
- Why can't we use one fair system?
- Should there be a referendum to choose one system once and for all?

Let's take a look at the results for the general election of 2005. The first past the post system was used.

This exercise shows you how you can use statistics in different ways.

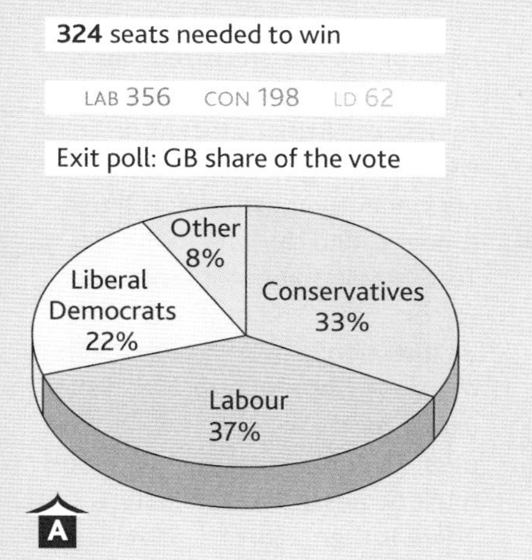

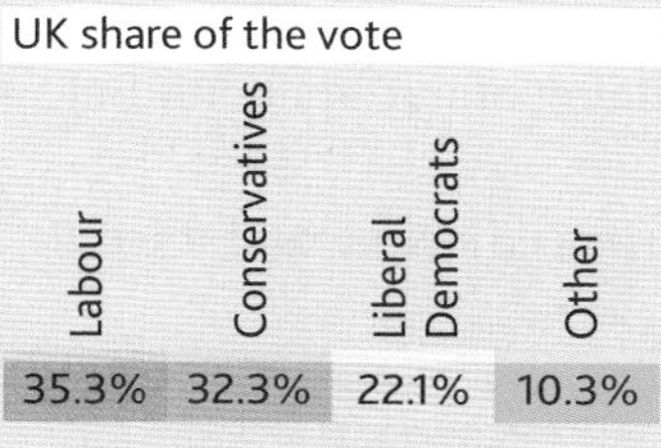

UK scoreboard

Party	Seats	+	–	Net
LAB	**356**	0	47	–47
CON	**198**	36	3	+33
LD	**62**	16	5	+11

Looking at the chart you can see that:

- The Labour Party won 356 seats with 35 per cent of the vote.
- The Conservative Party won 198 seats with 32 per cent of the vote.
- The Liberal Democrats won 62 seats with 22 per cent of the vote.
- Other parties won 30 seats with 10 per cent of the vote.

Do some simple maths:

- How accurate was the exit poll?
- Add up the number of seats won by all the other parties excluding Labour.
- Add up the percentage of votes cast for all parties excluding Labour.
- Therefore you know the percentage of people who did not vote for the Labour Party in the 2005 general election.
- What conclusions can you draw from this?
- Discuss the results as a whole class or in small groups.

6 Understanding diversity

6.1 Identity and diversity

The origins of **immigration** to Britain began with invaders as far back as the Romans, and then, at various intervals, the Angles and Saxons, the Vikings and the Normans, who were the last invaders. In the time since then a variety of Europeans have settled here, all adding to our culture and heritage. During the years of the slave trade some Africans settled around the major sea ports.

The highest levels of immigration came in the 1950s. After World War II there was a shortage of people to fill all the post-war jobs and rebuild the country. Many Polish people came and some Italians, but there were still shortages in the workforce. Jobs were advertised in the Commonwealth countries and there was mass immigration from the West Indies and India. This was the beginning of our multicultural society.

Immigration on this scale had not been experienced before and it led to many problems.

Racial **prejudice** was rife; racism and racial violence and riots occurred because the white population did not understand the black community. There were Acts of Parliament which placed conditions on entry to Britain and the number immigrating slowed. More Acts were passed; this time it was the Race Relations Act, and in 1976 the Commission for Racial Equality was established to combat racial discrimination.

Gradually the communities integrated and there was less tension as people accepted each other and began to appreciate and understand other cultures. This was achieved through a building up of mutual respect from working together and building normal social contacts, but, it took time.

The first non-white MPs were elected in 1987; there are now 12, but for equal representation according to the percentage of the population the number should be around 55.

The immigration problems today are very different. During the last 10 years especially there has been an influx of **asylum seekers** that has increased immigration figures; in 2000 there were 125,000 people allowed to settle in Britain. There has been much publicity about the numbers of illegal **immigrants** getting into the country and there have been much tighter controls imposed by the government. There has once again been an increase in racial tension.

The immigrants of the 1950s, 60s and 70s are now British citizens and are settled with children and grandchildren here. They are well integrated in their communities and some are now voicing their concerns about the new wave of migration.

The new migrants tend to live in the South of England, Greater London and the East of England, some around the larger, once industrial,

Objectives

To discover the origins and implications of diverse national, regional, religious and ethnic identities.

Information

In 2005 the government introduced requirements in the form of the British citizenship test which people seeking to become British citizens or those wishing to remain here permanently must take. The test is now called the 'Life in the UK Test'. It takes about 45 minutes to complete, and costs £34. The 24 questions cover many aspects of British life, and requires the use of basic English language. To pass, 75 per cent of the questions must be answered correctly. There is then a formal citizenship ceremony.

Key terms

Immigration: the process of people moving into this country to live and work.

Prejudice: when a person forms a bias opinion or belief that is not based on personal experience.

Asylum seeker: a foreigner who wishes to live in Britain because they have been abused in their own country.

Immigrant: a person born in a foreign country who wishes to live and work in Britain for a short time or permanently.

towns in the Midlands, Yorkshire, Humberside and the North East. This has caused problems where there is a high proportion of migrants who do not speak the language, and who rely on aid when they first arrive, causing resentment from residents who see local services such as health, housing, and education as being overstretched. As the influx slows down and migrants find employment and become part of the community tension decreases and there is less stress on local services.

Since the London bombing in 2005 when British Muslims were charged with acts of terrorism, there has been suspicion and mistrust on both sides. There are about 1.8 million Muslims in Britain (3 per cent of the total population). The overwhelming majority live peacefully and are just as appalled as the rest of us by acts of terrorism. The Muslim Council of Britain has urged cooperation with the police on matters related to terrorism. Muslims do not believe in violence and do not want the unwelcome attention the extremists have brought about.

Discussion activity

Look at a range of recent newspapers and find articles on immigration. Evaluate the content and identify any bias. List the main points from the text. In small groups discuss the content of the different articles and how the article is trying to influence the reader.

One example is the adapted article below from *The Sunday Times* in April 2008, written by Rageh Omaar.

AQA Examiner's tip

Know about **immigration** over the last 60 years and the effects it has had.

Know what is meant by 'a multicultural society', 'identity' and 'diversity'.

At least Britain is honest about immigration now

Adapted from www.timesonline.co.uk from The Sunday Times article on Sunday 6 April 2008

> *"Enoch Powell's explosive 'rivers of blood' speech in 1968 effectively closed down public debate about immigration for several decades. His inflammatory language made the topic radioactive, while at a stroke destroying his political career."*

> *"It has been a fascinating experience for me – a Briton born in Somalia barely a year before Powell's speech – to listen to these concerns. As an overseas reporter I have been more used to hearing villagers' grievances against another tribe of a different ethnicity. Yet in a sense these were familiar scenarios – whether I was talking to a white family who felt under siege in picture-postcard Lichfield or a second-generation black worker in Brixton who was complaining about Polish workers undercutting his business."*

A *Rageh Omaar*

6.2 Understanding diversity

Information

Before we begin to try to explain what we mean by 'Britishness' we will take a look at what we mean by being British. Britain is an island community formed by the Act of Union of 1707. Britain is composed of the home countries of England, Wales, Scotland and Ireland. In 1920 the Government of Ireland Act partitioned (separated) Northern Ireland from the Irish Free State, which became the Republic of Ireland (Eire) in 1937. Britain is the combination of these four constituent parts or countries and is really the United Kingdom of Great Britain and Northern Ireland or usually just the UK for short.

Objectives

To learn why 'identity' is important. What is 'Britishness'?

To understand prejudice and why tolerance is important.

What do we mean by 'Britishness'?

Do we mean that British people all have the same characteristics, the same way of life, believe in the same things, follow the same religion, have one culture, or is it something quite different? Do we mean that British people share the same sense of identity?

Britishness is a national identity that is made up of many different parts and comes together from diverse cultures down the centuries to the present day. When asked for your nationality, for instance, how would you reply? Depending on where you live or the culture you were brought up in, you may say that you are English, Welsh, Irish, Scottish or British first. A simple question, but already there is diversity and different identities beginning to emerge just from the part of Britain we live in. Each region will have its own particular identity and cultural background, perhaps a particular regional accent. All this identifies us in different ways, so we can be said to have multiple identities. If we believe in a particular religion or have a specific ethnic or cultural background there is another strand which builds up our identity.

links

Discrimination see chapter 9.

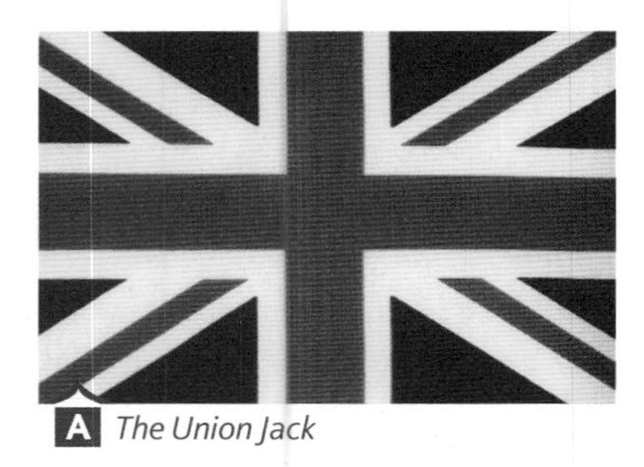

A *The Union Jack*

'Britishness' is a collection of different ideas and shared values that we can all associate with and aspire to. This would include a strong belief in our democracy, in fairness, justice and equality for all under the law, and with everyone's right to have their own opinion, even if we do not agree with that opinion.

In general we have accepted immigrants into Britain. Many contribute to the economy, society and the running of public services. In the last decade Britain has accepted many new people into the country from a great diversity of other countries and cultures, particularly from the countries who are new members of the European Union (EU).

However, if a large number of new people settle in one particular area it can cause problems; newcomers will have the effect of accentuating any difficulties and they may be blamed for the problems. This is particularly the case where there is unemployment, much use of social services and housing is not good. Then the inhabitants begin to resent the immigrants as they perceive them as taking the few jobs, getting the houses, overstretching the services and getting many state benefits. If this is coupled with the immigrants having difficulty with the

AQA Examiner's tip

Diversity is a topic that is likely to appear on the exam paper.

Form your own opinions on the topic and be able to justify them.

language and knowing little about the 'culture' then problems can arise and the community begins to be divided rather than cohesive.

It is at times like these when prejudice, **racism** and **discrimination** can occur. Many people have prejudices, but, if they recognise and understand their prejudice they can do something about it. For example, many elderly people believe the **stereotype** of young people as being ill-mannered and badly behaved and are prejudiced against them, but they do not actually know any young people, gathering their opinions from biased reports in the media. This incorrect assumption creates mistrust. If the old and young actually mixed a little more there would be acceptance of each other's positive qualities, and both groups would be **tolerant** of each other.

Labelling is a self-fulfilling prophecy. It is a concept that was popular in the 1970s and means that if you perceive a group as a crowd of troublemakers, there will probably be elements of their behaviour that are troublesome.

Key terms

Racism: a dislike or hostility towards a particular race, or believing one race is better than another.

Discrimination: treating someone unfairly because they are different in some way.

Stereotypes: a generalised view about a type of person or group of people.

Tolerance: acceptance of people or things as they are, even though you may not like or agree with them.

Labelling: a theory where terms or labels applied to a person or group may influence their behaviour.

Activity

1

a Make a list of some common stereotypes.

b Identify the different cultural or ethnic backgrounds within your community. Keep a note of them.

c Have you ever labelled a person or group because of a stereotype? Were you right?

d Do you have any prejudices? It's good to be able to recognise them.

e Discuss what racism means to you.

B *Tolerance and understanding*

6.3 British identity

Information

Types of economy

Generally the different types of economy are subsistence, market, planned and mixed.

A mixed economy is a mixture of a planned and market economy. This type of economy is prevalent in More Economically Developed Countries (MEDCs).

Objectives

To examine the nature of British identity.

AQA Examiner's tip

Use these pages and information from many media sources to form your own opinion of what is 'a British identity' or 'Britishness' and be able to justify it.

Key terms

Identity: how a person describes themselves as an individual.

The Prime Minister raised the question about Britishness and British **identity** in 2006 when he was Chancellor. He has returned to the topic since then and the media in general have kept it going. What this has done is to start a national debate about the whole topic of what it means to be British.

Now we are going to examine the concept further and look at British identity from a number of different aspects – social, political, economic and cultural.

Social

We all associate with others; some are family members, some neighbours, and some people we have met and formed friendships with. We belong to social groups because of school, work, religion, leisure pursuits or from following particular interests. All these people in their variety of groups and settings form our social network, where we interact with a wide range of people, creating opportunities to meet new people from different backgrounds. This encourages an understanding of others, tolerance of a range of opinions and possibly of other cultures. This gives us a social identity. British society has undergone changes during the last half century with many immigrants settling in Britain. Most have now integrated well in our communities and become part of our society and enriched it.

Political

The British political system has evolved over centuries, going back as far as Magna Carta which began to establish the rights of people. Modern politics cater for all shades of opinion, including some very extreme views with few supporters, which are tolerated even if not always agreed with. At times extreme opinions can be a source of tension and racism. The British political system is going through change; as we have seen in previous chapters, devolution, proportional representation, and discussions about changing the electoral system for parliament, the possibilities of an elected House of Lords, and a reduction in the voting age are all current issues. Our democratic system paved the way for many democratic systems worldwide. It is part of our heritage and definitely part of British identity.

Economy

The British economy is a mixed economy; it is the fifth largest in the world. In the last 30 to 40 years many services that were nationalised (owned and run by the government) especially the utilities, railways, coal, and telephone, have been sold to private companies. Our economy used to depend on a large manufacturing base; this has now been superseded by service industries and the major contributor to the economy is the financial industry. London is generally considered to be the financial capital of the world. In 2008 there was a reduction in economic growth, and by spring 2009 it was officially acknowledged the UK was in a recession, a period of negative growth. During your course keep track of the news; there will always be comment on the economic situation in the media. The British economy has seen many ups and downs and this is part of being British too.

Culture

When we think of culture we think of a mixture of different attributes; a nation's culture encompasses its language, dress, traditions, how society is organised, religion, rights and responsibilities, how children are reared, art, theatre, and literature. Our British culture again has developed through the ages and is not static. Being British means that we are a product of all the changes that have gone before to bring us to the present. The last 100 years has seen many changes with new cultures being accepted and enriching what was already here.

British identity

British identity is a true mixture of many different aspects; an accurate definition is very hard to give because there are so many variables. British identity must include our traditions and beliefs in democracy, freedom, fairness, and tolerance.

A *Dealing on the stock exchange*

Activities

1. Find out the definitions of the different types of economy and make a list of some countries that have these types of economy.
2. As a class or in small groups decide on your ideas of being British. What is British identity and what is Britishness? Keep some notes; they will be useful for revision.
3. As we have seen before, Britain is made up of the four home countries. England, Wales, Scotland and Northern Ireland all have their own separate identity, values, national cultures, emblems, traditions and national celebrations.

   Find out what some of these differences are – keep a record of what you find out or create a chart to show the information.

6.4 Opportunities and barriers

We have looked at the way immigration has changed during the last ten years and how this has brought a different set of problems relating to **inclusion** and integration. This applies to predominantly urban areas as most immigrants tend to cluster in urban rather than rural areas.

Britain today is one of the most culturally diverse societies in Europe and much has been done to encourage cultural diversity. However, is this at the expense of cohesion? We need to establish inclusive communities where a true sense of belonging is shared.

There are some communities where people live with limited integration into the wider society; these tend to be ethnic groups who are disadvantaged in some way according to the socio-economic indicators. To put it another way, the main barriers to citizens participating in their local communities are those of:

- language
- poor education, or low educational achievement
- poor housing
- poor health, due to an inability to access services
- lack of self-esteem
- lack of opportunity to integrate
- involvement in the criminal justice system – getting into trouble – breaking the law
- unemployment or lack of suitable job opportunities – possibly linked to low educational achievement
- low pay and low levels of disposable income.

To alleviate these disadvantages and encourage citizen participation there has to be a willingness to fund initiatives and follow up research on their effectiveness. The power to do this has to come from central government through the regional offices to the local communities where it matters.

Local authorities where such barriers exist have to create an environment that encourages citizen participation by putting adequate ongoing support in place so that community members have increased levels of self-esteem and know that their continued contribution is valued.

The Department of Communities and Local Government is in charge of all these strategies. One of these initiatives is Neighbourhood Renewal. Look back to chapter 3 – The economy, citizenship and community cohesion.

Improving Opportunity, Strengthening Society is a government strategy established in 2005. It aims to achieve racial equality and improve community cohesion.

Objectives

To investigate the opportunities and barriers to citizen participation.

Key terms

Inclusion: being included – not left out.

Activities

Find out more about what the government is doing:

1. Log on to the website **www.neighbourhood.gov.uk** and see what the Neighbourhood Renewal Unit is.
2. Log on to **www.communities.gov.uk**, look through this site to find out what this is about and plans for the future.
3. Find out more about the White Paper: Communities in Control.

REACH

This is a very important initiative from the Department of Communities and Local Government. Twenty five members of the black community, who had a wealth of experience in working with young black men to overcome the barriers they encounter, produced a report in 2007. The project aims to highlight positive black role models, to try to improve achievement at school, foster better home–school links and improve job prospects. This would increase opportunities to participate positively in the community.

The Race, Cohesion and Faiths Directorate

'The Race, Cohesion and Faiths Directorate works with other government departments to reduce race and faith inequalities in education, health, housing and the Criminal Justice System, as well as the labour market' (direct quote from Communities and Neighbourhoods at **www.communities.gov.uk**).

The White Paper

Communities in Control: real people, real power launched July 2008, is about giving local people control and influence in their communities.

It is part of the Community Empowerment, Housing and Regeneration Bill, which would involve more local people in local decisions about the services available to them. It is trying to break down the barriers and encourage citizen participation in local decision making, encouraging inclusion.

The Equality Standard and participation strategy will be fully discussed in the next chapter.

Measures to break down the barriers and create opportunities for citizens to participate are numerous. Those that will succeed are where local people from all the different groups are really consulted and listened to, and following these consultations strategies and structures are put in place to remove barriers, thereby encouraging citizen participation and helping community cohesion.

A

Activities

4 Find out who is the current Secretary of State for Communities and Local Government.

5 Follow the Bill mentioned opposite and see what happens to it as it passes through parliament.

6 Look at the list of bullet points – barriers to participation – and discuss measures to reduce or eliminate each one. Keep notes on the discussion.

AQA Examiner's tip

You could be asked to justify an opinion on how barriers could be removed or how citizen participation could be increased.

Chapter summary

What you should know:

From this chapter your knowledge should now cover:

Short course

- ✔ what identity is and why it is important
- ✔ an understanding of prejudice, discrimination, and stereotypes
- ✔ why tolerance is important
- ✔ an opinion on what is 'Britishness'
- ✔ an understanding of recent immigration

Full course

- ✔ what identity is and why it is important
- ✔ an understanding of prejudice, discrimination, and stereotypes
- ✔ why tolerance is important
- ✔ an opinion on what is 'Britishness'
- ✔ an understanding of recent immigration
- ✔ what is British identity – social, political, economic and cultural perspectives
- ✔ barriers and opportunities for citizen participation

Check your knowledge

You should be able to answer the following questions without looking back over the text. If you cannot answer all of the questions you need to learn the material more thoroughly.

1. What is immigration?
2. When did the first mass immigration into this country happen?
3. Where did the majority of immigrants come from?
4. Where did they settle?
5. Explain the term 'prejudice'.
6. Give an example of a stereotype.
7. What is discrimination?
8. What is an asylum seeker?
9. What is 'Life in the UK Test'?
10. Name the four home countries.

Further study

- Find two different newspaper articles on immigration – one supportive of it and one against.
- List at least six points for and against immigration.
- What policies do the political parties have on immigration?
- Form your own opinion and be able to justify it.
- An exam question may ask you to put a case for or against immigration.

Picture stimulus

An active group of teenagers have been campaigning for a new drop-in centre as there is nothing else for them in the neighbourhood. They have some support from a local Councillor but there is some opposition.

The Daily Globe

PROPOSED NEW FACILITIES FOR TEENAGERS

A community meeting last night.

Your task is to organise a role play of the community meeting to make the decision about a new facility. Divide the class into groups. Each group is to choose a representative to deliver a speech.

The following groups should be represented:

- teenage activists – include at least two members from different ethnic groups
- local residents a group in favour + a group against + an elderly group
- local Councillor
- Community Police Officer
- parent group
- neutral chairperson
- each group should prepare a 2–3 minute speech
- each member of the audience should prepare two questions
- carry out the role play of the meeting and take a vote at the end
- complete the article started in the cutting above.

7 Effects on community life

7.1 How migration can shape communities

Information

All migrants do not fit into the same category; there are many different reasons for migration:

- seeking asylum because of persecution due to religion or political beliefs or racism
- seeking work to send income back home to help families
- seeking employment and a better quality of life in another country
- seeking a good education
- wanting to live and work permanently or temporarily in another country.

These are often referred to as push or pull factors in immigration – asylum seekers are being pushed to leave their country as the conditions are intolerable or life threatening. The pull factors are better jobs, higher income, good education, etc.

Objectives

To investigate how migration can shape communities over time.

To investigate issues relating to a multicultural society.

Key terms

Host nation: the country the migrants live in.

Migration: the movement of people between different countries.

Multiculturalism: a mixture of different races, with many cultures and much ethnic diversity within a country/region/city/town/locality.

Pluralism: different beliefs/faiths/cultures existing within a society.

The perception of immigration used to be that over a period of time the migrants would adopt the language and culture of the **host nation**, they would integrate with the local society, have families and the the second and third generation would be completely assimilated by adopting the customs and lifestyle of the host nation. This happened with the **migration** of the 1950s and 60s. It is this that really started a pluralist society at least, or according to many was the start of a multicultural society. Certainly there has been an understanding, acceptance, and sharing of multiple cultures which have enriched the nation. In more recent times there have been more questions about Britain and whether we are a truly multicultural society.

In the last 15 years or so the views on migration have changed because migration has altered and the migrant population now tends to be more transient with fewer migrants settling for a long time. Some migrants now tend to take seasonal work and return to their homeland after a relatively short time. The internet makes communication with friends and family very easy and relatively cheap so migrants remain in closer contact with friends and family abroad and retain more of their own culture, without a sharing and integration process really beginning. Most migrants of this type, however, do speak some English.

Another smaller but often significant group of migrants do not wish to integrate into British society, remaining segregated within their own particular area and having little contact with the general population except when the children attend school.

Some immigrants are highly skilled, well educated and already have well-paid jobs waiting for them with accommodation already found.

At the other end of the spectrum, when migrants have low skill levels, no job to go to and no accommodation, there is a great difference in how quickly and how well they will settle. True asylum seekers may be traumatised by their experiences and may need special help to adjust to their new situation.

Contemporary issues in a multicultural society

We have people from many different countries living in Britain, some from Commonwealth countries, some from Africa, Asia, Australasia, and from all over Europe. All these peoples will have brought with them a different culture. Some will share the same religion but there will be followers of a number of different religions. Tolerance of religions and belief is important too, intolerance can cause a lot of tension.

Britain is trying to cope with the multitude of demands that all this makes on the public services and on the people already living here.

The contemporary issues facing society are really to do with the attitudes and prejudices of the host population and how well newcomers are willing to integrate. Naturally these are very mixed and vary not only within towns, cities, and regions but also within age groups and different ethnic groups. Generally where communities are secure and cohesive they tend to be more open and welcoming to migrants, more tolerant and understanding, knowing that newcomers have a contribution to make to the area and the local economy. In less stable communities there is often more resistance and suspicion of migrants. In such areas migrants tend to be resented, perceived as being given preferential treatment in housing, employment, health care and being a drain on resources in education, social services and state benefits.

A *Integration*

Case study

If a large number of highly skilled, English speaking, foreign people from a number of different countries arrive in a city, what is the effect going to be in the short term and over time?

If a large number of foreign people, mainly from one country, who speak little English, move into a town, what is the effect likely to be in the short term and over time?

Factors to consider and discuss:

- the degree of assistance required by the groups
- language difficulties – interpreters
- types and location of accommodation
- employment opportunities – qualifications – the local economy
- education for children
- health care
- contact with host population
- integration – would smaller numbers make any difference?

7.2 Shared perspectives and values

In the last chapter we have looked at and identified a number of issues about identity and common values that the majority of the population share as belonging to and being part of our British society. These common **perspectives** and shared values included:

- a strong belief in democracy
- fairness and equality of opportunity for all
- justice – the rule of law and equality for all under the law
- freedom of expression – the right to voice your own opinion
- freedom to participate in community activities
- freedom to belong to a political party.

Are there any others you would add to this list? Should tolerance be added?

The changes brought about by immigration during the last 50 years have given rise to some discrimination, with some groups being disadvantaged. Successive governments have implemented several policies to reduce discrimination and remove racism. How far they have been successful is a matter of great debate, with a great array of divergent views. It is up to you to make your own decisions based on accurate information and personal experience. Opinions are not right or wrong but they should be based in fact and should be justified.

The government has taken a series of actions and passed many laws to reduce discrimination and promote a more equal and cohesive society.

This really began with the Equal Pay Act 1970. The European legislation has been incorporated and the Human Rights Act was passed in 1998. The latest Act which will unify much of the legislation regarding discrimination is the Equality Act of 2006.

In 2007 the Equality and Human Rights Commission (EHRC) was set up under the Equality Act 2006. The EHRC was formed by the joining together of the Commission for Racial Equality, the Equal Opportunities Commission and the Disability Rights Commission.

The following quote is taken directly from the homepage of their website:

> *"The Equality and Human Rights Commission champions equality and human rights for all, working to eliminate discrimination, reduce inequality, protect human rights and to build good relations, ensuring that everyone has a fair chance to participate in society."*

Objectives

To identify shared perspectives and values.

To discover government actions to reduce discrimination.

Key terms

Perspective: in this sense we mean a particular view or opinion.

links

Look at chapter 9 and the different laws on equality and discrimination there.

AQA Examiner's tip

- Know, understand and be able to explain some of the government's actions mentioned in this chapter.
- Form and be able to justify your own opinion on what has been done to reduce discrimination, and what more could be done.

In 2001 the Equality Standard for local government was introduced to implement equality within all areas of local government. This Standard tried to ensure that at the local level equality was at the heart of all policies, procedures and practices. It included equality in terms of age, gender, race, disability, sexual orientation and religion and tried to see that it existed throughout all departments and referred to services the local authority provided and to the people they employed. The Standard tried to make the services provided more accessible to all people and to build in anti-discrimination policies throughout all sections of local government.

In 2007 a participation scheme was added to the Standard, to encourage Councils to work with local groups to increase the opportunities for citizen participation in the type and range of services provided as well as in formulating more inclusive policies for better **community cohesion**

Acts of Parliament need to be implemented within communities for them to be really effective and make a difference. It is only by working at a local level that change will be brought about and real differences made within communities. The process of consultation, asking people about their concerns and their opinions on a range of issues will aid in sharing expectations, experience and cultural diversity. This procedure should improve equality at all levels and thereby improve community cohesion because there will be a greater perception of shared values. This creates a feeling of shared ownership of the facilities available, because they will have been created through consultation, cooperation and an increased shared understanding.

Key terms

Community cohesion: enabling people within an area to have shared values and understanding by providing good facilities and the same opportunities for all.

Activity

1 The Government Equalities Office is a new department which aims to ensure equality throughout the government. It is introducing the Equalities Bill in the 2008 Parliamentary session.

a Find out more about this new Office and look at what the new Bill is proposing.

b Look at your school's equal opportunities policy and discuss it.

c Is discrimination an issue in your community? Discuss how it could be removed.

A *Working together*

7.3 The impact of migration

Many immigrants that first came to Britain between 1950 and 1970 have settled here as permanent residents and have integrated into the host population. This was not easy; at first there was a lot of tension, racism and some riots. There is still racism in some areas. The earlier migrants may now identify themselves as British but retain their ethnic identity too.

During this period there were plenty of opportunities for employment and migrants were not seen to be taking jobs away from the host community. Housing was a problem in some areas that had been devastated during the war years, this was a problem for the host population too. The **indigenous** population were not used to so many people from abroad; there were issues (mistrust, ignorance, prejudice, racism) from many sections of the community. As employment was not hard to find, people began to mix at work and the slow process of integration began. The Equal Opportunities Commission and Commission for Racial Equality did huge amounts to reduce racism and discrimination through new legislation. Gradually, with more interaction, a shared understanding of different cultures took place, communities became more settled as housing improved and tolerance increased as people accepted different ethnic groups.

In the last 20 years the nature of immigration has itself changed and has had a different impact on the country. There has been much media publicity about illegal immigrants and particularly the numbers entering Britain. This has created some tension in the larger urban areas where most migrants settle.

The new migrants come from a greater number of different countries, especially since the enlargement of the European Union (EU) and there is far more population movement internationally than there used to be. The mixture of diverse cultures has greatly increased, as has the diversity in religion. Not all migrants speak English and this has an impact on communities and the levels of social interaction and the support that is needed. There are many courses to help people learn English (English for Speakers of other Languages [ESOL]) where often people from diverse backgrounds meet and socialise through learning a common language. There is also the need to socialise with the indigenous community too. Many migrants have said how important community organisations and facilities are in bringing people together such as sport and leisure facilities, adult education centres, schools and facilities for young people.

Employment is now far more of an issue because there are fewer jobs available and there is a perception that migrants take jobs from indigenous workers. This causes tension.

Other groups of migrants who have low skill levels may not be employed for a while and when they are it is often in low paid work with little job security and no prospects. This is another cause of tension. There is some evidence to show that some migrants do not find suitable employment according to their skills and qualifications causing that person much dissatisfaction.

Objectives

To investigate the impact migration has had on cultural, social and employment issues.

Key terms

Indigenous: a citizen naturally belonging to that country.

AQA *Examiner's tip*

Learn the facts and understand diversity.

Information

The Joseph Rowntree Foundation is an independent organisation that carries out research on a national basis into social problems and disadvantage.

To find out more visit the website: **www.jrf.org.uk**

Research activity

1 a Find out about the UK Border Agency from www.ba.homeoffice.gov.uk

b Write a news item about recent events

Another factor which has become more of an issue this century is that of religion. The terrorist attacks in Britain have given rise to tension and mistrust on racial and religious grounds. Discrimination because of religion is more prevalent now. This is one new and very different impact. There is an assumption in some areas that racial identity or ethnicity also denotes a particular religious belief; this is a stereotypical view.

Some situations inflame tension and cause extremism on both sides. It is fuelling the unrest about immigration policy. This is why the Equalities Standard, especially the participation element, is important, in order to create further opportunities for diverse groups to meet and participate in local decision making for the benefit of all within the community.

Information

In 2008 the government has introduced new measures to control immigration:

- a system of gathering points so that people are given permission to enter Britain if they have the skills this country needs. It is called a Points Based System
- fingerprints are taken from people who apply for a visa. So far 3,500 identity 'swaps' have been discovered
- penalties in the form of substantial fines for businesses employing illegal immigrants
- November 2008 saw the introduction of new ID cards for all foreigners.

In 2007 over 63,000 failed asylum seekers and foreign criminals were deported.

2007 saw the lowest number of asylum applications since 1993 (23,430). In these 14 years the number of applications had reduced by 75 per cent.

Information taken from the UK Border Agency.

A *Migrant workers waiting at Calais to enter Britain*

Activity

1 We have become a multiethnic, multicultural society. Some would say a pluralist society; others would say a multicultural society where different cultures lead parallel lives.

a Discuss and decide which you think is the most appropriate description of British society today.

b Organise a formal debate within your class – 'This house believes that prejudice and racism depends on where you live.'

7.4 Cohesive communities

Equality

The concept of equality is really based in the simple definition of equal opportunities for all (regardless of colour, race, religion, belief, sexual orientation, age or disability).

This is the ideal, but is it reality? How can equality be achieved when there is such a great diversity of people, cultures and beliefs?

There are so many issues to be dealt with and society is changing at an ever-increasing pace, with a faster movement of people and temporary migrant workers creating transient communities.

As we have seen before there are many laws and organisations working to reduce and remove some of the barriers. These barriers include language differences which hinder adequate communication between people, along with attitudes, prejudice, stereotypes, racism, discrimination and extremism.

Cohesive communities

We have discussed community cohesion in chapter 3, so you should have an understanding of the terminology. Nationally there is a wide variety of communities and varying degrees of community cohesion. The degree of cohesion will depend upon a range of factors:

- the location – urban or rural, the size of the population
- in urban areas whether migrants are in one locality or spread throughout the town/city
- the numbers of newcomers and the number of ethnic groups – both new and already settled
- type and quality of accommodation
- range of community facilities available for different age groups.

Most problems occur where there are large numbers of people from different ethnic backgrounds in one area, especially if the area needs regeneration, that is, better housing, more community facilities, improved public buildings and services. Many people in such areas are unhappy and tension rises when one group is perceived to be given priority or to be receiving more help. This is where all the measures we have talked about before are needed to combat perceived inequalities and provide more community facilities where social interaction can occur to begin to create some sense of belonging and understanding between peoples and increase community cohesion.

Objectives

To explore equality in a changing diverse society.

To investigate why some communities are more cohesive than others.

To discover opportunities to celebrate diversity and challenge racism.

Activity

1 Consider these barriers and what you have learned about the measures that exist to combat them. Discuss your views on how effective they are.

AQA Examiner's tip

- Be able to describe a number of opportunities to celebrate diversity and how racism and discrimination can be challenged.
- Understand the concepts, and be able to justify your own views.
- Be prepared to present a case in an examination question.

links

See chapter 3 pages 46–47 about community cohesion.

Celebrating diversity and challenging discrimination

One way in which racism has been challenged is in sport. Years ago a campaign was started to rid football of racism. When black players first joined prominent football clubs there was a lot of racism displayed towards them. The 'Kick it Out' campaign has made a difference and now it is only when British teams go abroad to play in international matches that racism raises it ugly head. The campaign has been very successful and has increased tolerance in all spheres of life not just football.

Schools have many responsibilities; two of them are to promote equal opportunities and community cohesion. How is this managed? It is managed by giving all pupils equal opportunities to study all subjects, by using up-to-date textbooks, by using displays around school, holding events to show how gender should not influence career choices, and by promoting awareness, and increasing knowledge and understanding of many cultures and religions. Schools have done much to celebrate cultural diversity in their local communities by encouraging speakers from different ethnic and religious backgrounds to talk to pupils, and by taking pupils out of school on visits. By involving pupils and their families to participate in and share special multicultural events – displays and demonstrations of foods, customs, dress, dances, etc. this encourages more understanding and community cohesion. By encouraging young people to challenge racism and discrimination on any grounds schools are helping to develop confident, well-informed, tolerant young people who will help to create happy, peaceful, cohesive communities based on knowledge and understanding not stereotypical prejudice.

A *Inclusion*

Activities

2 When Paul Ince was appointed to manage Blackburn Rovers, the headlines were about him being the first black manager in the English Premier League. Was this celebrating a lack of prejudice or was it drawing attention to the fact he is the only one and some prejudice still exists? Discuss.

3 The 2008 Olympic Games saw remarkable successes for Team GB; racism was not an issue. If racism is not an issue in sport, why is it an issue in everyday life?

4 Look at your school policy on equal opportunities and discuss how it is implemented. What issues does it cover?

5 Is your school community a cohesive one – do you think pupils have shared values and a sense of belonging?

6 What are the shared values? Is there a good community spirit in your school? Why? Why not?

Chapter summary

What you should know:

From this chapter your knowledge should now cover:

Short course

- ✔ an understanding of migration and how it can affect communities
- ✔ contemporary issues in a multicultural society
- ✔ knowledge of a range of shared values
- ✔ some government actions to reduce discrimination

Full course

- ✔ an understanding of migration and how it can affect communities
- ✔ contemporary issues in a multicultural society
- ✔ knowledge of a range of shared values
- ✔ some government actions to reduce discrimination
- ✔ the impact of migration on cultural, social and employment issues
- ✔ equality in a diverse society
- ✔ why some communities are more cohesive than others
- ✔ opportunities to celebrate diversity and challenge racism

Check your knowledge

You should be able to answer the following questions without looking back over the text. If you cannot answer all of the questions you need to learn the material more thoroughly.

1. What is migration?
2. Define pluralism.
3. What is a host nation?
4. Give four reasons why people migrate.
5. Explain multiculturalism.
6. List four shared values.
7. What is the EHRC?
8. What is the aim of the EHRC?
9. Name two Acts of Parliament concerned with discrimination.
10. List four areas where discrimination may occur.

Further study

- Design an anti-discrimination poster.
- Write an article about how discrimination could be reduced in your community.
- Follow the path of the Equalities Bill and see what happens to it during your course.
- Find out what measures have been introduced during your course relating to immigration.
- Look up some statistics on how many people have migrated to Britain in the last five years and which countries they came from. How has this changed over time?

Now consider both sides of this situation and the many forces at work in such a community where there is a sudden large influx of foreigners or there are many foreigners from many different countries.

A *Integration*

Migrants come here to live and work. They have to:

- find jobs
- find accommodation, not always easy to find and often in deprived areas
- find schools for their children
- find out about health care
- adapt to a new climate
- adapt to a different way of life
- learn a new language.

They meet with prejudice, discrimination and racism.

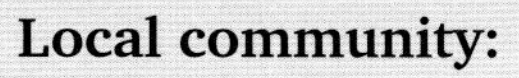

Local community:

- not used to foreigners
- feel threatened by so many strangers
- do not understand the new people in their community or why they have come here
- resent change
- resent immigrants and their ways
- think jobs may be at risk
- think that immigrants are taking priority in education, housing, health care and benefits
- do not understand race and religious differences.

Can you add any other issues?

Discuss the different aspects of this and what has happened and what should happen to resolve the situation.

THEME 3 Fairness and justice

In this Theme you will learn about rights and responsibilities, how the justice system works and the role of the media in society.

The four chapters are:

8 Rights and responsibilities of the British citizen

9 The citizen and the law

10 The criminal justice system in Britain

11 Why does the media matter in Britain?

8 Rights and responsibilities of the British citizen

In this chapter we will look at the rights we have and responsibilities we face as British citizens by looking at key legislation that includes United Nations declaration and European laws.

A *Freedom of speech in action at Speakers' Corner, Hyde Park, London*

Concepts

What are rights? What rights have I?

Rights and responsibilities – legal, political and human rights

Key terms

rights politics legal human freedoms United Nations declaration European law convention checks legislation balances entitlement freedom of speech freedom of association freedom of movement freedom of assembly charter rapporteur

9 The citizen and the law

In this chapter we will look at civil law and how it relates to young people by examining different types of British laws.

B *The signing of the Magna Carta in 1215*

Key terms

society freedom fairness equality wellbeing social system justice respect participation common law criminal law civil law justice system mediation arbitration negotiation ombudsman acquittal conviction civil liberties victimization direct discrimination indirect discrimination harassment commission

Concepts

Should we be free to do what we want?

What makes a fair society?

Freedom Fairness Equality

Civil liberties

10 The criminal justice system in Britain

In this chapter we will look at a number of issues relating to criminal law and the criminal justice system with specific reference to young people.

Key terms

legal framework justice
rule of law police magistrates
solicitors barristers judges
juries youth offending teams
probation service prison service
punishment treatment
sentencing deterrence
rehabilitation reparation
custodial community fines
courts social exclusion
criminal responsibility
retribution

Concepts

The legal framework – protecting the citizen

Justice

Rule of law

C *Symbol of Justice, Criminal law courts, London*

11 Why does the media matter in Britain?

In this chapter we will look at issues surrounding the media and its responsibilities to individuals and the general public.

Key terms

media censorship civil liberties
freedom of the press
responsibilities fair reporting
restrictions public opinion
reflection creation distortion
influence advertising
using the media mass media
propaganda spin opinion poll

Concepts

The media

Censorship

Freedom of the Press

D *Children are influenced by the media*

8 Rights and responsibilities of the British citizen

8.1 What are rights and responsibilities?

The concept of rights and responsibilities is complex. Basically a right is an **entitlement** or a **freedom**. However, your right to be cared for becomes a responsibility for your parents and your school. This type of right is an entitlement. Your right to be free from exploitation becomes a responsibility for society and the law. This type of right is a freedom. You have rights in many aspects of your life, but with these rights you accept the duty to act responsibly. A major part of being a good citizen is a full knowledge of your rights and accepting responsibility for your opinions and actions.

Objectives

To know what legal and human rights and responsibilities are and how they relate to citizens.

To understand legislation – why laws, charters and conventions are made.

Information

- The rights of children in the UK are protected by laws and **conventions**.
- The rights of children in the UK are covered by The Children Act 1989 and The Children Act 2004. The Acts are concerned with the welfare of the child. They state that the opinion of the child should be taken into account.
- The United Nations (UN) Convention on the Rights of the Child became part of international law in 1992.
- For a convention to be part of international law it must be signed by at least 20 countries.

Key terms

Entitlement: a right given to an individual by law.

Freedom: ability to do something without restraint.

Convention: name given to an international agreement.

Politics: is the means by which groups make decisions.

Basic rights and liberties of a British citizen

British citizens have the following basic rights and freedoms:

- freedom:
  - of movement
    conscience in matters of religion and **politics**
    expression
    association, including the right to protest peacefully
  - from arbitrary arrest or unjustified police searches
    social freedoms – such as the right to:
  - to marry, divorce, procure abortions or have homosexual relations
  - to vote and stand for election
  - to have a fair trial
  - to own property
- the right not to:
  - be coerced or tortured by agents of the state
  - be subjected to surveillance without due legal process.

A *The right to protest peacefully*

In addition to these rights, as a British citizen, you have political rights, legal rights, and human rights. **Political rights** include the right to vote, the right to stand for election and the right to peaceful protest. **Legal rights** include the right to a fair trial, the right to be represented in court and the right to be assumed innocent until proven guilty. **Human rights** include the right to life, the right to education and the right to freedom from discrimination. You will also have rights in other aspects of your life as a consumer or an employee.

What are human rights?

B *In some countries people are beaten, tortured or imprisoned without trial*

Human rights are rights given to all human beings, whatever our nationality, place of residence, sex, national or ethnic origin, colour, religion, language, or any other status. We are all equally entitled to our human rights without discrimination. These rights are all interrelated and interdependent. All human rights are indivisible, whether they are civil and political rights, such as the right to life and equality before the law; economic or social and cultural rights, such as the right to work, and to receive education.

Universal human rights are often expressed and guaranteed by law, in the forms of treaties, conventions and international law. International human rights law lays down obligations on governments to act in certain ways or to refrain from certain acts, in order to promote and protect human rights and fundamental freedoms of individuals or groups.

Human rights are inalienable. They should not be taken away, except in specific situations and according to due process of the law. For example, the right to liberty may be restricted if a person is found guilty of a crime by a court of law.

There are many organisations in the world that check that people are given their basic rights. These organisations are mainly NGOs (non-governmental organisations). They include Amnesty International, Liberty, Oxfam, ActionAid, Save The Children, Christian Aid, Water Aid and many more.

Activity

Some people think that CCTV in the street is in opposition to our rights and freedoms as British Citizens. What do you think? Discuss this in groups.

Key terms

Legal: means founded upon law or accepted rules.

Human: means having the nature or attributes of a human being.

Declaration: a formal statement, generally in writing that makes a position very clear.

Information

'Interrelated', 'indivisible', 'interdependent', and 'inalienable'.

Interrelated means they are mutually connected.

Indivisible means cannot be divided. Interdependent means mutually dependent.

Inalienable means cannot be taken away or transferred to someone else.

These are the technical words used in the Universal **Declaration** on Human Rights adopted by the United Nations in 1948. You can use the internet to find out more information about this declaration.

8.2 Understanding rights and responsibilities

There are many people involved with your care. It will not be possible to highlight the work of all of these people in this chapter. We will focus on some of the people involved in your care at school. Secondary schools have many employees (teachers, administrative staff, caretakers, technicians, teaching assistants, cleaners, managers). They provide a learning opportunity for hundreds of children. The rights and responsibilities of the main groups responsible for the care of children at school are outlined below.

	Rights	Responsibilities
Parents	Free education for their children from age five to sixteen Choose the school they want their children to attend Decide which religion their children will follow Determine medical treatment for their children Decide on discipline and punishment	Provide a home for children to live in and care for them Feed and clothe their children Give appropriate medical care Ensure children attend school and behave in an acceptable manner Teach children a moral code that shows them what is right and what is wrong Support school with homework, pupil attendance and behaviour
Pupils	A safe learning environment A balanced curriculum which meets individual needs Good standard of teaching Details of progress made and advice on how to make improvements	Attend school regularly and arrive on time Behave in a reasonable manner Follow school rules Arrive prepared for lessons Work hard Respect other people in the school community
Teachers	A safe place to work Expect pupils to behave appropriately and try to succeed Payment for their work Training and development opportunities	Keep up to date with their subject Teach well Make classroom environment stimulating Assess/mark pupils' work Inform pupils and parents about progress made Implement school standards/values/rules
Governors	Make decisions about how school funding is used Make the policies by which the school is managed Determine the rules for the school's operation Appointment of school staff Receive appropriate training Support from Local Education Authority	Review the policies of the school Monitor school procedures Appoint staff and manage welfare issues Establishing the ethos of the school Develop the reputation of the school Allocate the school's budget to meet school's targets Monitor school spending and progress Report to parents

A

Activities

1 Read the table carefully. Choose one group and discuss the rights of this group in pairs.

2 Which group do you feel has the greatest responsibilities and why?

3 Governors are appointed or elected to serve a school. Find out how many governors there are on the governing body of your school. What are the categories of governor, for example, teacher, parent, etc?

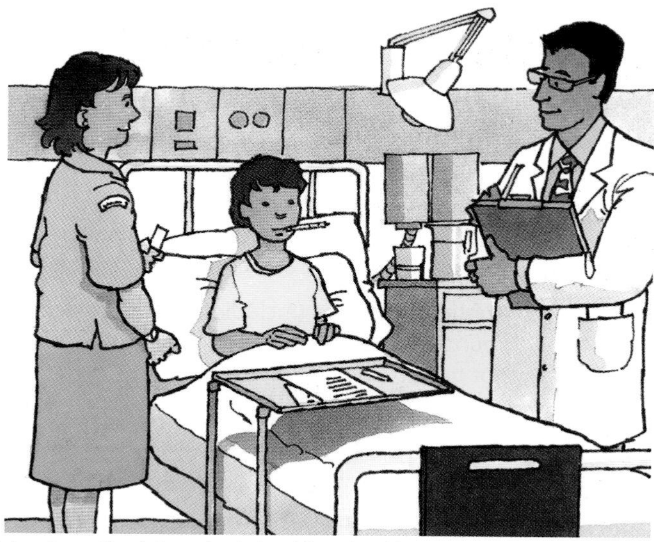

B *Children have the right to basic health and welfare*

The Rights of the Child

However, meeting children's rights is also meeting their basic needs so that every child in the world is given the opportunity to develop to their full potential. Children have special needs which they cannot meet themselves if they are to become fully functioning adults. They need protection and nurturing. These needs are met by the UN Convention on the Rights of the Child that was adopted in 1989. The UK government accepted this **convention** into law in 1991.

The convention spells out for governments what standards they should keep. It has four basic principles:

1 the right to non-discrimination
2 the right to have the child's best interest considered in all actions concerning children
3 a child's right to life, survival and development
4 a child's right to be heard.

The Convention on the Rights of the Child covers the following subjects:

- definition of children as all persons less than 18 years of age, unless the legal age of majority in a country is lower
- general principles, including the right to life, survival and development, and the requirement to give primary consideration to the child's best interests in all matters affecting them
- freedom of expression, thought and association, access to information and the right not to be subjected to torture
- family environment and alternative care, including the right to live with and have contact with both parents
- basic health and welfare, including the rights of disabled children, the right to health and health care, social security, child care services and an adequate standard of living
- education, leisure and cultural activities, including the right to education and the rights to play
- special protection measures covering the rights of children at risk.

Key terms

Convention: name given to an international agreement.

links

The articles outlined in the UN Convention on the Rights of the Child are in the Reference Section page 221.

Activities

4 Put the subjects covered by the convention into an order.

5 Put the points you consider the most important first.

6 Discuss the order you have chosen with someone else. Give reasons for your choice.

8.3 Human Rights law in the UK

Case study

Campaigns for human rights in the UK

The Human Rights Act became law in 1998. It strengthens the convictions embodied in the European Convention on Human Rights in two ways:

- It makes it clear that as far as possible the courts in this country should interpret the law in a way that is compatible with Convention rights.
- It places an obligation on public authorities to act compatibly with Convention rights.

Under current anti-terror laws you can be locked up and repeatedly questioned by police for up to 28 days without being charged. Pre-charge detention refers to the period of time that an individual can be held and questioned by police before being charged with an offence. Liberty launched the 'Charge or Release' campaign. For individuals suspected of terrorism, the maximum period is currently 28 days. This is seven times the limit for someone suspected of murder.

Amnesty International believes that a further extension beyond 28 days is unjust, unnecessary and will not, as the government has argued, make us any safer.

What do you think is an appropriate length of time to hold a suspected terrorist subject for questioning? Remember to consider the point that many people who are arrested are not charged.

A *Liberty Charge or Release campaign poster*

Every child matters

In addition, in June 2003 the government appointed the first Minister for Children, Young People and Families, a move which was recommended by the UN in 2002.

In September 2003 the government published the Green Paper 'Every Child Matters' which made provision for the creation of a new post of Children's Commissioner for England (the Children's Commissioner). The Commissioner will have a role with the Minister for Children in the development of all policies and programmes relating to children.

Information

Interpreting the law compatibly means that courts must make sure that a person's rights under the Convention are not breached in a judgement.

Public authorities (including the police and local councils) have an obligation to act in a way that does not breach Convention rights.

Case study

Human Rights Watch (HRW) wrote to the Premier League in 2007 to challenge Thaksin Shinawatra's right to own Manchester City. It thinks he was not a 'fit and proper person' under Football Association (FA) laws. Thaksin, who was the Thai prime minister from 2001 to 2006, denies the allegations. It is alleged that during his time as Thai prime minister, he presided over extra-judicial killings during the 'war on drugs'. HRW says 2,500 people were killed during one three-month period at the start of 2003. HRW alleges that Thaksin told the Thai military to employ any means to suppress an insurgency in the south of Thailand and suppressed the Thai media.

The human rights abuses have never been proven.

- Do you think it is acceptable for anyone suspected of human rights abuses to own a football club? Discuss this in small groups.

B *Thaksin Shinawatra – former owner of Manchester City*

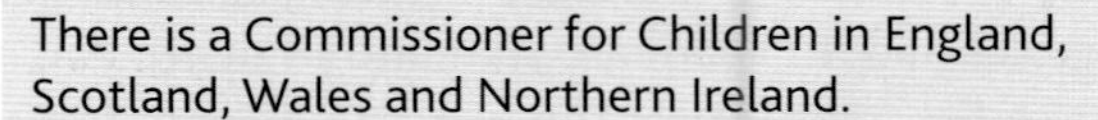

There is a Commissioner for Children in England, Scotland, Wales and Northern Ireland.

Find out who is Commissioner for Children in your part of Britain.

C *What constitutes a child's wellbeing?*

Every Child Matters proposed a new approach to the handling of issues relating to the wellbeing of children and young people from birth to age 19.

The programme places better outcomes for children firmly at the centre of all policies and approaches involving children's services. These outcomes are:

- be healthy
- stay safe
- enjoy and achieve
- make a positive contribution
- achieve economic wellbeing.

Every Child Matters led to the creation of a development plan. The Children's Plan sets out a series of targets for all areas of children's lives:

- At age 5, 90 per cent of children will be developing well across all areas of the early years foundation stages.
- At age 11, 95 per cent of children will have reached expected levels in literacy and numeracy.
- At age 16, 90 per cent will have achieved the equivalent of five good GCSEs.
- At age 19, the majority of children will be ready for higher education with at least 6 out of 10 children achieving the equivalent of A-levels.
- Child poverty will be halved by 2010 and eradicated by 2020.
- There will be clear improvements in child health, with the proportion of overweight children reduced.
- The number of first time young offenders will be reduced by one quarter by 2020.

Activities

1. Find out the name of the commissioner of children for your country.
2. Write to the commissioner and ask a question about their role and how it helps you.
3. Find out more about 'Every Child Matters'. List five responsibilities of the Minister for Children and the commissioner.
4. Who is the current Minister for Children?
5. Go to the website of the Minister for Children and see what the role involves. You may want to send a message.
6. Discuss the targets of the Children's Plan. Do you think they can be achieved?
7. Do you think that every child matters? Give reasons for your answer.

8.4 Human rights and the European Union

With the expansion of the European Union and the general acceptance of the need for good human rights protection in the world, the European Union decided it was necessary to strengthen the protection of fundamental rights in the light of changes in society, social progress and scientific and technological developments by making those rights more visible in a charter. This charter pays due regard to the traditions and international obligations of the member states.

Key terms

Charter: a document that bestows certain rights on the people or country it covers.

The European Union **Charter** of Fundamental Rights sets out in a single text, for the first time in the European Union's history, the whole range of civil, political, economic and social rights of European citizens and all persons resident in the EU. It was signed in Nice in December 2000.

The rights set out in the charter are divided into six sections:

- Dignity (Articles 1–5)
- Freedoms (Articles 6–19)
- Equality (Articles 20–26)
- Solidarity (Articles 27–38)
- Citizens' rights (Articles 39–46)
- Justice (Articles 47–50).

A *The signing of the Charter of Fundamental Human Rights*

They are based, in particular, on the fundamental rights and freedoms recognised by the European Convention on Human Rights (1950), the constitutional traditions of the EU Member States, the Council of Europe's Social Charter, the Community Charter of Fundamental Social Rights of Workers and other international conventions to which the European Union or its Member States are parties.

The European Union recognises the rights, freedoms and principles set out in the charter. As such it gives the rights set out in the charter to all residents of the European Union. This charter differs from the rights set out in the UN declaration in that it gives rights with respect to work and life. These rights are set out in chapter 4 of the EU declaration, Solidarity. An outline of the rights is given here:

- right of access to placement services
- protection in the event of unjustified dismissal
- fair and just working conditions
- prohibition of child labour and protection of young people at work
- family and professional life
- social security and social assistance
- health care
- environmental protection
- consumer protection.

The European Union Charter of Fundamental Rights makes it clear that it considers that enjoyment of these rights entails responsibilities and duties with regard to other persons, to the human community and to future generations.

links

The articles outlined in the European Charter of Fundamental Rights is given in the Reference Section page 222–223.

Discussion activity

Chapter 4, Solidarity, gives EU citizens equal rights to employment across the European Union. Is this a good thing? Discuss.

The role of the international community in human rights

The **United Nations** Human Rights Council is an international body within the United Nations System. Its stated purpose is to address human rights violations. The Council is the successor to the United Nations Commission on Human Rights. The 47-seat Human Rights Council is a subsidiary body of the General Assembly. The 47 seats in the Council are distributed among the UN's regional groups.

The Convention for the Protection of Human Rights and Fundamental Freedoms required the EU to set up a mechanism for the enforcement of the obligations entered into by Member States. Three institutions were entrusted with this responsibility: the European Commission of Human Rights (set up in 1954), the European Court of Human Rights (set up in 1959) and the Committee of Ministers of the Council of Europe. The right of individual complaint is one of the essential features of the system today.

How does the UN keep a check on child issues?

The UN has a special expert (**Rapporteur**) on the sale of children, child prostitution and child pornography, and a Special Representative of the **Secretary General** on the impact of armed conflict on children. Many UN representatives must make reference to children's rights when they report their findings. These representatives include experts on the right to education; on torture; on executions; on violence against women; on freedom of religion or belief; and on contemporary forms of racism, racial discrimination and related intolerance; on human rights and extreme poverty. There are also country-specific experts who focus on the human rights situations in particular countries and who can receive individual complaints. Some of the people who work for the UN see terrible acts of violence during the course of their work.

B *UN representatives working in Zimbabwe*

Activities

1 From the human rights listed in the declarations, the Act and the charter, make a list of the ten rights that you consider the most important. Find out what are the most important rights to your class or group.

2 Hold a class debate on the motion.

'This house believes that people have too many rights.'

You will need to divide into two groups. One group needs to write a list of points for the motion. The other group will write a list of points against the motion.

You must keep to the list of points you have made when you debate.

Key terms

United Nations: an international organisation that aims to facilitate cooperation throughout the world.

Rapporteur: appointed by a body like the United Nations to investigate an issue or a situation and report back to that body.

Secretary General: the chief administrator of the United Nations.

8.5 The issue of responsibility

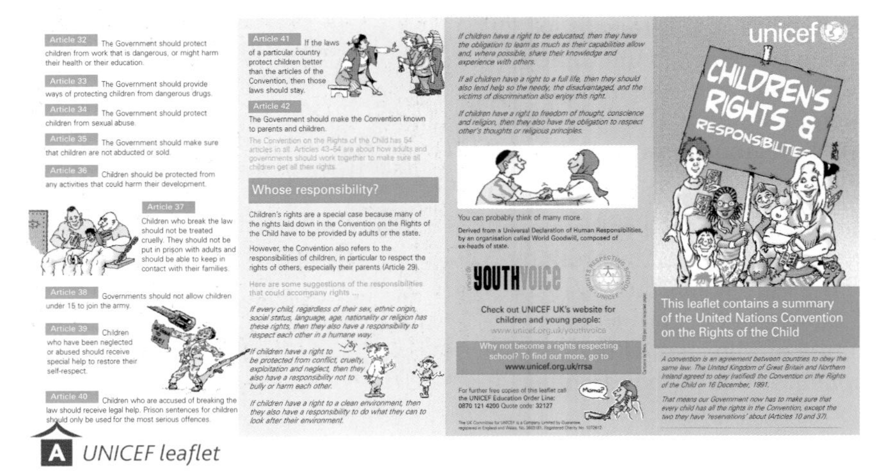

Article 32 The Government should protect children from work that is dangerous, or might harm their health or their education.

Article 33 The Government should provide ways of protecting children from dangerous drugs.

Article 34 The Government should protect children from sexual abuse.

Article 35 The Government should make sure that children are not abducted or sold.

Article 36 Children should be protected from any activities that could harm their development.

Article 37 Children who break the law should not be treated cruelly. They should not be put in prison with adults and should be able to keep in contact with their families.

Article 38 Governments should not allow children under 15 to join the army.

Article 39 Children who have been neglected or abused should receive special help to restore their self-respect.

Article 40 Children who are accused of breaking the law should receive legal help. Prison sentences for children should only be used for the most serious offences.

Article 41 If the laws of a particular country protect children better than the articles of the Convention, then those laws should stay.

Article 42 The Government should make the Convention known to parents and children.

The Convention on the Rights of the Child has 54 articles in all. Articles 43–54 are about how adults and governments should work together to make sure all children get all their rights.

Whose responsibility?

Children's rights are a special case because many of the rights laid down in the Convention on the Rights of the Child have to be provided by adults or the state.

However, the Convention also refers to the responsibilities of children, in particular to respect the rights of others, especially their parents (Article 29).

Here are some suggestions of the responsibilities that could accompany rights ...

If every child, regardless of their sex, ethnic origin, social status, language, age, nationality or religion has these rights, then they also have a responsibility to respect each other in a humane way.

If children have a right to be protected from conflict, cruelty, exploitation and neglect, then they also have a responsibility not to bully or harm each other.

If children have a right to a clean environment, then they also have a responsibility to do what they can to look after their environment.

If children have a right to be educated, then they have the obligation to learn as much as their capabilities allow and, where possible, share their knowledge and experience with others.

If all children have a right to a full life, then they should also lend help so the needy, the disadvantaged, and the victims of discrimination also enjoy this right.

If children have a right to freedom of thought, conscience and religion, then they also have the obligation to respect other's thoughts or religious principles.

You can probably think of many more.

Derived from a Universal Declaration of Human Responsibilities, by an organisation called World Goodwill, composed of ex-heads of state.

YOUTHVOICE

Check out UNICEF UK's website for children and young people:
www.unicef.org.uk/youthvoice

Why not become a rights respecting school? To find out more, go to www.unicef.org.uk/rrsa

For further free copies of this leaflet call the UNICEF Education Order Line: 0870 121 4200 Quote code: 32127

unicef

CHILDREN'S RIGHTS & RESPONSIBILITIES

This leaflet contains a summary of the United Nations Convention on the Rights of the Child

A convention is an agreement between countries to obey the same law. The United Kingdom of Great Britain and Northern Ireland agreed to obey (ratified) the Convention on the Rights of the Child on 16 December, 1991.

That means our Government now has to make sure that every child has all the rights in the Convention, except the two they have 'reservations' about (Articles 10 and 37).

A *UNICEF leaflet*

The UN Convention gives children rights, but it also refers to the responsibilities of children with particular reference to respecting the rights of others, especially their parents. Article 29 states that:

> *Education should develop each child's personality and talents to the full. It should encourage children to respect their parents and their own and other cultures.*
>
> *From United Nations Children's Fund (UNICEF) leaflet CHILDREN'S RIGHTS AND RESPONSIBILITIES*

This UNICEF leaflet suggests that:

- If children have the right to be educated then they have the responsibility to learn as much as their capabilities allow and, where possible, share their knowledge and experience with others.
- If children have the right to a full life, then they should also lend help so the needy, the disadvantaged, and the victims of discrimination also enjoy this right.
- If children have the right to be protected from conflict, cruelty, exploitation and neglect, then they also have the responsibility not to bully or harm each other.

Consider your responsibilities

Discuss the responsibilities outlined in the three statements above in pairs or small groups.

Consider what the ending of these statements might be:

- If children have the right to a clean environment, they have the responsibility to ....
- If children have the right to freedom of thought, conscience and religion, children have the responsibility to ....
- If every child, regardless of sex, social status, ethnic origin, language, age, nationality or religion has these rights, then they have the responsibility to ....

Activities

1. What does UNICEF stand for?
2. Create a poster highlighting the importance of the Rights of the Child.
3. Children often complain that they are not taken seriously and that no one listens to them. What do you think? Write a short report on your experiences of this issue.
4. Article 12 of the convention says that adults must take your opinion into account in accordance with your age and maturity. How can you show adults that you are mature enough to have your opinion count?

Terrorism and civil liberty

Governments have a duty to take steps to protect citizens from terrorism, but this does not justify forgetting democratic values.

After the attack on the World Trade Center in 2001 and the bombings in London in 2005, the government needed to introduce measures for national security. We should note that:

- pre-charge detention has been increased from 14 days to 28 days, with further extensions planned
- new speech offences impact on free speech rights and
- our right to protest has been curtailed.

B *The twin towers in New York are attacked*

Many people believe that strong measures are needed. Others argue that:

- repression and injustice, through the denial of non-violent speech and protest is likely to help extremism by marginalizing the people we need in the fight against terrorism; and
- restrictive practices undermine the values that separate us from the terrorist, the very values we should be fighting to protect.

We need to strike a balance between finding the measures to combat terrorism and protecting **civil liberties** and human rights.

Civil liberties and human rights are closely related. Your civil liberties include:

- **freedom of association**
- **freedom of assembly**
- freedom of religion
- freedom of speech
- the **right to due process**, to fair trial, to own property and to privacy.

The formal concept of civil liberties dates back to the Magna Carta of 1215. Many of your civil liberties are protected by the EU and UN legislation on human rights.

Key terms

Civil liberties: set limits for government so that it cannot abuse its power and interfere with the lives of its citizens.

Freedom of association: the individual right to join with other individuals to collectively pursue and defend common interests.

Freedom of assembly: used in the context of the right to protest.

Right to due process: (more fully **due process of law**) is the principle that the government must respect all of a person's legal rights.

Activities

5 Find out about the Magna Carta. Why was this document created?

6 Some people say that the government has set too many restrictions on the individual and that we live in a 'Nanny State'. Find out about this and discuss it in groups.

7 Which of your civil liberties do you consider the most important? Give reasons for your choice.

8 Visit a civil liberties website. What are the current campaigns mentioned here?

9 Martin Luther King Jr was a champion of civil liberties in the USA. He believed in non-violent demonstration. Find out how this was achieved.

Chapter summary

8

What you should know:

You should know about:

Short course

- ✔ what are rights and responsibilities
- ✔ different types of right – human, political, legal
- ✔ the rights and responsibilities of parents, pupils, teachers and governors
- ✔ what human rights are
- ✔ understanding rights and responsibilities
- ✔ the Rights of the Child
- ✔ the United Nations Declaration on the Rights of the Child
- ✔ human rights law in the UK
- ✔ The Green Paper: Every Child Matters
- ✔ a Minister for Children
- ✔ a Commissioner for Children

Full course

- ✔ the issue of responsibility
- ✔ human rights and the European Union
- ✔ the role of the international community
- ✔ human rights and the UK
- ✔ how the UN checks on human rights
- ✔ terrorism and civil liberty

Check your knowledge

You should be able to answer the following questions without looking back over the text. If you cannot answer all of the questions you need to learn the material more thoroughly.

1. What are human rights?
2. Explain what a right is.
3. Give two rights and responsibilities of school pupils.
4. Name two non-governmental organisations concerned with human rights.
5. List four responsibilities of parents.
6. List four areas of protection given under the UN Declaration.
7. What year was the Human Rights Act passed by the UK Parliament?
8. What is a convention?
9. Name two topics that Every Child Matters hopes to improve?
10. What is UNICEF?

Further study

Choose one of these to study

- This study is looking at the rights of the child.

Go to the UNICEF website

Choose an area of concern:

- Poverty
- Child labour
- HIV/AIDs and children
- Child protection
- Child survival and development.

Find out what UNICEF are doing about your chosen topic.

Find out how big a problem it is and where it is occurring.

Decide what you feel about this and what you could do about it.

- This study is looking at human rights.

Go to the Amnesty International website

Choose one of the areas of current concern for the organisation.

Find out what Amnesty International feels about your chosen topic.

Decide what you feel about it and what you can do about it.

- This study is looking at basic rights.

Go to the WaterAid website

- Choose a country from the where we work section.
- Read about the work WaterAid is undertaking in your chosen country.
- Find out what needs to be done to make the water safe in this country.
- Decide what you feel about it and what you can do about it.
- For your chosen area of study you should:
  - Make a report or
  - Prepare a talk or
  - Make a poster for display or
  - Discuss it with someone or
  - Write a letter to your MP or
  - Prepare a PowerPoint presentation or
  - Write a poem or
  - Draw a picture or
  - Write in support of the NGO.

Your teacher may have some other ideas for your work.

Picture stimulus

A *Food queue in Africa*

- Which of the child's basic rights are not being met?
- Which of the child's human rights are unlikely to be met?
- What do you think the world authorities should be doing about improving the life of this child?
- What are you going to do to improve the lives of millions of children like this one?

9 The citizen and the law

9.1 Should we be free to do what we want?

In an ideal world, where everything and everyone was equal, where everyone respected each other's right to be free and to live according to whatever creed and practice they chose, then the answer to this question would be, 'Yes, we should be free to do what we want.' However, history has many stories about the injustice and inhumanity one individual or group has shown to another.

In past times, you were expected to protect yourself, your family, your property and your land. As a result, the strong people in **society**, the people in **authority**, prospered and the weaker became bound to serve them. There was no one to turn to when you needed help or disagreed with the way you were treated. Sometimes people rebelled against their masters or the government and changes took place. Over the ages, people took their disputes and injustices to tribunals or courts so a judgement could be made. This forms the basis of our law today. If we lived in a society without laws, we would live in **anarchy**.

Activity

1 Look at some of these punishments from the past. You will find out more from history books or the internet.

- Chopping off the hand or fingers for theft
- Flogging someone to get a confession
- Locking in the stocks or pillory for a minor offence
- Gouging the eyes out of a Peeping Tom
- Branding a person with a hot iron
- Burning at the stake for witchcraft, heresy and treason
- Ducking stool for talkative women

In a land without laws, these could be some of the punishments given to you. Who is there to stop it? Discuss this in groups. Role play some of these trials.

AQA Examiner's tip

It will be helpful in an exam if you know what is fair in a society and if you have your own opinion of why fairness is necessary.

Objectives

To understand the concepts of fairness, freedom, justice and equality.

To understand and know of how the civil law affects the lives of young people.

To understand British law and the difference between civil and criminal law.

Key terms

Society: the term given to a large social group having a distinctive cultural and economic organisation.

Authority: the right to influence, control or direct the actions of other people.

Anarchy: a state of lawlessness and disorder where there is no government and no laws.

A *Public punishment in the Middle Ages*

What makes a fair society?

There are a number of social, economic, environmental and structural factors that affect the lives of individuals and their communities. The **wellbeing** of individuals is governed by factors such as the quality of housing, one's level of health, and the ability to have some control of one's own life.

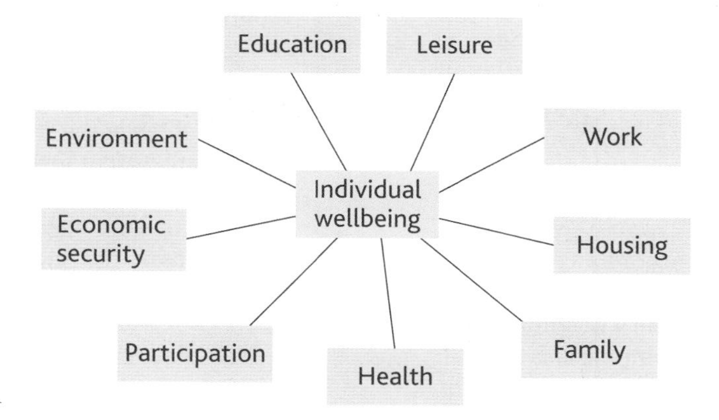

Individuals, families and communities are subject to complex interactions at different levels of the **social system**. Individuals are affected by:

- direct relations with others
- decisions and interactions in their local communities; and
- decisions at national level that drive the distribution of resources and people's access to them.

A fair society seeks to enhance the economic and social wellbeing of people through a system of inclusive policies. This creates the foundations for a prosperous and inclusive society which values **fairness** and **justice**.

The most important elements of a just and fair society are:

- respect: recognising the intrinsic worth of all individuals. Every human being has a unique worth and all people are entitled to be treated with respect
- participation: opportunities for active participation. There are three key features of active participation:
  - people have choices about how they live, and have the means to make those choices;
  - people perceive themselves as active agents;
  - people are active participants in decision-making process
- wellbeing: quality of life. Wellbeing is essential for and contributes to a just and fair society. Justice and fairness are essential to a sense of personal and community wellbeing
- fairness: equity for all. Everyone has equitable access to social, economic and political resources and information. Communities value difference and are inclusive of diverse groups
- just social structures. Government institutions and service providers are accountable, open and transparent. People receive equal treatment and protection under the law.

Key terms

Wellbeing: a positive state of mind, brought about by the simultaneous satisfaction of personal, organisational, and collective needs of individuals and communities.

Social system: the parent system that includes social structures like family, law, religion, class, and economy.

Fairness: achieving the right balance of interests without regard to one's own feelings and without showing favour to one person against another.

Justice: a term used to refer to fairness though this is usually related to the administration of law within a society.

Activity

2 Look at the important elements of a just and fair society listed here. Put these in order. List the one you think is most important first. Give reasons for your choice.

9.2 What are the laws that govern us?

Law consists of **common law** and **statute law**. Statute law is usually more helpful for consumers, because most consumer laws extend the rights people have in common law by laying down specific conditions.

In practice, there's little difference between law in England and Northern Ireland but Scotland is different – the courts have different names and follow different procedures. Some English laws don't apply to Scotland and vice versa.

Common law

The common law of England was developed in accordance with basic moral principles. These principles include honesty, keeping your word, fairness, respect for property, concern for one's neighbours and responsibility for one's spouse and children. The emphasis is upon the duty and responsibility of the individual. No society can function efficiently or humanely without these values.

A *Civil law dispute – a boundary issue*

Civil law

Civil laws are not abstract legal problems familiar only to lawyers, or discussed only in tribunals and civil courts. They are in most part the problems of 'everyday life' – the problems people face living in a modern society. Over time we have established an extensive range of rights and obligations related to child support, education, employment, debt, health, housing, and welfare benefits. These problems involve numerous issues of basic social wellbeing. They also form the basis of civil law.

Civil law involves a dispute between individuals or groups.

The civil justice system

Civil justice in England and Wales is administered mainly by the County Courts and the High Court. In Scotland, the bulk of civil business is handled in the sheriff court. County Courts also handle family proceedings, such as divorce, domestic violence and matters affecting children.

Activities

1. Can you name some groups or organisations you know or are a member of that have rules or laws?
2. Choose three of the organisations that you have discussed. Find out what happens to a member when he/she breaks the rules.

Key terms

Common law: the law based on decisions made by judges over the years.

Statute law: the law made by parliament.

Mediation: an intervention conducted by some impartial party for the purpose of bringing about a settlement to a dispute.

Negotiation: the process of achieving agreement through discussion.

Arbitration: the hearing and determination of a dispute by an impartial referee agreed to by both parties.

Ombudsman: a person in a government agency to whom people can go to make complaints.

Acquittal: a verdict of not guilty.

Conviction: the verdict that results when a court of law finds a defendant guilty of a crime.

Most civil disputes do not go to court at all, and most of those which do, do not reach a trial. Many are dealt with through statutory or voluntary complaints procedures, or through **mediation** and **negotiation**. **Arbitration** is also common in commercial and building disputes. **Ombudsmen** have the power to determine complaints in the public sector and, in some private sector activities – for example, banking and pensions.

Criminal law

English criminal law derives its main principles from the common law. 'Criminal' means that the behaviour is considered to be wrong, damaging to individuals or to society and is unacceptable. The criminal law presumes that each individual is innocent until proven guilty. The level of proof that is required is that the evidence presented should establish the person's guilt 'beyond reasonable doubt'. All systems of criminal law are based on the principle that the innocent should go free and only the guilty should be punished. Without punishments and the institutions designed to measure and carry out punishments, there can be no criminal law.

The criminal justice system

The criminal justice system is the mechanism by which action is taken to deal with those suspected of committing offences. The criminal justice system refers to the whole process from the initial investigation of a crime through to **acquittal** or to **conviction** and sentence in the criminal courts.

Activity

3 Which of these cases is civil and which is criminal?

theft, divorce, debts, perjury, murder, bankruptcy, argument about a will, custody of children, speeding, forgery, robbery, possession of drugs, boundary dispute, cruelty to children.

Make a table to display your answer.

The table should have three headings: Case, Type of Offence, Definition of Offence.

Use a dictionary or the internet to find your definitions.

AQA *Examiner's tip*

You will need to know the distinction between civil and criminal law to answer questions in the exam.

links

You will find out about the criminal justice system in chapter 10.

B *The distinction between civil and criminal law*

	Civil Cases	Criminal Cases
The aim and purpose of the law	To uphold the rights of individuals	1 To maintain law and order 2 To protect society
The cases are dealt with in different courts	County Court High Court	Magistrates' Court Crown Court
Who starts the case?	The individual whose rights have been affected	The State through the police or the Crown Prosecution Service
The legal name for that person	The claimant	The Prosecutor
The standard of the proof of the case	On the balance of probabilities	Beyond all reasonable doubt
The person responsible for making the decision	The judge	Magistrates or jury
The decision of the court	Liable or not liable	Guilty or not guilty
Powers of the court	Compensation The judge sets the level of compensation	1 Prison 2 Fine 3 Community sentence 4 Discharge The magistrates/judge set the sentence.

9.3 Civil law and the young

Adoption

If you are an orphan or given into care under the age of 18, you can be adopted if you are not married or in a registered civil partnership. As a child, you will have little say over who adopts you, but you should be consulted by the adoption agency or social services department involved in the adoption. If you are under 18, you have no legal right to know the identity of your birth parents.

A *Children being adopted should be consulted by social services*

Changing your name

You cannot change your name until you are 16 years old. Between 16 and 18 you can complete a change of name deed with parental consent.

Local authority care

You can only be taken into care if you are under 18 and the local authority has obtained a court order. You have a right to know why you are in care, under what law, and how long you are likely to remain there. You can be accommodated by a local authority without a court order if a parent requests it or gives permission. However, the local authority must take your wishes into account.

Marriage

If you are 16 or 17 and want to get married in a registry office you need the written permission of a parent. If they refuse permission, in England and Wales you can apply to a Magistrates' Court, County Court or the High Court for permission to marry. In Northern Ireland you apply to the County Court. Anyone aged 18 or over can be married without parental permission. This is also the case for civil partnerships.

Parents aged under 16

Mothers aged under 16

If you are under 16 and have a baby, you have the same legal rights and responsibilities towards the child as any mother.

Fathers aged under 16

As a father aged under 16, you may want to have a formal relationship with your child by applying for a parental responsibility agreement, residence order or contact order.

Wills

If you are under 18, you cannot make a valid will unless you are in the armed forces or a seafarer. No one under the age of 18 can act as a trustee, executor or administrator of a will.

links

There is an age-related law that tells you what you can do and when in the reference section on page 216.

AQA Examiner's tip

Knowledge of **civil liberties** and how they affect people may be a useful examination topic.

Case study

Civil liberties and young people

The mosquito and you

Based on technology that was originally designed to scare away vermin, the 'mosquito' is a device that emits a very high-frequency buzzing sound that cannot be heard by people over the age of 25. This device is now being used to deter young people from particular areas, with a sound that is described as 'distressing' or 'unbearable'. There are estimated to be 3,500 such ultra-sonic dispersal devices in use across the country.

B

Should we be concerned?

1 The device will affect those who are behaving in the same way as those who are misbehaving.

2 It exposes young people to extreme discomfort but not adults.

3 It cannot determine who is making the noise; it targets all young people.

A campaign against the Mosquito was launched in the European Parliament in May 2008. The issue was taken up by the European Youth Forum, and, since then, it has been raised at the European Union Youth Council.

Activities

1 Liberty considers this device to be a violation of civil liberties. What do you think? Give reasons for your answer. It calls its campaign against this device 'Buzz off'. Some local councils have banned this device. Has your council? Find out. You could write to your local Councillor and let him/her know how you feel.

2 If an action deliberately excludes someone we call it discrimination. Do you think this device is discriminatory to the young? How would society feel if it targeted old people?

3 Find out about the European Union Youth Council and what it does.

Information

Liberty is a non-governmental organisation protecting civil liberties and promoting human rights.

9.4 Types of discrimination

There are four types of discrimination: direct discrimination, indirect discrimination, victimisation and harassment.

Objectives

To understand equal opportunities law and its operation in Britain.

Direct discrimination

Direct discrimination occurs when a person treats you less favourably than he or she would treat, or treats, some other person. Sometimes direct discrimination is very obvious, but it can be subtle.

Information

Since December 2003 it has been unlawful to discriminate against somebody in the workplace on the grounds of their religious or other belief.

Indirect discrimination

Indirect discrimination aims to challenge practices and procedures which appear to apply in the same way to everyone but which in practice have different, unfair effects on certain groups. Indirect discrimination is defined in the employment context as being the application of a specific provision or practice, which places a group or individual at a disadvantage, in a way that cannot be justified.

links

You will find a definition of discrimination in chapter 6 page 77.

Victimisation

Victimisation occurs when one person treats you less favourably than he or she treats, or would treat, someone else in those particular circumstances.

Harassment

Harassment is unwanted conduct that has the purpose or effect of violating someone's dignity or creating an intimidating, hostile, degrading, humiliating or offensive environment for them.

What is race discrimination?

The Race Relations Act aims to prevent discrimination on the grounds of race. Items that are covered include discrimination on the grounds of race, colour, nationality, ethnic and national origin in the fields of employment, the provision of goods and services, education and public functions.

Most people think of race discrimination as being less favourable treatment on the grounds of colour or race. However, discrimination on the grounds of nationality, ethnic or national origins is equally unlawful.

Information

The Race Relations Act became law in 1976.

A *Discrimination in action*

What is age discrimination?

Age discrimination occurs when a person faces negative attitudes or is treated differently or receives a different standard of service simply because of their age.

Older people have a right to receive equal treatment and opportunity in all aspects of life. Age discrimination is not always easy to recognise. It can be mistaken for many other things, such as bad manners or poor standards. Age discrimination could be overt or more subtle, on purpose or accidental; it can be down to individuals, or part of an organisation's culture.

Information

The law on age discrimination came into force on 1 October 2006. It covers employment training and education but does not provide protection against discrimination in the health service and social care.

What is disability discrimination?

The Disability Discrimination Act (DDA) of 1995 was extended in 2005 to give disabled people additional protection. This Act aims to end the discrimination that many disabled people face. It gives disabled people rights in the areas of employment, education, access to goods, facilities and services (including larger private clubs and transport services), buying or renting land or property.

The Act requires public bodies to promote equality of opportunity for disabled people. It also allows the government to set minimum standards so that disabled people can use public transport easily.

Information

The UN Convention on the Rights of Persons with Disabilities provides a recognised international standard for disabled people's human rights in one document. The UK was among the first 82 countries to sign the convention on 30 March 2007.

What is sex discrimination?

Equal opportunities laws aim to ensure that people are employed, paid, trained and promoted only because of their skills, abilities and how they do their job. It's unlawful for an employer to discriminate against you because of your sex or because you are married. It's also unlawful to discriminate against you because you've had, are having or intend to have, a gender change.

Sex discrimination at work is unlawful in all parts of employment. The law covers recruitment, terms and conditions, pay and benefits, status, training, promotion and transfer opportunities, right through to redundancy and dismissal.

However, in some cases, a job can be offered to someone of a particular sex, because of what is called a 'genuine occupational qualification'. Examples could include:

- some jobs in single-sex schools
- jobs in some welfare services
- acting jobs that need a man or a woman.

Information

The Sex Discrimination Act became law in 1975. The 1970 Equal Pay Act makes it unlawful for employers to discriminate between men and women in terms of their pay and conditions where they are doing the same or similar work.

AQA *Examiner's tip*

You should know about the types of discrimination and where you might find discrimination.

Activities

1. Find out who the current Secretary of State for Equality is.
2. Go to the website (**www.equalityandhumanrights.com**) and find one current issue needing resolution. Discuss this in small groups. What do you think is fair?
3. Give an example of direct discrimination, indirect discrimination, victimisation and harassment. Try to do this for each type of discrimination.

9.5 UK law on equality and discrimination

The UK laws on equality do not allow discrimination and provide the means for individuals to lodge complaints when they experience unlawful discrimination. The UK has laws prohibiting discrimination on the grounds of race, religion and belief, sex, sexual orientation and transgender status, disability and age.

Key terms

Commission: a special group set up to consider some matter of importance.

The Commission for Equality and Human Rights (CEHR)

This single organisation was established in 2007 from three existing **commissions**:

- Commission for Racial Equality
- Disability Rights Commission
- Equal Opportunities Commission.

The CEHR will take on all of the powers of the existing commissions. In addition it has powers to actively promote equality for all. The CEHR will be responsible for tackling all forms of discrimination and ensuring all equality laws are enforced. Promotion of human rights will also be included within the commission's power.

The government hopes that a single commission will have many benefits, including:

- bringing together equality experts and acting as a single source of information and advice
- being a single point of contact for individuals, businesses and the voluntary and public sectors
- helping businesses by promoting awareness of equality issues, which may prevent costly court and tribunal cases
- tackling discrimination on multiple levels because some people may face more than one type of discrimination; and
- giving older people a powerful national body to tackle age discrimination.

Activity

1. Do you think one commission is better than three? Give reasons for your answer.

Case study

Joanna

Joanna works in the same office as you where everyone does the same job and has the same level of qualification. However, the workers are all on individual contracts and salaries. Kevin shows Joanna his wage slip and he is earning £50 a month more than her even though he has not been there as long as she has.

- What would you do to support Joanna?

A

Case study

Harry

Harry lives in Cherrytree Retirement Home in Smalltown. The staff in the care home treat him like a child. They make decisions for him and don't ask his opinion on issues that concern his welfare. He is a slow eater and they often remove his food before he has finished with it.

- Is the law enough to protect Harry in this position? What could you do to help?

B

Case study

Liz

Liz is an experienced city bank worker. She was subjected to sly comments from her fellow workers when she announced her pregnancy and noticed a change in her supervisor's attitude. On her return from maternity leave, she discovered that some of her duties had been transferred to other colleagues, as a result of which she was limited in the amount of work she could generate. She complained, but nothing was done about it. Six months later, she was selected for redundancy over the person her work had been transferred to, on the basis that she had generated less work.

- What would you do to support Liz?

C

Activity

2 Discuss each case study in groups. Answer these questions.

a What is the nature of the problem?

b What could be the possible causes of the problem?

c What does the law say?

d What advice and support from professional or voluntary agencies is available?

Case study

Ahmed

Ahmed works in a busy printing firm. His new supervisor insists on holding his team meeting to review the week's performance between 11.30am and 12.30pm on a Friday. The meeting regularly over-runs. Ahmed is a Muslim and he attaches particular importance to Friday mid-day prayers. He has asked for the meeting time to be changed but nothing has happened.

- What would you do to support Ahmed?

D

Chapter summary

What you should know:

From this chapter your knowledge should now cover:

Short course

- ✔ whether we should be free to do what we want
- ✔ what makes a fair society
- ✔ what the laws are that govern us
- ✔ common law
- ✔ civil law and the civil justice system
- ✔ criminal law and the criminal justice system
- ✔ the distinction between civil and criminal law
- ✔ civil law and the young
- ✔ civil liberties and young people

Full course

- ✔ types of discrimination
- ✔ what race discrimination is
- ✔ what age discrimination is
- ✔ what disability discrimination is
- ✔ what sex discrimination is
- ✔ UK law on equality and discrimination
- ✔ the Commission for Equality and Human Rights

Check your knowledge

You should be able to answer the following questions without looking back over the text. If you cannot answer all of the questions you need to learn the material more thoroughly.

1. Name three things needed in a fair society.
2. What do we mean by justice?
3. What is common law?
4. What do we mean by civil liberties?
5. What does an ombudsman do?
6. List three distinctions between civil and criminal law.
7. What are civil liberties?
8. List three topics covered by civil law for young people.
9. What does the NGO Liberty do?
10. What kind of court hears civil law cases?

Further study

Choose one of these to study

- This study is looking at age discrimination.

Go to the Age Concern website

Choose an area of concern:

Care needs Pensioner poverty
Council Tax Feeding in hospital
Financial issues

- Find out what Age Concern is doing about your chosen topic.
- Find out how big a problem it is and where it is occurring.
- Decide what you feel about this and what you could do about it.
- This study is looking at sex discrimination.

Go to the Terence Higgins Trust website

Choose one of the areas of current concern for the organisation.

- Find out what the Terence Higgins Trust feels about your chosen topic.
- Decide what you feel about it and what you can do about it.
- This study is looking at justice issues.

Go to the Ministry of Justice website

- Choose a topic from the news section.
- Read about the work the Ministry of Justice is undertaking in your chosen topic.
- Find out what needs to be done.
- Decide what you feel about it and what you can do about it.
- For your chosen area of study you should:
  - Make a report
  - or Prepare a talk
  - or Make a poster for display
  - or Discuss it with someone
  - or Write a letter to your MP
  - or Prepare a PowerPoint presentation
  - or Write a poem
  - or Draw a picture or
  - Write in support of the NGO/organisation.

Your teacher may have some other ideas for your work.

Picture stimulus

A *The right to peaceful protest*

- What is happening here?
- Why is this person being arrested if we have the right to peaceful protest?
- What type of court will this person be heard in?
- Discuss how a peaceful protest might go wrong and how the authorities view protests like this one.

10 The criminal justice system in Britain

10.1 What is the point of criminal law?

Criminal law seeks to protect the public from harm by inflicting punishment upon those who have already done harm and by threatening with punishment those who are tempted to do harm. The harm that criminal law aims to prevent varies from case to case.

- It may be physical harm, death, or bodily injury to human beings; the loss of or damage to property; child pornography or disturbance of the public peace and order.
- It could be something as serious as a terrorist attack and danger to the government. Conduct that threatens to cause, but has not yet caused, a harmful result may be enough to constitute a crime.

The criminal justice system

The criminal justice system (CJS) is one of the major public services in the country. It employs over 400,000 staff across its agencies:

- the Police Service
- the Crown Prosecution Service
- Her Majesty's Court Service
- The National Offender Management Service (comprising prisons and probation) and
- the Youth Justice Board.

A *The police are in the front line of the criminal justice system*

Objectives

To understand what the criminal justice system is and how it works.

Activity

1 The CJS is there to support members of the public but most people in England and Wales think the justice system is stacked in favour of the rights of criminals. Discuss this in groups. Do you think that the CJS is protecting the public or the criminals?

Who is responsible for the criminal justice system?

Within central government, three departments are jointly responsible for the criminal justice system and its agencies. They are:

- the Ministry of Justice (MoJ), which is responsible for criminal law and sentencing, for reducing reoffending and for prisons and probation. This office oversees Magistrates' Courts, the Crown Court, the Appeals Courts and the Legal Services Commission
- the Home Office, which is responsible for policing, security and counter-terrorism, borders and immigration, passports and identity
- the Office of the Attorney General, which oversees the Crown Prosecution Service, the Serious Fraud Office and the Revenue and Customs Office.

Youth Justice Board

The Youth Justice Board for England and Wales is a public body. Its aim is to prevent offending by children and young people. It delivers this by:

- preventing crime and the fear of crime
- identifying and dealing with young offenders
- reducing re-offending.

Activity

5 Visit the Youth Justice Board website (www.yjb.gov.uk/) and find out if it is fulfilling its aims. How do you think that improvements can be made? You could write a letter to your MP, the Minister for Justice or the Home Secretary to let them know how you feel.

Youth crime

Youth crime harms communities, creates a culture of fear and damages the lives of some of our most vulnerable young people.

Reducing youth crime and improving the **youth justice system** is a central part of the government's effort to build safer communities and to tackle the problem of **social exclusion**.

What causes youth crime?

These are some of the major risk factors that increase the chances of young people committing crimes:

- poor attainment at school, truancy and school exclusion
- troubled home life
- drug or alcohol misuse and mental illness
- deprivation such as poor housing or homelessness
- peer group pressure.

Activity

6 In groups, discuss the factors that increase the chances of young people offending. Which factor do you consider is the most likely to cause a person to offend?

Activities

2 Find the name of the current Home Secretary.

3 Visit the Home Office website (www.homeoffice.gov.uk) and find out some details of its current work from one of its links.

4 Prepare a presentation on your chosen subject or make a poster for display.

Information

The Youth Justice Board was established under the Crime and Disorder Act 1998. The Youth Justice Board along with the police service, courts, prison and probation services are part of the criminal justice system that is managed by local criminal justice boards across England and Wales.

AQA Examiner's tip

You should know what the criminal justice system is and what it does with reference to young people.

Key terms

The youth justice system: the section of the criminal justice system that deals with young offenders.

Social exclusion: being unable to access the things in life that most of society takes for granted, such as decent housing, adequate information and support, and the ability to exercise basic rights.

10.2 The law and young offenders

Those aged 17 or under, who have committed an offence, are classified as 'young offenders'. A wide range of sentences is available to the youth justice system for young offenders, and imprisonment is a last resort.

Objectives

To investigate how the law applies to young offenders.

Age of 'criminal responsibility'

Ten is the legal age of '**criminal responsibility**'.

- Children under the age of ten are not considered to have reached an age where they can be held responsible for their crimes so they can't be charged with any criminal offence.
- Children aged 10–14 can be convicted of a criminal offence if it can be proved that they were aware that what they were doing was seriously wrong.
- After the age of 14, young people are considered to be fully responsible for their own actions in the same way as an adult would.

Activity

1 In groups discuss criminal responsibility. Do you think the age is correct? Do you think that changes should be made? Give reasons for your decisions.

Key terms

Criminal responsibility: when a young person is held responsible for his/her own behaviour and can be found guilty in a court.

Anti-Social Behaviour Order (ASBO): a statutory order. A breach of this order can lead to imprisonment or legal action.

Child Safety Orders: only apply to children under 10 years of age. Under a Child Safety Order a social worker or officer from the youth offending team (YOT) supervises the child.

A *Young people offending*

Behaviour orders and warnings

When young people first get into trouble for committing minor offences, or for anti-social behaviour, they can be dealt with outside the court system. For anti-social behaviour, the police and local authority can use pre-court orders, such as **Anti-Social Behaviour Orders** (ASBOs) or **Child Safety Orders**. For first- or second-time minor offences, the police can use Reprimands and Final Warnings.

AQA Examiner's tip

You should know about behaviour orders and why they are given.

The courts

The Youth Courts

The Youth Court is a section of the Magistrates' Court. It deals with almost all cases involving young people under the age of 18. This section of the Magistrates' Court is served by youth panel magistrates and district judges. They have the power to give detention of up to 24 months, as well as a range of sentences in the community.

Youth Courts are less formal and they are more involved with the young person appearing in court with their family. Youth Courts are essentially private places and members of the public are not allowed in. The victim (or victims) of the crime can attend the hearings of the court if they make a request to the court.

Crown Court

In very serious cases, a young person charged with an offence will have to appear in a Crown Court, rather than a Youth Court. The cases a Crown Court is likely to deal with include:

- serious offences including murder, rape and robbery
- offences that could be heard either in a Magistrates' Court or Crown Court if the offender was an adult
- appeals against sentences given in Magistrates' Courts or Youth Courts.

Sentencing young offenders

The main aims of sentencing are to protect the public and punish the offence. Sentences for young offenders are set in a way that can punish, reduce re-offending and provide a means to pay back to the community.

The young offender may receive the following sentences by a court:

- discharge
- fine
- Reparation Order, for example repairing damage caused to property or cleaning up graffiti
- Community Punishment, for 16–17 year olds. This might involve working with the elderly or conservation work
- Community Rehabilitation, for 16–17 year olds. This might include programmes to address offending behaviour
- Curfew Order, requiring the offender to remain in a specified place for set periods of time
- Drug Treatment and Testing Order, for individuals with drug misuse issues
- Referral Orders – given to all young offenders (aged 10–17) pleading guilty and convicted for a first offence.

Attendance centre orders

Male and female offenders between the ages of 10 and 25 can also be given an attendance centre order. This is an alternative to community sentence or detention. Offenders usually take part in group exercises and are offered help to develop skills and confidence to help them explore why they offend.

AQA *Examiner's tip*

You may be asked to give examples of sentences for young offenders in the exam.

links

You will find an Overview of the Criminal Justice System in the Reference Section pages 217–218.

Activities

2. Some people believe that community based sentences are too easy on offenders. What do you think?
3. Find out what some of these sentences might involve.
4. Are they as easy as people think?
5. Organise a class debate.

   'This house believes that all young offenders should be detained when they commit their third offence.'

10.3 The people in the legal system

Objectives

To explore the people and structures responsible for the legal system.

Barristers

A *A Barrister*

Barristers are specialist legal advisers and court room advocates. They are independent and objective and trained to advise clients on the weaknesses as well as strengths of their case. They have specialist knowledge and experience which can make a substantial difference to the outcome of a case. A limited number of senior barristers are made Queen's Counsel (QC) usually as a mark of outstanding ability.

Information

Queen's Counsel are normally instructed in very serious or complex cases. Most senior judges once practised as QCs.

Solicitors

B *A Solicitor*

A solicitor's role is to give specialist legal advice and help. Solicitors are the main advisers on all matters of law to the public.

A solicitor's job is to provide clients with skilled legal advice and representation, including representing them in court. Most solicitors work in private practice, which is a partnership of solicitors who offer services to clients.

Judges

C *A Judge*

A judge is an official who presides over a court. The judge has powers to conduct the case in the court and make judgements including the type of sentence given to a convicted person. Judges are appointed by the Lord Chancellor and they are trained to undertake their roles. All judges must sign a judicial oath which is a promise of duty of care.

Information

The Lord Chancellor is a member of the cabinet and is responsible for judges, the courts and the legal system.

AQA Examiner's tip

You may be asked to describe the work of one of the key people in the criminal justice system in an examination

Juries

A jury is a sworn body of people brought together to give a considered, impartial verdict in a court of law. The jury will give its verdict on the defendant's guilt after hearing the evidence given. It is guided on the law by the judge. Jurors usually try the more serious criminal cases such as murder, rape, assault, burglary or fraud. These trials take place in the Crown Court. However, jurors are needed in a civil case such as libel. All juries consist of 12 people between 18 and 70 years of age, selected at random from the register of voters.

D *A Jury*

The structures of the legal system

The police

The police are responsible for investigating crimes, arresting or reporting people reasonably suspected of committing crimes, and in preparing the prosecution case. As well as general policing, officers can be trained in special duties such as counter-terrorism; surveillance; child protection; and investigating major crime such as fraud, rape, murder, and drug trafficking.

E *The police*

Youth Offending Teams (YOT)

This is a team of professionals from a wide range of public services that includes the police, Probation Service, social services, health, education, drugs and alcohol misuse and housing officers. There is a YOT in every local authority in England and Wales. Each team has a manager who is responsible for the administration and conduct of the team.

The principal aim of the team is to prevent offending by children and young people, through the following objectives:

- the swift administration of justice so that every young person accused of breaking the law has the matter resolved without unnecessary delay
- confronting young offenders with the consequences of their offending, for themselves and their family, their victims and their community and helping them to develop a sense of personal responsibility
- intervention which tackles the particular factors (personal, family, social, educational or health) that put the young person at risk of offending
- punishment proportionate to the seriousness and persistence of offending
- encouraging reparation (pay back) to victims by young offenders
- reinforcing the responsibilities of parents.

The Probation Service

The National Probation Service (NPS) is a law enforcement agency and public authority, and is actively committed to the rehabilitation of offenders released from prison and support to those given community sentences. In addition, the service supervises imprisoned people who have been given a statutory licence supervision in the community as an integral part of the sentence. Protecting the public is a main priority of the Probation Service so great care is taken to manage offenders on their release from prison and when they are in the community.

The Prison Service

Her Majesty's Prison Service serves the public by keeping in custody those committed by the courts. Its duty is to look after prisoners with humanity and help them lead law-abiding and useful lives in custody and after release. The service's aim is to protect the public by holding prisoners securely and to provide safe and well-ordered establishments in which prisoners are treated humanely, decently and lawfully.

Activity

Create a court scene. Decide on three offences that would be heard in a Crown Court. Make sure that the 'actors' have been given the correct information about what is expected of their roles. You will need a judge, a jury, a defendant, prosecution barrister and witnesses, defence barrister and witnesses. Remember to be appropriate with your language and actions. Your teacher may like to act as the court usher.

F *A youth offending officer*

G *A probation officer*

H *A prison officer*

10.4 The issues about sentencing and appeals

Types of sentence

Whenever a criminal offence has been committed and the offender is found guilty, it is up to the judge to find a proportional sentence to punish/rehabilitate the offender. When judges or magistrates pass a sentence they not only look at the sentences available, they also have to consider what they are aiming for with the sentence they give. In general the aims of sentencing are divided into different categories: **retribution**, **deterrence**, **rehabilitation** and **reparation**.

Custodial sentences

Imprisonment is the most severe penalty that is available to the courts. It is generally only available for the more serious offences. Additionally, each offence has a maximum prison term, which is usually set out by an Act of Parliament. There are mandatory minimum sentences for serious repeat offenders (meaning that they can't be sentenced to less than a specified amount of time in prison). Any time an offender has spent in custody before their trial usually counts as time towards their sentence. In general terms, this type of sentence matches the theories of retribution and deterrence.

Community sentences

Community sentences mean that the offender has to do a certain amount of unpaid work for the community. If the offender is employed, they are expected to do the work in their own time. If they are under a 'community rehabilitation order' they will be under the supervision of a probation officer. In general terms, this type of sentence matches the theories of reparation and rehabilitation.

Activity

1. a Go to the Home Office website (www.homeoffice.gov.uk). Find the statistics for sentences given by 1) Magistrates' Courts and 2) Crown Courts. Make a bar chart to show the types of sentence given by each court. Compare the charts. What are the differences?
   b Why do you think this has happened?

Appeals

Any person convicted by a Magistrates' Court can appeal to the Crown Court against their conviction, and/or the sentence imposed. Appeals are investigated by the Criminal Cases Review Commission to ensure that there are no **miscarriages of justice**.

How effective is our criminal justice system?

An effective criminal justice system is the basis of our society. Our legal system and police services are rightly esteemed throughout the world. But, as the threats to our way of life are evolving ever more rapidly, we need to ensure that the system continues to protect us all.

Objectives

To investigate the issues surrounding sentencing.

Key terms

Retribution: the theory that the offender deserves punishment.

Deterrence: the theory justifies a punishment in order to discourage the offender and other people from committing the particular offence or other offences.

Rehabilitation: the theory that the sentence is intended to reform the offender's behaviour.

Reparation: aims to make some compensation to society, the victim and/or the victim's relatives.

Miscarriage of justice: when a person is convicted or punished for a crime that he or she did not commit.

AQA Examiner's tip

Knowledge of sentences and the reasons for them is a popular examination topic.

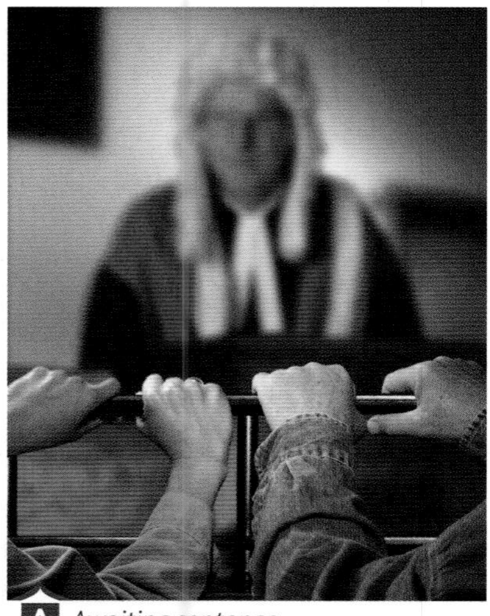

A *Awaiting sentence*

To check that we are being effective we look at public confidence in criminal justice agencies, public fear of crime, the crime rate and the number of criminals as indicators of success. In our system people want to:

- feel safe
- have value for money
- ensure human rights are being met, and
- see offenders brought to justice.

Activity

2 Do you think that the criminal justice system does its job? What would you change? Give reasons for your answer.

Case study

The Intensive Supervision and Surveillance Programme (ISSP)

This is an intensive programme used by Youth Offending Teams across the UK in place of custodial sentences. It is not seen as a soft option for offenders. It involves intensive supervision combined with surveillance.

B *Electronic tagging device*

The supervision:

- is a planned intervention focusing on offending behaviour
- offers support for the young person and family, to help achieve change
- is a minimum of 25 hours per week during the first 3 months (education, training, individual sessions)
- is a minimum of 1 hour per day during months 3–6.

The surveillance:

- involves daily tracking and monitoring by ISSP team: accompanying young people to appointments, providing support and advice, and following up non-attendance. Missed appointments are followed up within 24 hours
- arranges voice verification: timed telephone contacts to check young person's whereabouts
- involves tagging: electronic monitoring of the young person to reinforce night-time curfew.

The police monitor the movements of young offenders at key times to reinforce the programme as well as sharing information with the ISSP team.

Information

Northern Ireland's legal system is broadly similar to that in England and Wales.

Activities

3 Some people consider the Intensive Supervision and Surveillance Programme to be an easier option than sitting in a prison cell. What do you think?

4 Is tagging a young person at night-time a breach of their civil liberties? What do you think?

5 Discuss these points in groups.

10.5 Tackling youth crime

The Home Office website starts its section on youth crime with this statement.

> *Youth crime harms communities, creates a culture of fear and damages the lives of some of our most vulnerable young people.*
>
> *Reducing youth crime and improving the youth justice system is a central part of our effort to build safer communities and to tackle the problem of social exclusion.*

Objectives

To explore the type of activities being undertaken to reduce youth crime.

To look at an outcome of anti-social behaviour.

Case study

Operation Reclaim in Glasgow

A *Sporting activities are used as a means of engaging young offenders*

Operation Reclaim is a pioneering project started by Strathclyde Police. Reclaim is a diversionary project that promotes integration and tolerance whilst developing the skills and qualities of the young people who participate in the various activities offered by the project. The project is managed by Sidekix Ltd.

In the north of Glasgow there are five areas. They are outlined in the statistics below. Crimes of disorder have reduced by the following percentages since Operation Reclaim was extended to all people regardless of colour, religion or culture in May 2007. Everyone is welcome. Reclaim is about integrating people from all backgrounds and breaking down the racial and territorial barriers in the north of the city.

Crime reduction:

- Red Road – down by 44.5 per cent
- Sighthill – down by 57 per cent
- Royston – down by 50 per cent
- Quarrywood – down by 34 per cent
- Springburn – down by 24.5 per cent.

These are official Strathclyde Police figures.

Information

Sidekix Ltd is a sport/activity, personal development and events management company that provides high quality staff, equipment, activity programmes and service.

Activities

1. The Operation Reclaim project is funded by National Lottery funds. Do you think it is a good use of good causes money? Give reasons for your answer.
2. Your local Youth Justice Board will run a scheme to help young people in your area. Find out about what is available where you live.
3. The Youth Offending Team for your area or the local police station will be able to tell you about statistics for your area. Write and ask for information.

Case study

Kelly

Newtown is a rural community, with a mixture of social and private housing. Facilities and opportunities for young people are very limited with young people often travelling long distances to reach suitable activities.

Kelly is a 14-year-old girl who first came to the attention of police early in 2007 when she received a verbal warning for breaking into an abandoned industrial building with a group of young people she hung out with. Her nuisance behaviour continued to escalate and became noticeably worse later in 2007. She received a reprimand for assaulting another young person and a final warning for criminal damage. Residents, local businesses and her mother complained about her behaviour. The main problems were identified as:

B

- hanging around in inappropriate places in the evenings (public buildings, school grounds)
- swearing and being abusive to members of the public
- drinking alcohol with friends in public places
- poor school attendance and disruptive behaviour in school
- not coming home at night – her parents were concerned
- not considering her own behaviour to be a problem.

In March 2008, the police ABC officer referred Kelly to the Newtown Youth Project.

What happened to help Kelly?

- **Police:** Drew up an acceptable behaviour contract (ABC) on 3 March 2008. Referred Kelly to the youth project.
- **Youth project worker:** Worked with Kelly weekly over five months. Put in place an intervention plan to address her behaviour and offer her support with home and school.
- **School/Education:** Carried out an assessment to establish Kelly's support needs and steps to improve her attendance.

What happens now?

In July 2008, the Home Office published a Youth Crime Action Plan. It was designed to approach the issue from a number of different perspectives. It calls for cross-governmental cooperation to address this serious and troubling problem. The government is committed to tackling youth crime and reducing the fear of youth crime.

Activities

4. Why was Kelly allowed to misbehave for a year and end up in trouble with the police before action was taken to help her? Discuss in pairs.
5. What can be done to stop other children in this area from displaying unacceptable behaviour? Write down five things that might make things better for the young people in this area. Who might be able to make your suggestions a reality? How would you go about making these things happen?
6. Do you think that the intervention used for Kelly was successful? Give reasons for your answer.

Activity

7. Go to the Home Office website (**www.homeoffice.gov.uk**). Find out what happened to the Youth Crime Action Plan. What is the government doing about youth crime now?

Chapter summary 10

What you should know:

From this chapter your knowledge should now cover:

Short course

- ✔ what the point of criminal law is
- ✔ the criminal justice system
- ✔ the Youth Justice Board
- ✔ youth crime and its causes
- ✔ the age of criminal responsibility
- ✔ behaviour orders and warnings
- ✔ the courts – Youth Court and Crown Court
- ✔ sentencing young offenders

Full course

- ✔ the people in the legal system
- ✔ the structures in the legal system
- ✔ types of sentence
- ✔ how effective the criminal justice system is
- ✔ tackling youth crime
- ✔ what happens now?

Check your knowledge

You should be able to answer the following questions without looking back over the text. If you cannot answer all of the questions you need to learn the material more thoroughly.

1. What is an ASBO?
2. Name two sections of the criminal justice system.
3. What is social exclusion?
4. What is the name of the current Home Secretary?
5. Which section of the criminal justice system is responsible for prisons?
6. Give two causes of youth crime.
7. What is the age of criminal responsibility?
8. When is a young offender sent to Crown Court?
9. List three sentences a court may give to a young offender.
10. What is the youth justice system?

Picture stimulus

A *Youth offence*

- Look at the picture carefully. Do you think this is the person's first offence?
- What do you think the person will be charged with when they are caught?
- Do you think the range of punishments for this crime compensate for the damage caused?

Further study

The effects of sentencing on society

B *The effects of sentencing on society*

Sentences		Age (years)			
		10-17	18-20	21+	All ages
Total sentences	1996	74,507	152,298	1,198,472	1,425,277
	2006	93,806	142,694	1,176,440	1,412,940
Custodial sentences	1996	6,497	14,750	64,002	85,249
	2006	6,183	13,897	75,937	96,017
Community sentences	1996	25,123	22,752	84,762	132,637
	2006	61,498	24,879	104,460	190,837
Fines	1996	16,962	95,330	949,201	1,061,493
	2006	11,599	80,910	861,653	954,162
Other measures	1996				139,114
	2006				134,281

Go to the criminal justice system website (**http://lcjb.cjsonline.gov.uk/**).

- Choose your area from the map of England and Wales.

Answer one of the polls your criminal justice board is currently holding.

From the options, choose Meet the Team. Who is your board chairperson? Choose one topic from the criminal justice system and:

- Make a report
- or Prepare a talk
- or Make a poster for display
- or Prepare a PowerPoint presentation
- or Write a poem
- or Draw a picture about this topic.

Your teacher may have some more ideas for you.

Activity

1. a Look at the above table. Note the increase in the number of custodial sentences. What does this mean for the prison service?

   b Which type of sentence has increased the most? Why do you think this has happened?

   c Look at the Probation Service website. Why has re-offending reduced?

11 Why does the media matter in Britain?

11.1 What is the media?

The media is the biggest provider of information in the modern world. The media includes:

- television
- radio
- videos/cds/dvds
- magazines
- newspapers
- books
- the interent
- advertisements and
- the cinema.

Objectives

To explore the concepts of media and mass media and their influence on society.

Information

Psychologists believe that from our earliest years, the media, in one form or another, influences our thoughts or attitudes and, to some extent, our behaviour.

The mass media

A *Mass media is circulated widely*

The **mass media** includes the distributors of news and entertainment across media such as:

- newspapers and magazines
- television and radio broadcasting.

The mass media can be used for various purposes:

- reporting the news, both locally and nationally
- advocacy, both for business and social concerns including advertising
- enrichment and education
- entertainment
- public service announcements.

The media has a responsibility to report information fairly but the people who control the transmission of information determine how the information is presented.

Key terms

Mass media: a term used to denote a section of the media designed to reach a very large audience.

Activity

1. Give details of three public service campaigns shown on the television. Make a poster to advertise one of these campaigns. Does this type of service work?

Mass media influence

In the last 50 years media influence has grown in line with the advance of technology – first there was the telegraph, then the radio, the newspaper, magazines, television and now the internet. We live in a society that depends on information and communication to keep us informed about issues we relate to, for example, work, entertainment, health care, and education.

In life, most of our decisions, beliefs and values are based on what we know for a fact from our own experience. However, on a daily basis, we rely on the media to get the current news and facts about what is happening in the world. We put our trust in the media to give us news, entertainment and education. However, the influence of mass media is so great that we need to understand how it works and consider each item of news so that we form our own opinion.

How mass media influence works

Of all the media distribution channels, the most influential has been the television. We are constantly exposed to thousands of images on a daily basis. Years ago there was more diversity in companies, but they have merged into huge industries that have the power to shape public opinion.

The media makes billions of pounds by selling advertising. We buy what we are told is good, after seeing thousands of advertisements. We make our buying decisions based on what we saw on TV, in newspapers or magazines. We trust the product based on what other people we know are buying. However, their decision is often based on media exposure. The media uses celebrities to persuade teenagers and children what is acceptable in terms of fashion, sports equipment, soft drinks, perfume deodorant, etc.

B *Celebrities receive sponsorship to promote products*

Information

Five companies own 95 per cent of all the media that we get every day. They own major theme parks, movie studios, television and radio broadcast networks, integrated telecommunications, wireless phones, video games software, and more.

AQA *Examiner's tip*

You should know the different types of media and how the media works.

Activities

2 Name five brands of product that are promoted by sports personalities.

3 Name five television programmes that are sponsored. Name the firms or products that sponsor them.

4 Have you or has someone you know created a problem for a parent by insisting on a certain toy, game or piece of clothing? Why did this problem arise? Why did the person insist on that product? Why was a similar product not good enough?

11.2 Freedom of the press

Freedom of the press, like freedom of speech, is one of our civil liberties. It differs from other liberties in that it is both individual and institutional. It applies not just to a single person's right to publish ideas, but also to the right of print and broadcast media to express political views and to cover and publish news.

A free press is one of the foundations of a democratic society. Indeed, as society has grown increasingly complex, people rely more and more on newspapers, radio, and television to keep abreast with world news, opinion and political ideas. One sign of the importance of a free press is that when anti-democratic forces take over a country, their first act is often to control the press. This is known as **censorship**.

Media, reporting and propaganda

We are used to reading newspapers and listening to news broadcasts on the television. But is the information we receive the truth, the whole truth and nothing but the truth, or something less?

One learns to expect partial truth, selective memory and strategic omissions from governments that 'manage' information to present their official positions in the best possible light (that is, **propaganda**), but when the free media participates in the management and filtering process, it raises serious concerns.

To have meaning and value, information must be accurate, objective and reasonably complete. Hence, a cornerstone of democracy is freedom of the press and objectivity of the press.

What is the Press Complaints Commission (PCC)?

The Press Complaints Commission is an independent body that deals with complaints from members of the public about the editorial content of newspapers and magazines. All complaints are investigated under the accepted Code of Practice, which binds all national and regional newspapers and magazines.

The Press Complaints Commission is charged with enforcing the Code of Practice.

All members of the press have a duty to maintain the highest professional standards.

Information

- The Code of Practice was designed by the newspaper and magazine editors. It was accepted by the PCC on 1 August 2007.
- The Office of Communications (Ofcom) is responsible for the regulation of broadcasting.

Objectives

To explore the issues of press freedom and media reporting.

To understand restrictions placed on the press and the role of the Press Complaints Commission.

Key terms

Freedom of the press: allows the press to publish thoughts, beliefs or opinions without interference from the government.

Censorship: is the control of information and ideas circulated within a society.

Propaganda: specially created information that aims to make people think a certain way.

Activity

- Do you think the British press always reports information fairly? Write five sentences in support of your view.
- Using a medium of your choice produce a piece of propaganda aimed at selling something. For example, you might attach a drink to a footballer or a type of food to a singer.

AQA *Examiner's tip*

You may be asked in the examination to say what the Press Complaints Commission is and what it does.

Features of the Code of Practice

The press must make sure that the following rules are applied:

- Information should be accurate and should not be misleading.
- A fair opportunity should be offered for reply to inaccurate reports.
- It must be recognised that everyone is entitled to respect for his or her private and family life.
- Journalists must not engage in intimidation, harassment or persistent pursuit.
- In cases involving personal grief or shock, enquiries and approaches must be made with sympathy and discretion and publication handled sensitively.
- Young people should be free to complete their time at school without unnecessary intrusion. A child under 16 must not be interviewed or photographed on issues involving their own or another child's welfare unless a custodial parent or similarly responsible adult consents. Pupils must not be approached or photographed at school without the permission of the school authorities. The press must not, even if legally free to do so, identify children under 16 who are victims or witnesses in cases involving sex offences.

There may be exceptions to a person's right to privacy in the clauses marked * where the situations can be demonstrated to be in the public interest.

The public interest involves matters that are held to affect a considerable number of people. It must not only be something that people are merely interested in knowing about.

Information

There are also rules covering *hospitals, *reporting of crime, *using hidden cameras or listening devices, discrimination, paying witnesses in criminal trials and *paying criminals.

Case study

Harry Potter author, Ms JK Rowling complained to the Press Complaints Commission that an article in the *Daily Mirror* headlined 'The JK Rowling Story: Day Three' intruded into her privacy in breach of Clause 3 (Privacy) of the Code. The article contained a photograph of her London property, with the name of the road on which it was located. Her solicitors said that there was sufficient information to identify its exact location in breach of the Code.

The complaint was upheld. The Commission recognised that high profile individuals may be exposed to security problems if their precise addresses are published. Indeed, the newspaper itself noted that Ms Rowling had 'gained her fair share of stalkers and obsessive fans'.

- Do famous people and their families have the right to privacy? Discuss.

A *JK Rowling won an appeal against the* Daily Mirror

Discussion activity

Discuss the following in groups:

- The newspaper industry regulates itself through the Press Complaints Commission. Do you think this is the right way to do it?
- How would you decide what was in the public interest? Put your answer in writing.

11.3 The media and public opinion

In general terms, the media are likely to lead **public opinion** in a direction favoured by their sponsors. The public opinion that is often created by the mass media is that of the passive recipient of information rather than the active participant in a defining political and social system.

Public opinion plays an important role in the political arena. Many **opinion polls** are undertaken to determine how the public feels about important issues particularly at the time of elections. The media is one of the biggest users of polls. In this way the media is seeking to reflect public opinion in its reports. However, the reporting of an opinion poll in the media can influence how people think about an issue. In this situation it is possible to put a **spin** on the information in such a way that public opinion could be distorted.

When we interpret a poll, it is important that we look at the size of the sample and what sort of person was used in the sample. Otherwise the sample may not represent us.

Objectives

To investigate the role of the media in the formation of public opinion.

To consider the role of the media in the reporting of terrorism and world conflict.

Key terms

Public opinion: the belief held by the majority of adults – the popular view.

Opinion poll: a survey of public opinion using a sample of the total adult population to show how people think.

Spin: a way of presenting information in an attempt to control the public's response.

Activity

1 Should the media try to control public opinion or report facts factually and without bias? Does the media distort, reflect or create public opinion? Discuss in groups.

Case study

On 5 April 2005, Prime Minister, Tony Blair went to Buckingham Palace to request that the Queen dissolve parliament and that a general election be held. The general election would be on 5 May. The results of opinion polls for national newspapers are shown here.

Type of Poll	*Labour*	*Conservatives*	*Lib democrats*	*Others*
NOP *(Independent)*	33%	34%	21%	10%
Populus *(Times)*	37%	35%	19%	9%
MORI *(Financial Times)*	34%	39%	21%	6%
ICM *(Guardian)*	37%	34%	21%	8%

The actual result was

Labour	*Conservatives*	*Lib Democrats*	*Other*
36%	30%	22%	12%

A *These figures are from www.historylearningsite.co.uk*

- Why do you think the poll figures were wrong in estimating the Conservative vote?
- Do you think public opinion polls should be conducted face to face, on the telephone, by post or on the internet? Give reasons for your answer.

Terrorism and the media

The primary goal of terrorism is to attract attention. Over long periods of time group differences and rejection become deeply ingrained and can lead to protracted conflict and hatred between groups.

What's in a name? Experts can't agree on a definition of the word 'terrorism'. A key objective of any political campaign is publicity, which requires attracting media coverage. This is true for governments and their opponents. The journalistic challenge is to avoid using the term 'terrorist' indiscriminately, or to apply it equally to each case regardless of whether the violence is perpetrated by a government or a militant group.

Words do matter. The term 'terrorist' carries a stigma and is used specifically to condemn an organisation. Other words used for the same purpose include: Marxist, communist, extremist, and fascist. When these words appear, it's wise to be alert for propaganda.

AQA Examiner's tip

You should form your own opinion of the media and how it affects the public and be able to give reasons for your opinion.

Activity

2 Use a dictionary and find a definition of 'terrorist' and 'terrorism'. Use this to write your own definition of the two words. Share your definition with someone. Are your definitions the same?

The media and world conflict

Freedom of the press entails:

- having access to people and events
- the ability to collect news and information
- the ability to distribute information and
- meeting the rights of citizens to receive information.

In the case of political disputes, violent conflict and war, each of these elements is at risk. Often we will find that the first casualty of war is truth.

B *Pentagon in Washington, USA, is attacked*

With freedom comes responsibility and challenge. Correspondents are just people, people who struggle to remain balanced and objective. Faced with the tragedies of conflict, it's difficult to remain a detached observer, though this is what we expect them to do. Under pressure to deliver compelling and captivating reports, it must be difficult for controllers to resist the temptation to sensationalise what is happening.

C *Suicide bombing in Iraq*

Television networks and newspaper publishers face their own set of challenges. These challenges include:

- the requirement for financial performance
- the pressure for ratings and readership, and
- the constraining influences of governments, politicians, advertisers and interest groups.

The ethical and operational challenges to maintain a press freedom and effective flow of information are enormous. For the citizen receiving the news, the task of sorting the facts and truth are no less daunting.

D *Bombed tank in Georgia*

11.4 Politicians and the media

> *Politicians and the media have a lot to answer for ... The remedy is simple: governments should play it straight, and the media should play it fair.*
>
> *Tony Wright MP Chair of the Commons Public Accounts Committee (from www.guardian.co.uk/politics)*

Objectives

To investigate how politicians and other groups use the media.

The relationship between politics and the media has never been easy. They have different jobs so it does not matter if the relationship is one of occasional conflict. Politicians and journalists should be open and honest and not be influenced by media owners who have a purely commercial interest in the outcome of events.

Politicians are often critical of the way the media reports politics claiming that they over-simplify issues, exaggerate the impact and focus too much on scandals or disagreements between politicians.

The media often accuse politicians, particularly the government, of over-complicating matters and trying to manipulate the media for their own benefit.

Information

Political parties use the television to make party political broadcasts and buy space in newspapers and magazines to promote party policies and campaigns.

Case study

Individual politicians use the media to highlight personal and party policy. In 2008, Conservative leader, David Cameron, used the media to show his commitment to green issues by summoning the media to photograph and film him cycling to the House of Commons. This backfired in two ways:

1 It was found that he cycled to work but then had his car follow with his briefcase. This caused much comment and criticism and required the Conservative Party to speak in his defence.

2 He was seen to ignore red lights and cycle the wrong way up a one-way street.

This gave an opportunity for political opponents and interest groups to criticise his behaviour. Mr Cameron apologised for his mistakes.

- Do you think politicians should pull publicity stunts like this one? Did Mr Cameron make his point or was it lost in the criticism? Discuss in groups.
- Look at the national media. Choose an article that shows a politician using the media to make a point. Write a report about the incident. Was the event successful?

A *David Cameron cycles to parliament*

Politicians and the internet

Is this the future? There is no denying that the internet has the potential to change the way that politicians do their job. It can open up the opportunity for comment to the general public. However, it will only succeed if the internet is universally available and the system is used and read regularly.

How other agencies use the media

The media is essential to success in any campaign. Whether you are a person trying to bring about change in your local community or whether you are an international organisation, you will need to use some form of media to bring your point to the attention of the wider public and find a response to your appeal.

The Non-governmental Organisation (NGO) community and charities consider the media to be important in their efforts to effect change and influence public opinion. They believe that good relationships with journalists are an integral part of any effective media outreach campaign. The media can help these organisations by:

- creating an environment of political pressure
- conveying general information
- serving as a public education tool
- countering popular misconceptions
- comment on an issue, and
- providing an alternative viewpoint.

NGOs develop a clear and specific message that includes:

- the situation the campaign is addressing
- the solution the group proposes
- the action that the public can take to help solve the problem.

Individuals can make a difference too. Working together, like-minded people can change society's views and make changes to procedures and laws.

Activity

- Do you think politicians and the citizens they represent will use this new technology as a means of interaction? What are the benefits of internet communication? Discuss.
- Go to **www.adampriceblog.org.uk** to see how this Plaid Cymru member uses his blog.

Information

NGOs give advice on how to issue a press release and hold a radio and television interview. All major NGOs and charities have websites to give details of their activities and campaigns.

Case study

Families Need Fathers

In May 1974, two fathers, Alick Elithorn and Keith Parkin, got together and decided to do something about the problems they faced with family law during the breakdown of their marriages. They knew that a change in society would require concerted effort by a group of like-minded people. So they founded an organisation and called it Families Need Fathers (FNF).

The *Guardian* supplied the opportunity for this charity to launch its message in June 1974. Today, the organisation is principally concerned with the problems of maintaining a child's relationship with both parents during and after family breakdown and it is the principal society providing advice on children's issues for separated and divorced parents.

B *A new father*

Chapter summary

What you should know:

From this chapter your knowledge should now cover:

Short course

- ✔ what the media is
- ✔ the mass media
- ✔ mass media influence
- ✔ how mass media influence works.
- ✔ freedom of the press
- ✔ media reporting and propaganda
- ✔ what the Press Complaints Commission is
- ✔ features of the Code of Practice

Full course

- ✔ the media and public opinion
- ✔ terrorism and the media
- ✔ the media and world conflict
- ✔ politicians and the media
- ✔ politicians and the internet
- ✔ how other agencies use the media

Check your knowledge

You should be able to answer the following questions without looking back over the text. If you cannot answer all of the questions you need to learn the material more thoroughly.

1. Name three sections of the media.
2. What is the mass media?
3. What is the name of the broadcasting regulator?
4. What is the Press Complaints Commission?
5. Name two things the mass media is used for?
6. What is censorship?
7. What is freedom of the press?
8. What does 'in the public interest' mean?
9. What is propaganda?
10. Name two rules from the Code of Practice that deal with children.

Further study

Manipulating the media – the Beijing Olympics opening ceremony

A *This girl mimed*

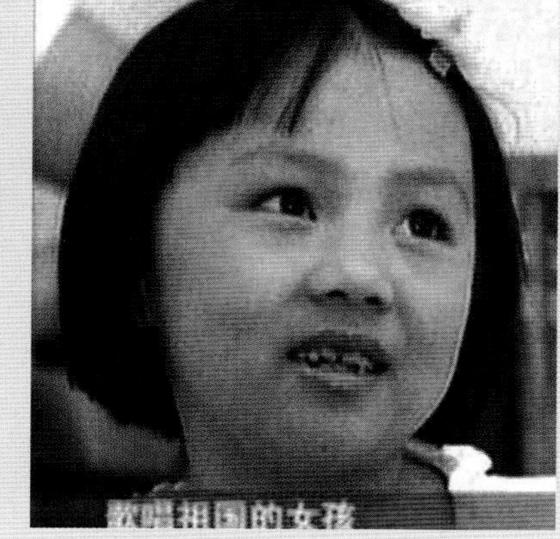

This girl sang the anthem

The cute, tiny, pigtailed nine-year-old mouthed her words before a worldwide audience.

The seven-year-old was considered unsuited to the lead role because of her buck teeth.

Gilbert Felli, the International Olympic Committee's (IOC's) Olympic Games executive director, was uncomfortable when he was asked if this was the right message to be sending to the children of the world: that appearance, not skill, is what counts. What do you think of the decision to substitute beauty for skill?

- Go to the website of your regional newspaper.
  - Choose the campaigns and events section.
  - Choose one of these and read about it.
  - Decide what you feel about it and what you can do about it.
- Choose an issue that is bothering young people in your school, your club or your team.
  - Find out why people are so upset. Interview two people about the issue.
  - Decide what you feel about it and what you can do about it.
- For your chosen area of study you should:
  - Make a report
  - or Prepare a talk
  - or Make a poster for display
  - or Discuss it with someone
  - or Write a letter to your MP
  - or Prepare a PowerPoint presentation
  - or Write a poem
  - or Draw a picture.

Your teacher may have some other ideas for your work.

Picture stimulus

B *Stop knives, save lives campaign and Amir Khan*

- In 2008, the Daily Mirror launched a campaign called 'Stop Knives, Save Lives'. Go to the Mirror website (www.mirror.co.uk/) and see if this campaign is still running. What other issues does the Daily Mirror support?
- The campaign was launched as a result of knife crime in the UK. The young man on the shirt is Ben Kinsella. Visit the website (www.benkinsella.org.uk/). What will the money from donations be used for?
- Do you think that more celebrities should attach themselves to charities like this one?

THEME 4 Global issues and making a

The five chapters are:

- **12** Dealing with important global issues
- **13** The global economy and world trade
- **14** Sustainable development – facing the challenges
- **15** The UK's role in world affairs
- **16** Influencing international issues

Key terms

globalisation global inequality
World Trade Organization G8
fair trade ethical trade
inequality and injustice
aid programmes multi-lateral
free trade bi-lateral fairness
trading practices
multinational companies
supranatural Primary
Secondary Tertiary
world economic system LEDCs
MEDCs agencies world bank
IMF poverty and hunger
child labour global resources
individual consumers

In this Theme you will learn about international organisations, the global economy, the UK's role within the world community, sustainable development and other important global issues including conflict and poverty.

12 Dealing with important global issues

In this chapter you will look at the role of international bodies in dealing with conflict and genocide. In the short course, you will see how conflict arises and how difficult it is to resolve. The full course deals with the issue of genocide and the problems it leaves behind.

A *Dealing with conflict*

Concepts

United Nations European Union Commonwealth
The issue of conflict International conflict and cooperation
Human rights abuses Understanding genocide and war crimes

Key terms

International bodies global issues disagreement conflict resolution prevention crisis management cooperation extremism reasons mediation use of force sanctions human rights abuses NGOs targeted aid/support genocide war crimes tribunals international court armed conflict protection victims

13 The global economy and world trade

In this chapter you will look at the issues surrounding world trade. You will see that what seems fair to one country is often seen as unfair in another. You will see how certain types of trade bring different things to the world's rich and the world's poor.

B *G8 leaders meeting*

Concepts

How does the global economy work?
Globalisation Global inequality World Trade Organization/G8
Fair/ethical trade Fairness

14 Sustainable development – facing the challenges

In this chapter we will look at a number of issues relating to the challenges facing the global community in relation to environmental concerns.

Concepts

Interdependence

Sustainability

Local agenda 21

C *Deforestation is one cause of global warming*

Key terms

challenges sustainability local Local Agenda 21 global issues biodiversity Environmental issues climate change fossil fuels population growth greenhouse effect acid rain global warming renewable energy wind power interdependence commodity biofuels

15 The UK's role in world affairs

In this chapter you will look at the UK's role and relationships with international groups and organisations. You will look at the reasons why the UK joins with other groups and the benefits and problems that arise from membership.

D *Flags of European Union*

Concepts

The UK's role in:
The United Nations The European Union The Commonwealth, and International Organisations

Key terms

European Union UN Commonwealth Relationships IMF World Bank NATO G8 functions cooperative trade membership genetic modification differing viewpoints consumer issues reasons for membership trade discussions challenges

16 Influencing international issues

In this chapter you will look at how pressure groups and Non-governmental Organisations (NGOs) influence international issues and how an individual can make a difference. You will look at participation and volunteering in the community.

Concepts

The individual and making a difference

Participation

Pressure groups and NGOs

'Global village'

Global citizenship

E *NGOs from around the world give assistance and advice*

Key terms

pressure group NGOs individuals methods media international issues understanding choices differences natural disaster participation volunteering climate change campaign development goals poverty global citizenship global village

12 Dealing with important global issues

12.1 Understanding conflict

Underlying causes of conflict

The way a society is organised can create both the causes of **conflict** and the conditions in which it's likely to occur. People need to be treated equally and justly or conflict will erupt. Human beings have basic needs. Everyone needs to be recognised as an individual with a personal identity and everyone needs to be able to feel safe. When these needs aren't met, conflict ensues. People must learn that different cultures do not, inevitably, pose a threat and then they might learn to manage differences cooperatively and peacefully.

Objectives

To understand the issue of conflict and how it can be managed.

Key terms

Conflict: a dispute: a disagreement or argument about something important.

The issue of conflict

Our case study will concentrate on conflict that is expressed in group violence and war. The issues explored will mostly be those that arise between peoples and nations, but you will find that they can all be translated into local terms, to match the conflicts that you may know about personally. Conflicts arise:

- when people are competing for the same resources such as land
- when the people are unhappy with how they are governed. The most common conflicts occur when a particular group wants to be independent from a government or when the government oppresses them and doesn't respect or meet their basic needs
- when people's beliefs clash. Religious and political views are particularly sensitive, because people often depend on these for a sense of identity and belonging, and
- when ethnic differences are not sensitively handled. People's ethnicity gives them a sense of identity and belonging, and threats to this can cause violent responses.

A *Armed citizens in a conflict*

Indeed, conflicts of all kinds most frequently arise when people feel threatened – regardless of whether the threat is real. It is harder to soothe and reassure people when they are frightened or angry.

Handling conflict

A lot of research has been and is being done to find the best ways of dealing non-violently with conflicts in all their stages, whether they are interpersonal, local, national or international. The aim is to transform conflicts from destructive forces into violence-free, constructive ones. Most techniques for handling conflict involve the intervention of individuals or teams of individuals who aren't involved in the dispute themselves.

In international conflict, some interveners are voluntary peace workers or members of aid agencies, non-governmental organisations (NGOs) and support agencies. Sometimes interveners are diplomats from other countries, or representatives of international organisations such as the European Union (EU) or the United Nations (UN). Neutral member states of the region in conflict also have a part to play.

B *UN Peacekeeping troops on escort duty*

Prevention

Some peace-makers and teams concentrate on spotting areas in which conflict looks likely to break out, and then monitor them closely. At the same time they help the conflicting sides to work out their disputes without use of violence.

Although this work may well prevent the outbreak of violence, it cannot resolve the conflict until the underlying causes have been dealt with. This requires long-term projects to identify the causes correctly and provide the sort of support needed to put things right. The right kind of support also needs to be given.

Information

UN Peacekeepers wear blue caps so they can be easily identified.

Crisis management

If violence is imminent but hasn't yet broken out, an intervener acceptable to both sides has a chance to remind them of the destructive risks they are running, and to express concern about people getting hurt. This approach may slow the move towards violence, but the issues disputed have not been dealt with and violence may still break out at a later date. If violence has already started, then the interveners' work is primarily an effort to keep it to a minimum and to deal with the damage it is causing.

Sometimes, outside intervention has been military. Military intervention causes long-term damage and often makes the conflict much harder to resolve. The introduction of armed intervention simply adds another combatant to the conflict and reinforces the idea that violence can resolve it. Any military intervention must carry the promise of help with reconstruction.

AQA *Examiner's tip*

You should be able to explain the reasons for the conflict and give your own opinion about the causes and the possible outcome.

links

You will find the stages of a conflict outlined in the reference section on pages 217–218. Use this guide to describe what stage the conflict outlined in the following case study has reached and whether a resolution is likely.

Activity

1. What examples of conflicts, local or national, can you think of which:
   - a seem to have arisen from issues to do with resources?
   - b seem to have arisen from issues to do with management/authority/government?
   - c seem to have arisen from differences of belief?
   - d seem to have arisen from ethnic differences?

Research a conflict in your local area – collect information and map the history of the conflict. Perhaps the conflict you are researching hasn't yet ended. If it has, do you think that the risks of renewed conflict have been dealt with?

12.2 Conflict

Israel-Palestine

About the conflict

The Israeli-Palestinian conflict is a major source of **Arab** and Muslim grievances against the West in general and the US in particular. Many believe that Israel has strengthened its influence over American politics and Middle East policy. Up until 2000, the US was often seen as an independent broker, working to resolve the Middle-East conflict, but in recent years America has been perceived as lending support to Israeli policies in the Occupied Territories. Failure to resolve the Israeli-Palestinian conflict continues to strengthen anti-western **extremism** throughout the Middle East.

Israel as a nation state was confronted by a political and paramilitary organisation called the Palestine Liberation Organization. This organisation was accepted as the legitimate representative of the Palestinian people by the **Arab League** in 1974.

This conflict has been waged over many years and within each country there are now many different groups claiming to represent the wishes of the majority. Some of these groups are extremist in nature. Both parties hold very different views about how these issues should be resolved and what constitutes fairness and justice.

East Jerusalem is mainly Arab. Some Arabs chose Israeli citizenship rather than leave and have been granted freedom of speech, religion and the right to vote, though they would prefer to be Palestinian.

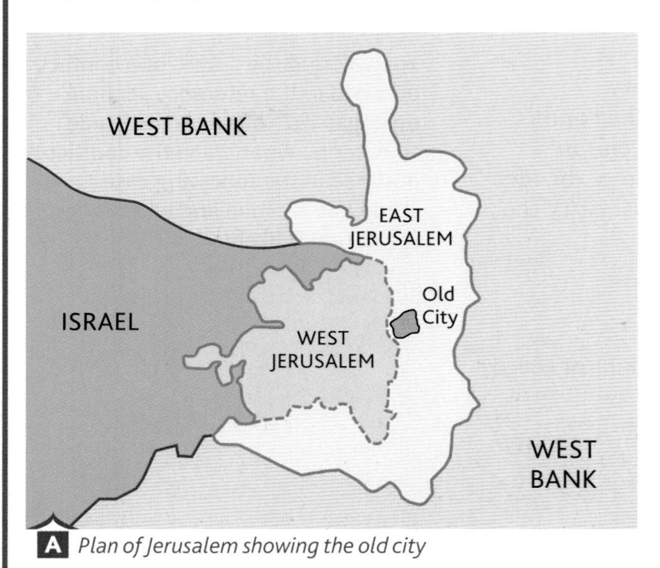

A *Plan of Jerusalem showing the old city*

Key terms

Arab: a person whose first language is Arabic.

Extremism: a term used to describe the actions of individuals or groups outside the political centre of a society.

Arab League: formed in 1945 for the purpose of securing Arab unity. Today, the League has 22 members.

Timeline

A brief history of events

From the beginning of history the area that became Palestine was settled and ruled by different peoples. The name 'Palestine' derives from one group of early inhabitants of the coastal plain, the Philistines. Among their neighbours were the **Jews**, who lived in the hills inland from the 10th century BC, and ruled several kingdoms, until their subjugation by the Roman Empire around 70 AD. This began the modern Diaspora, scattering the Jewish people in lands away from 'Palestine'.

638 AD: A Christian Palestine was conquered by the Arabs and became an Islamic country; the majority of its people adopted the new faith and the Arabic language.

1517: Palestine became part of the Turkish Ottoman Empire, and remained so until its capture by the British in 1917.

1897: The first **Zionist** Congress, convened by Theodor Herzl in Basle, declares the right of the Jewish people to a homeland.

1917: Balfour Declaration by the British Government, supporting the Basle proclamation.

1920: The British take over Palestine and recognise Hebrew as an official language, alongside English and Arabic. There are 800,000 Arabs and roughly 80,000 Jews in Palestine at that time.

Timeline – *continued*

1945: The number of Jews massacred in Europe by the Nazis and their allies is estimated at 6 million.

29 November 1947: The UN General Assembly (GA) asks for the creation of a Jewish State in Palestine.

1948: Declaration of Independence of the State of Israel. Jerusalem is divided between Israel and Palestine. About half of the population of 1,400,000 **Palestinians** are forced to leave or flee their country.

1950: Israel announces the Law of Return, allowing any Jew to acquire **Israeli** nationality and to live in Israel. There are 700,000 new arrivals between 1948 and 1951. Palestinian refugees are refused by the Israeli government the right of return they have under international law.

1967: The Six Day War breaks out in June: the Israeli army conquers the Sinai peninsula, including the Gaza strip, the West Bank of the Jordan (including East Jerusalem), and the Syrian Golan Heights. Jewish **settlers** begin to move into the new territory, against international law.

1973: Yom Kippur War. Israel attacked by Egyptian and Syrian armies. The USA supports Israel. Peace treaties are signed.

1982: Israel invades Lebanon. Troops not withdrawn until May 2000.

December 1987: Resistance of the Palestinians within the **occupied territories** intensifies and the **intifada** (uprising) begins.

13 September 1993: Signing of the so-called Oslo Agreement, a declaration of principles for a peace process, by Itzhak Rabin (then Israel's Prime Minister) and Palestinian leader Yasser Arafat.

1998: Agreement between Israel and the **Palestine Liberation Organization** (PLO) signed which requires, among other things, the withdrawal of Israeli troops from 13 per cent of the West Bank. The number of Jewish settlers in Palestinian territory grows to over 130,000.

2000: The peace process comes under increasing strain. New intifada begins after the intrusive visit to the Al-Aqsa Mosque by Ariel Sharon, now Israel's Prime Minister.

Sources: Land Before Honour, Kitty Warnock
Making Peace, Oxfam

B *Arabs living in East Jerusalem*

Key terms

Jew: someone whose mother is Jewish or who has converted to the religion of Judaism. Many Jews do not practise their religion. They have been given the right to live in Israel. This is a source of contention in the peace process.

Zionist: a person who believes that Jews have the right to a nation state. Most of the political parties in Israel are Zionist.

Palestinian: someone whose family originates from what was Palestine before 1947. Most Palestinians are Muslim, a large number are Christian.

Israeli: a citizen of the state of Israel. This includes Jews and Palestinians (sometimes known as Israeli Arabs), 18 per cent of Israeli citizens are Palestinians who can vote but are not asked to serve in the army and are denied access to many benefits in housing, employment and social security.

Settlers: almost 300,000 Jews have settled in the occupied territories since 1967. This is against international law and one of the main obstacles to the peace process.

Occupied Territories: the West bank, Gaza strip and East Jerusalem, which were taken over by Israeli military occupation in the Six Day war of 1967.

Intifada: the Palestinian uprising (meaning 'shaking off' in Arabic) which began in 1987 against Israeli military occupation and continued until the peace process began in 1993. A second intifada began in 2000.

Palestine Liberation Organization (PLO): an umbrella organisation founded in 1964 to represent the different Palestinian resistance groups. The largest, Fatah, was led by Yasser Arafat.

Knesset: the parliament of Israel.

Source: Making Peace, Oxfam

Case study – continued

The Temple Mount is a site of importance for Judaism and Islam. It is one of the most contested religious sites in the world.

In Judaism, Midrash (Hebrew teachings) holds it was from here that the world expanded into its present form, and this was where God gathered the dust He used to create the first man, Adam. Two Jewish Temples were built here. Jews believe that the Third Temple, which they hope will be the final one, will also be located here.

In Islam, the site is revered as the location of the Islamic prophet Mohammed's journey to Jerusalem and ascent to heaven. The site is the location of the al-Aqsa mosque and the Dome of the Rock, the oldest Islamic structure in the world.

C *Temple Mount – an area of great dispute in the Israel-Palestine conflict*

What does Israel want?

short-term

- that the other stops attacking

medium-term

- talk on the basis of a further temporary agreement
- full Palestinian cooperation in stopping attacks on Israel
- end of any troublemaking comments from Palestinian controlled areas

long-term

- an undivided Jerusalem as the Israeli capital
- an agreement on the end of conflict
- 5–10 per cent of the West Bank to go to Israel
- a Palestinian state with no army allowed
- no right to return of Palestinian refugees.

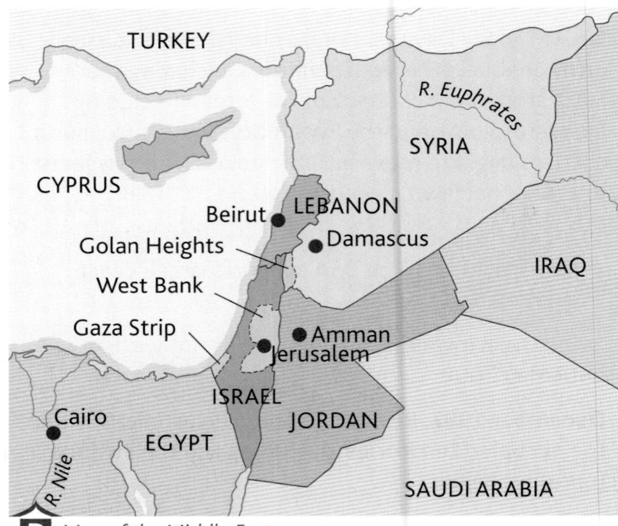

D *Map of the Middle East area*

What does Palestine want?

short-term

- that the other stops attacking
- the end of border closures and the handing over of all tax money owed them

medium-term

- an end to all Israeli settlement building and a stop to the taking of land
- begin peace talks again, where they left off in January 2001
- release all Palestinian prisoners

long-term

- an independent state with East Jerusalem as the capital
- compensation and limited right of return for the 3.7 million Palestinian refugees.

The situation is made more difficult as some Palestinians do not want Israel to exist or Jews to live there. Likewise some Israelis want to keep Palestinian land for themselves.

E *Map of Israel and disputed territory*

The role of the UN in this conflict

Though the Security Council has primary responsibility for the maintenance of international peace and security, it has not been able to address and resolve the Israel-Palestine conflict. The Council has taken no significant action since 1967, when it passed Resolution 242 calling on Israel to relinquish the territories acquired during its war with Syria and Egypt. Resolution 242 called upon the Arab states to end their war against Israel and to engage in direct peace talks. The General Assembly has taken a more active role in the conflict, repeatedly taking action and often calling on parties to respect human rights.

Within the UN the United States has used its influence to keep the issue off the Security Council's agenda and it has repeatedly used its veto power on Israel's behalf while Arab members of the UN have used the General Assembly as a forum for isolating Israel. There have been many discussions about this problem at the UN and there have been many resolutions asking for a solution to the conflict in the Middle East.

After the second intifada, which resulted in a massive loss of life, the reoccupation of territories, military incursions, suicide attacks, rocket and mortar fire, and the destruction of property, Israel began the construction of a West Bank separation wall, located within the Occupied Palestinian Territory. This was ruled illegal by the International Court of Justice in 2004. In 2002, the Security Council adopted resolution 1397 affirming a vision of two States, Israel and Palestine, living side by side within secure and recognised borders. In 2003, the Middle East Quartet (United States [US], European Union [EU], Russia, and the UN) released a detailed Road Map to a two-State solution, endorsed by Security Council resolution 1515.

However, there is still conflict between Israel and Palestine. A lot has been done, but a lot more needs to be done.

How the international community deals with conflict

The international community responds to threats of conflict in many ways. Heads of state will meet to discuss the problem and their representative will meet the aggressor to diffuse the issue. Depending on where the conflict has taken place the representative could be from the European Union, the Commonwealth or a trading partner. The aggrieved country will be supported usually by UN staff monitoring their living conditions and the grant of aid. The aid will be given for specific reasons. It is known as targeted aid.

In addition, the matter will be referred to the United Nations Security Council. This body was set up after World War II in 1945. It has five permanent members – Russia, France, China, Britain and the USA and ten temporary members. The five permanent members have the right to veto decisions of the Council. Decisions are made on a majority vote unless the right to veto has been used. The Security Council's role is:

- to discuss threats to international security
- to suggest solutions or
- to propose action.

Action will usually include trade sanctions or the removal of aid to a country. In rare cases a boycott will be employed. As a last resort, the option of military intervention is available.

Activities

1. Look at the bullet list on page 148 showing Palestinian and Israeli demands for resolution of the conflict. List three areas of disagreement. How do you think these contentious issues can be resolved?
2. In August 2008, the Israelis released 198 of their estimated 9,000 Palestinian prisoners. Israel said the release was designed to give a boost to the slow-moving peace talks. By December 2008 there was armed conflict between Israel and the Palestinian group Hamas, in the Gaza strip. This included rocket attacks, bombing, air strikes and ground troops. Many people, mainly Palestinian civilians, died. Can you suggest a way to end this long-running conflict? Discuss in groups.
3. Which countries do you think can help to bring this conflict to a peaceful outcome?
4. Imagine you have been forced to leave your home because the UN had given someone else the right to your land. Write about your feelings – this could be a report, a story, a diary entry or a poem.
5. How can a solution to the contest for Temple Mount be found?
6. The right to veto has caused problems for the UN on many occasions. Should the right to veto be removed from the permanent members of the Security Council?
7. Write a newspaper article about an aspect of this conflict that interests you.

12.3 Understanding genocide

> *“In Germany they first came for the communists; and I didn’t speak up because I wasn’t a communist. Then they came for the Jews; and I didn’t speak up because I wasn’t a Jew. Then they came for the trade unionists; and I didn’t speak up because I wasn’t a trade unionist. Then they came for the Catholics; and I didn’t speak up because I wasn’t a Catholic. Then they came for me – and by that time there was nobody left to speak up.”*
>
> *Martin Niemoller*

The term ‘genocide’ did not exist before 1944. It is a very specific term, referring to violent crimes committed against groups with the intent to destroy the existence of the group. Human rights, as laid out in the 1948 United Nations Universal Declaration of Human Rights, concern the rights of individuals.

The Jewish Holocaust has been ingrained in the world’s collective memory, but it is not the only case of genocide. Armenians, Chechens and Kosovans, have all suffered a similar human devastation. In Africa, Rwanda has not yet recovered. In Russia the purges of the Stalin era were among the worst cases of crimes against humanity.

Genocide, as defined by the United Nations in 1948, means any of the following acts committed with intent to destroy, in whole or in part, a national, ethnic, racial or religious group, including:

- **a** killing members of the group
- **b** causing serious bodily or mental harm to members of the group
- **c** deliberately inflicting on the group conditions of life calculated to bring about its physical destruction in whole or in part
- **d** imposing measures intended to prevent births within the group
- **e** forcibly transferring children of the group to another group.

It is important for the international community to recognise genocide and take action to stop it.

Activity

1 Here are some of the genocides in recent history. Research one of these and make notes about what happened to whom and where. Why do you think this genocide occurred? What could have been done to prevent it?

- Stalin’s Purges and Forced Famine [1932–1938]
- Armenians in Turkey [1915–1918]
- The Nazi Holocaust [1938–1945]
- Bosnia-Herzogovina [1992–1995]
- Sudan [1983–present]

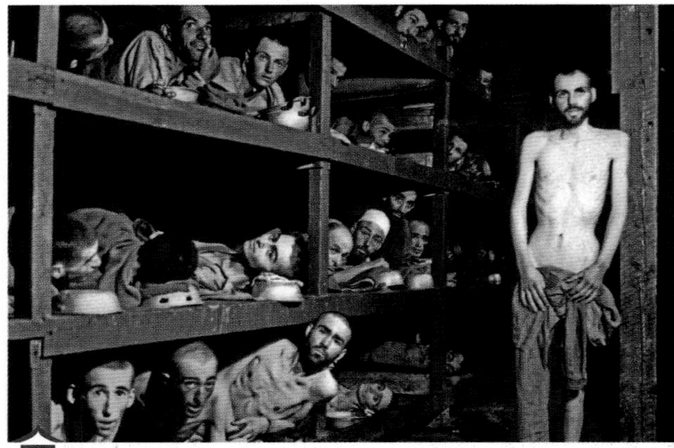

A *Jewish prisoners in Buchenwald Concentration Camp at the end of World War Two*

B *Thousands died in the 1992–1995 conflict in Bosnia*

What is a war crime?

Article 147 of the Fourth Geneva Convention defines war crimes as:

- wilful killing, torturing or subjecting to inhuman treatment
- wilfully causing great suffering or serious injury to body or health
- wilfully depriving a protected person of the rights of fair and regular trial
- action not justified by military necessity and carried out unlawfully and wantonly.

This is an accepted definition of war crime.

Information

The concept of war crimes is the idea that an individual can be held responsible for the actions of a country or that nation's soldiers. This concept was first used in the trials of Nazi soldiers at Nuremburg at the end of World War II.

Case study

War crimes and Yugoslavia

A brief history of Slobodan Milosevic

Yugoslav President Slobodan Milosevic led his country on a course of conflict.

During his 13 years of power, the people of Yugoslavia saw their country torn apart, and hundreds of thousands of people die. The Croatian war claimed some 20,000 lives, the Bosnian war 100,000 and the Kosovo war some 10,000.

C *Slobodan Milosevic*

From 1991 to 1999, he presided over internal conflicts and mass murder. He was the first European head of state to be prosecuted for genocide and war crimes. He was charged with crimes against humanity in 2001. Milosevic was tried in court at the Yugoslav war crimes tribunal in The Hague. His trial was nearing its end when he died of a heart attack in 2006.

Radovan Karadzic

Former Bosnian Serb leader Radovan Karadzic was one of the most wanted men in the world for thirteen years. He was arrested in July 2008 for genocide and war crimes. He will be charged with crimes against humanity for his leadership of the Serbian campaign (supported by Slobodan Milosevic) of ethnic cleansing in Bosnia in 1992–95 which left 100,000 dead and 2 million Bosnian refugees.

D *Radovan Karadzic*

Information

Radovan Karadzic was arrested in 2008 so the details of his trial were not publicly known when this book was written.

Activities

2 Why do you think it took so long to arrest Radovan Karadzic? Use the internet to answer this question.

3 Find out about the trial of Radovan Karadzic. Why do you think trials of this nature take so long to reach a judgement in court? Write a report on the trial.

4 Do you think the leader of a group is responsible for the actions of his supporters to the extent that he can be tried as an individual for war crimes? Discuss in groups.

12.4 Rwanda

Case study

Facts about Rwanda:

Location	Central Africa
Capital	Kigali
Population	9.9 million
Altitude	1,829 m
Climate	mild all year
Wild life	gorillas, antelope, chimpanzees, eagles, water birds
Flora	eucalyptus, acacia, palm, orchid

Rwanda is one of the smallest countries in Central Africa and is comprised of two main ethnic groups, the Hutu and the Tutsi. Rwanda was part of German East Africa. Although the Hutus account for 90 per cent of the population, in the past, the Tutsi minority was considered the aristocracy of Rwanda and dominated Hutu peasants for decades, especially while Rwanda was under Belgian colonial rule. The Rwandan king was a Tutsi.

A *Map of Rwanda and neighbouring countries*

Timeline

1946: Ruanda-Urundi becomes UN trust territory governed by Belgium.

1957: Hutus issue manifesto calling for a change in Rwanda's power structure to give them a voice commensurate with their numbers; Hutu political parties formed.

1959: Tutsi King Kigeri V, together with tens of thousands of Tutsis, forced into exile in Uganda following inter-ethnic violence.

1961: Rwanda proclaimed a republic.

1962: Rwanda becomes independent with a Hutu, Gregoire Kayibanda, as president; many Tutsis leave the country.

1963: Some 20,000 Tutsis killed following an attack by Tutsi rebels based in Burundi.

1973: President Gregoire Kayibanda ousted in military coup led by Juvenal Habyarimana.

1978: New constitution ratified; Habyarimana elected president.

1988: Some 50,000 Hutu refugees flee to Rwanda from Burundi following ethnic violence there.

1990: Forces of the Rwandan Patriotic Front (RPF), mainly Tutsi, invade Rwanda from Uganda.

1991: New multi-party constitution promulgated.

Genocide

1993: President Habyarimana signs a power-sharing agreement with the Tutsis in the Tanzanian town of Arusha, ostensibly signalling the end of civil war; UN mission sent to monitor the peace agreement.

April 1994: Habyarimana and the Burundian president are killed after their plane is shot down over Kigali; RPF launches a major offensive; extremist Hutu militia and elements of the Rwandan military begin the systematic massacre of Tutsis. Within 100 days around 800,000 Tutsis and moderate Hutus are killed; Hutu militias flee to Zaire, taking with them around 2 million Hutu refugees.

A brief history of the conflict

Ethnic tensions in Rwanda were significantly heightened in October 1993 upon the assassination of Melchior Ndadaye, the first popularly elected Hutu president of neighbouring Burundi. A United Nations peacekeeping force of 2,500 soldiers was then dispatched to Rwanda to preserve the fragile cease-fire between the Hutu government and the Tutsi rebels. On 6 April, while returning from a meeting in Tanzania, a small jet carrying the presidents of Rwanda and Burundi was shot down by ground-fired missiles as it approached Rwanda's airport at Kigali.

Immediately after these deaths, Rwanda was plunged into political violence as Hutu extremists began targeting prominent opposition figures who were on their death-lists. Beginning on 6 April 1994, and for the next hundred days, up to 800,000 Tutsis were killed by Hutu militia using clubs and machetes, with as many as 10,000 killed each day. The killings then spread throughout the countryside as Hutu militia, armed with machetes, clubs, guns and grenades, began indiscriminately killing Tutsi civilians. Victims were easily identified as everyone in Rwanda carried identification cards specifying their ethnic background, a practice left over from colonial days. These 'tribal cards' now meant the difference between life and death.

Among the peacekeepers were ten soldiers from Belgium who were captured by the Hutus, tortured and murdered. As a result, the United States, France, Belgium, and Italy all began evacuating their own personnel from Rwanda. Back at UN headquarters in New York, the killings were initially categorised as a breakdown in the cease-fire between the Tutsi and Hutu. The UN Security Council responded to the worsening crisis by voting unanimously to abandon Rwanda. The remainder of UN peacekeeping troops were pulled out, leaving behind a tiny force of about 200 soldiers for the entire country.

The Hutu, now without opposition from the world community, engaged in clubbing and hacking to death defenceless Tutsi families with machetes everywhere they were found. The Rwandan state radio, controlled by Hutu extremists, further encouraged the killings by broadcasting non-stop hate propaganda and even pinpointed the locations of Tutsis in hiding. Many Tutsis took refuge in churches and mission compounds. These places became the scenes of some of the worst massacres. Hospitals also became prime targets as wounded survivors were sought out then killed. In some local villages, militiamen forced Hutus to kill their Tutsi neighbours or face a death sentence for themselves and their entire families.

Confronted with international TV news reports depicting genocide, the UN Security Council voted to send up to 5,000 soldiers to Rwanda but it failed to establish any timetable and thus did not send the troops in time to stop the massacre. The killings ended after armed Tutsi rebels from neighbouring countries managed to halt the genocide in July 1994. By then, over one-tenth of the population, an estimated 800,000 people, had been killed.

B *Evidence of the massacre*

The genocide in Rwanda – The role of the United Nations

The United Nations failed to take the actions needed to prevent or stop this genocide [Refer to the official report presented to the Security Council in December 1999 by an Independent Inquiry, chaired by Mr Ingvar Carlsson, former Prime Minister of Sweden].

In November 1994, the Security Council, acting under Chapter VII of the UN Charter, passed resolution 955 in order to bring those responsible for the massacres to justice. It established the Rwanda Tribunal (UN International Criminal Tribunal for Rwanda, ICTR). The Tribunal was given the power to prosecute persons responsible for serious violations of **international humanitarian law**, genocide and crimes against humanity in Rwanda and neighbouring countries between 1 January and 31 December 1994.

For security reasons, the Rwanda Tribunal was established in the small Tanzanian town of Arusha, a two hour flight away from Kigali. There were many administrative shortcomings in the early stages including poor communication with the people and government of Rwanda.

The convictions set legal history for the crime of genocide. The conviction of Jean Kambanda, Prime Minister, during the 1994 events was the first time a Head of Government was convicted for such offences. He was sentenced to life imprisonment.

C *Jean Kambanda at the International tribunal*

Information

The International Red Cross describes **international humanitarian law** as a set of rules which seek, for humanitarian reasons, to limit the effects of armed conflict. It protects persons who are not participating in the hostilities and restricts the means and methods of warfare. The rules were determined by Geneva Conventions.

Information

Other Rwandan leaders were tried, for example Jean-Paul Akayesu was the Mayor of Taba, an area administered by the town of Gitarama.

UN International Criminal Tribunal for Rwanda

Some facts:

- The ICTR is made up of three independent structures: the Trial Chambers, Prosecution and Registry.
- The first suspect arrived at Arusha detention centre in May 1996 and the first ICTR trial began in January 1997.
- The ICTR submitted its Completion Strategy to UN headquarters in July 2003.
- As of December 2007 it had completed 35 cases; 27 are ongoing.
- Six suspects are still awaiting trial, while 16 wanted fugitives remain at large.

D *Jean Paul Akayesu was found guilty by the tribunal*

Where are we now?

Rwanda's UN-backed genocide court was due to finish its work in 2008 but critics and survivors say it has not prosecuted enough of those responsible for the slaughter. There are issues being raised and questions being asked.

- Over the last decade, the tribunal has completed fewer than four cases a year on average, prompting anger from survivors who say too few suspected ringleaders have been dealt with.
- The Rwandan government does not want the tribunal's mandate extended, preferring all pending files be handed to its jurisdiction.
- Rights groups have criticised moves to transfer cases to Rwanda, questioning the independence of its courts.

The survivors' group Ibuka acknowledged some of the concerns but said that victims felt removed when justice was being dispensed in another country. Ibuka is an umbrella organisation for the survivor organisations in Rwanda, representing them at national and international levels. Ibuka means 'remember'. Ibuka was created in 1995 in order to address:

E *Memorial of Rwanda genocide*

- issues of justice
- confronting memories, and
- social and economic problems faced by survivors.

The message from the Rwanda Tribunal to the people of Rwanda and to the rest of the world is clear:

- Acts like mass murder or mass rape are not acceptable in any situation. Those who are breaking the law will be punished.
- To have obeyed an order does not constitute an excuse. All individuals have their own value and also their own responsibility.

Issues for discussion

- Why has the tribunal taken so long to reach decisions?
- Why does the UN take so long to act in emergency situations?
- Why was this tribunal held in a different country rather than The Hague?
- Why did the UN fail to stop the massacres in Rwanda? Why did the Security Council withdraw UN personnel from the area? How can this type of trouble be prevented or controlled in the future?
- If trials about massacres in Britain had taken more than ten years to complete, what response do you think there would be from the British public? Why has this been considered acceptable for the people of Rwanda?
- Do you think the tribunal has done enough to answer the wrongs done to the victims of this genocide?

If you feel very strongly about any of these issues you could write to your MP, or the Foreign Secretary or the Secretary General of the United Nations.

Activity

1 Go to the official website of the Republic of Rwanda (www.gov.rw/). Choose the tourism section. Read about Gorillas and Tourism. Make a poster to advertise Rwanda as a destination.

a Write a report for a newspaper describing the situation in Rwanda. Write it from the point of view of a reporter who is witnessing events as they happen.

b Find out about Ibuka. Go to www.hope-survivors.org.uk/ What work is this organisation doing today?

c Find the names of the following:

- your MP
- the Foreign Secretary
- Secretary General of the United Nations.

Chapter summary

What you should know:

From this chapter your knowledge should now cover:

Short course

- ✔ the underlying causes of conflict
- ✔ the issue of conflict
- ✔ handling conflict
- ✔ prevention
- ✔ crisis management
- ✔ an understanding of the Israel-Palestine conflict
- ✔ the geography of the region
- ✔ the role of the United Nations in this conflict
- ✔ how the international community deals with conflict

Full course

- ✔ an understanding of genocide
- ✔ what genocide is
- ✔ what a war crime is
- ✔ an understanding of the conflict in Rwanda
- ✔ the genocide in Rwanda
- ✔ the role of the United nations in this conflict
- ✔ the role of the UN International Criminal Tribunal
- ✔ what is happening now in Rwanda

Check your knowledge

You should be able to answer the following questions without looking back over the text. If you cannot answer all of the questions you need to learn the material more thoroughly.

1. What is a conflict?
2. Give two situations where conflict can start.
3. Who are usually the first people to act when a conflict arises?
4. How can conflict be prevented?
5. What is extremism?
6. What does PLO stand for?
7. What and where is Temple Mount?
8. Name the countries in the Middle East Quartet.
9. What does the UN Security Council do?
10. Name the five permanent members of the UN Security Council.

Further study

- Go to the Genocide Watch website (**www.genocidewatch.org/**).

  Choose an area of concern.

  In July 2008, the prosecutor of the International Criminal Court filed genocide charges against the Sudanese President, Omar al-Bashir, accusing him of masterminding attempts to wipe out African tribes in Darfur with a campaign of murder, rape and deportation.
  - Find out what happened with this prosecution. Did this prosecution stop the mass killings and dislocations and pressurise Sudan into negotiating settlements in good faith?
  - Decide what you feel about this and what you could do about it.
- Go to the Amnesty International website (**www.amnesty.org/**).
  - Choose one of the areas of current concern for the organisation. This topic should include a conflict or what is happening to people as a result of conflict.
  - Find out what Amnesty International feels about your chosen topic.
  - Has the conflict left people displaced? Do people need humanitarian aid? Have people's human rights been met?
  - Decide what you feel about it and what you can do about it.
- Go to the UN Peacekeeping website (**www.un.org/Depts/dpko/**).
  - Choose a country from the Current or Past Operations section.
  - Read about the work the UN is undertaking in your chosen country.
  - Find out what needs/needed to be done to make this country safer.
  - Do you think the UN action was all that was needed to help this country?
  - Decide what you feel about it and what you can do about it.
- For your chosen area of study you should:
  - Make a report
  - or Prepare a talk
  - or Make a poster for display
  - or Discuss it with someone
  - or Write a letter to your MP
  - or Prepare a PowerPoint presentation
  - or Write a poem
  - or Draw a picture
  - or Write in support of the NGO.

Your teacher may have some other ideas for your work.

Picture stimulus

A *An injured Georgian woman in Gori*

Look at this photograph carefully.

- What do you think is happening in this picture? Do you think this woman is in any way responsible for this action? Why do you think this happened? How do you think this woman is feeling? Who is likely to help her?
- What can be done to ensure that incidents like this don't happen?

13 The global economy and world trade

13.1 What is globalisation?

Over the years **globalisation** became more than simply a way of doing business, or running financial markets. **Multinational** companies with production plants around the world control more of the goods that are produced in global markets. This has enabled them to take advantage of cheaper labour and has given them access to local markets across the world.

Objectives

To understand the concept of globalisation and what it means to World Trade systems.

Key terms

Globalisation: the process by which the world has become interconnected as a result of increased trade and cultural exchange.

Multinational: a large corporation or company with offices and/or factories in several countries.

GM (genetically modified): means that the genes in a seed or food have been altered to produce something that does not occur naturally, for example, this might make the crops bigger or resistant to disease.

A *The globalised market*

How does the globalised market work?

It is modern communications that make it possible:

- for the British service sector to deal with its customers through a call centre in India, or
- for a sportswear manufacturer to design its products in Europe, make them in south-east Asia and sell them in north America.

What the critics say.

The critics of globalisation say it:

- has not improved the position for the world's poor
- presses Genetically Modified (GM) seed on to developing world farmers
- leads to low-paid sweatshop workers
- causes countries to sell off state-owned industry to qualify for International Monetary Fund (IMF) and World Bank loans
- causes job losses in industrialised economies like Britain and the USA, and
- allows European/American corporate companies to control business across the globe.

These are known as the negative aspects of globalisation.

What supporters say.

The supporters of globalisation think it:

- has brought better health opportunities to the world
- has made societies fight for more democracy and greater social justice
- improves the skill base of developing countries
- allows economies to concentrate on what they do best and raises incomes and
- allows us the chance to build a world where we better understand each other.

These are known as the positive aspects of globalisation.

What is World Trade and how does it work?

World Trade is the movement of goods and services between different countries in the world. Most countries rely on trade to bring a source of income. Trade agreements are used to regulate the import and export of goods between countries.

The World Trade Organization (WTO) is an international body connected to the United Nations (UN). Its purpose is to promote free trade by persuading countries to abolish import tariffs and other barriers. As such, it has become closely associated with globalisation. The WTO is the only international agency overseeing the rules of international trade. It polices free trade agreements, settles trade disputes between governments and organises trade negotiations. Countries and individual companies complain to the WTO if they feel that they have been treated unfairly.

Free Trade agreements

Free trade agreements were intended to allow goods to flow between countries unhindered by government-imposed restrictions like taxes and tariffs. Because free trade agreements are not regulated multinational companies have generated a strong power base. This trend has undermined the sovereignty of some nations and the economic stability of millions of workers.

Bilateral trade agreements

Bilateral trade agreements (which are between two countries) became popular because of opposition to multilateral agreements. However, bilateral agreements often result in economic domination by the more developed nation. Bilateral agreements do not create the type of markets that slow the development of many poorer nations.

Multilateral trade agreements

Multilateral trade agreements are agreements made amongst multiple countries. For this reason, they are very complicated to negotiate, but are very powerful once all parties sign the agreement. Because they are negotiated by companies trading with countries, they favour transnational corporations who aim to maximise their profits. They are monitored by the WTO. An example of an agreement is the anti-dumping agreement.

Activities

1. Look at the lists of positive and negative aspects of globalisation. Which of these do you think is true? Give reasons for your answer.
2. Find the names of five multinational companies. List the countries they operate in.

Information

Dumping occurs when foreign exporters sell their goods in international markets at prices lower than the price in their home market (referred to as 'normal value'), or at prices below the full cost of production. Dumped imports cause problems for domestic producers of the same product.

Activities

3. Here are the logos of five multinational companies. Name the companies.
4. Choose one of the companies and go to their website. Each one of these companies is doing something to help others. Find out what your chosen company is doing to help individuals or communities. Make a poster to show this.
5. Do you think trade agreements are designed to help developing countries or large companies? Discuss in groups.

13.2 The nature of the world's economic system

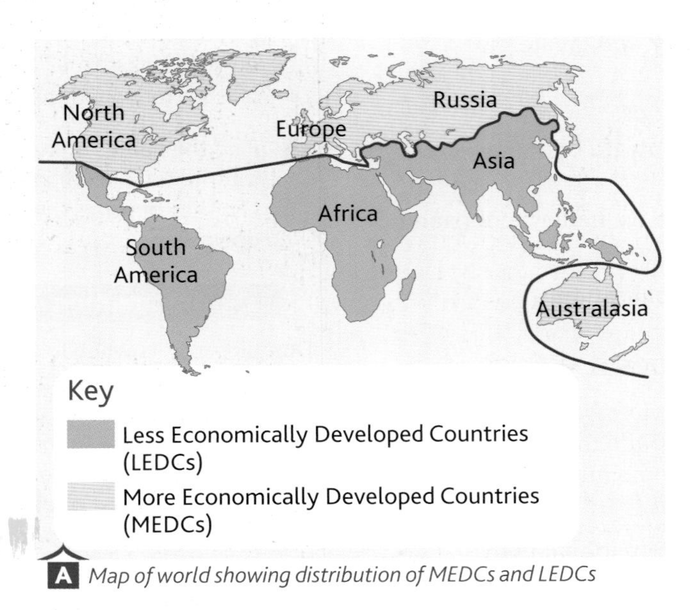

A *Map of world showing distribution of MEDCs and LEDCs*

Objectives

To explore the differences between developed and less developed countries.

Information

MEDC stands for 'more economically developed country'.

LEDC stands for 'less economically developed country'.

The difference between these countries is known as the development gap.

MEDCs and LEDCs

In a LEDC like Ethiopia you would expect to find that:

- birth rates would be very high
  death rates would have been falling for a number of years and would be now much lower
- population increase will be high and the total population will be growing at a high rate
- national disasters are a burden on all economies but for a poor country they can ruin decades of slow growth and set the country back in its development programme
- most people will work in the Primary sector with some working in the Secondary or manufacturing, though usually low-skilled manufacturing. There will be some growth in the tertiary/services sector but it will be the smallest sector
- education for most will be at a low level, and illiteracy will still be high
- health services will be of a low order and many people will die of diseases that in the UK have long been forgotten.

In a MEDC like the UK the opposite would be the case. You would expect to find that:

- birth and death rates would be low and the total population will be steady or in some cases declining
- national disasters would be coped with as we have the resources to cope and quickly recover
- most people work in the higher paid service industries typical of a developed country
- education and health standards would be high with people having a long life and relatively easy working conditions.

Information

- **Primary sector:** Involves the extraction and production of raw materials. (A coal miner and a fisherman would be workers in the primary sector.)
- **Secondary sector:** Involves the transformation of raw materials into goods. (A builder and a dressmaker would be workers in the secondary sector.)
- **Tertiary sector:** Involves the provision of services to consumers and businesses. (A shopkeeper and an accountant would be workers in the tertiary sector.)

Activity

Here are five LEDCs and five MEDCs. Add to the list to make ten of each.

LEDC: Sudan, Ethiopia, Bangladesh, Zimbabwe, Chad . . .
MEDC: USA, Canada, UK, France, Germany . . .

However, people in MEDCs still suffer from problems like high crime, pollution, overcrowding in cities, traffic congestion and diseases associated with our lifestyles like heart disease, obesity and cancers.

Issues surrounding globalisation

Fair Trade

Fair Trade means a trading partnership, based on dialogue, transparency and respect, that seeks greater fairness in international trade. Fair trade organisations have a clear commitment to fair trade. They are backed by consumers and are engaged in supporting producers, awareness raising and in campaigning for changes in the rules and practice of international trade. They can be recognised by the FTO Mark. They set standards for trade that include payment of a fair price, a good working environment and no child or forced labour.

B *The Fairtrade logo*

Information

The International Fair Trade Association (IFAT) is the global network of fair trade organisations with over 300 members in 70 countries. Two-thirds of IFAT members are located in developing countries.

Ethical trade

Ethical trade is a term for business practice that promotes more socially and/or environmentally responsible trade. Ethical trade and ethical sourcing means that a company accepts responsibility for the labour and human rights practices within its supply chain. This usually involves adopting a code of practice that sets out minimum labour standards that they expect their suppliers to comply with.

Aid programmes

Various types of aid are available:

1 Short-term aid is given after a natural disaster – flood, famine, drought, or earthquake.
2 Long-term aid is given to help a country improve the standard of living of the people by constructing large projects like hospitals, roads, bridges, schools, power stations and irrigation schemes.

Information

Aid can come from:

1 A country (UK) or an international organisation like the UN. This money comes out of our taxes.
2 Charities like Oxfam, Water-Aid, Save the Children, Red Cross, etc. This money comes from donations and appeals for aid.

Aid can also come in the form of technical advice, grants and loans. Grants help the receiving country as they don't have to be repaid.

C *The Red Cross at work*

Discussion activity

What kind of aid is best for a poor country? Discuss.

How does debt occur?

As with all borrowing the person/country you borrow from expects to be paid back and with interest. It is easy to borrow money based on the price of raw materials. The problem arises when the price of raw materials falls and the country has problems with the loan repayments. The interest charges grow and the country falls deeper in debt. For many LEDCs the interest on the loan repayments alone can be more than they can make in a year.

13.3 Key players in the world's economic system

The United Nations

The United Nations as the foremost **supranational** agency in the world keeps a close watch on how the world's economy will affect development. As national economies become more and more interdependent through information, trade, investment and financial ties, the UN helps to coordinate efforts in international cooperation. The UN:

- provides the ground rules for the global economy by setting standards
- prepares the ground for investment in emerging economies by promoting political stability
- addresses the downside of globalisation by fighting international crime, and works to solve global environmental problems like climate change.

The UN warns that a decline in world economic growth increases the challenges of the less-developed countries in their hope for progress towards millennium development goals (MDGs). It reports that any increase in food prices threatens to deepen hunger and malnutrition in the world.

The World Trade Organization

The World Trade Organization (WTO) is a global international organisation dealing with the rules of trade between nations. It is based in Geneva, Switzerland. It creates the WTO agreements, negotiated and signed by the bulk of the world's trading nations and ratified in their parliaments. These documents provide the legal ground rules for international commerce. They are essentially contracts, binding governments to keep their trade policies within agreed limits.

The International Monetary Fund

The International Monetary Fund (IMF) is an international organisation that provides financial assistance and advice to member countries. The IMF is responsible for the creation and maintenance of the international monetary system, the system by which international payments among countries take place. It tries to provide a systematic mechanism for foreign exchange transactions in order to foster investment and promote balanced global economic trade.

Information

The IMF gets its money from subscriptions paid by member states. The size of payment is determined by the size of its economy. This determines the voting rights of each country within the IMF.

Objectives

To understand what is involved in the operation of the world's economic system.

To understand who is involved in the world economy.

A *The home of the UN*

links

MDGs are defined in the case study on Make Poverty History in chapter 16 page 200.

links

You will learn about the WTO in chapter 14 page 186.

Key terms

Supranational: means beyond the borders or scope of any one nation, especially through organisations that encompass more than one nation.

The World Bank

The World Bank is a source of financial and technical assistance to developing countries around the world. It helps governments in developing countries reduce poverty by providing them with money and the technical expertise they need for a wide range of projects – such as education, health, infrastructure, communications and government reforms. It provides low-interest loans, interest-free credit and grants. The World Bank is like a cooperative in which 185 member countries of the International Monetary Fund (IMF) are shareholders. It is not a bank in the common sense. It is made up of two unique development institutions owned by member countries – the International Bank for Reconstruction and Development (IBRD) and the International Development Association (IDA). The IBRD focuses on middle income and creditworthy poor countries, while IDA focuses on the poorest countries in the world.

Activity

Find out more about the work of the World Bank. Go to **www.worldbank.org/**

- Find out what the World Bank is focusing on.
- Find out what the World Bank is doing in Africa.
- Choose one aspect of the bank's work and prepare a presentation.

The G8

The G8 is an informal grouping of the world's richest industrial countries whose leaders have an annual summit to discuss problems in the world economy. It doesn't have a headquarters, a budget or regular staff but it is one of the most influential groups in the world. The summits initially focused on economic problems, such as the oil crisis, but more recently the agenda has broadened out to include development, environment, and global security issues.

Information

The G8 nations are the United States, Japan, Germany, France, Britain, Italy, Canada and Russia. The group of eight countries make up more than half of the total world economy.

Group debate

'This house believes that the World Bank is a good thing for the world's development.'

The World Bank has its supporters and its critics. Here are some of the reasons given in the argument for the bank and against the bank.

For ...

- It has backed infrastructure projects that have brought clean water and electricity to millions.
- It loans or grants more than $11bn (£5.5bn) to around 300 development projects every year.
- World Bank loans give confidence to other investors and businesses and stimulate local economies.

Against ...

- The insistence on Western-style governance as a condition of loans promotes policies that hurt the poor.
- Refusing to deal with corrupt regimes only compounds the misery for their citizens.
- By supporting fossil-fuel development, it is contributing to global warming.

Divide into two groups. One group should research the arguments for the bank. The other group should research the arguments against the bank. The statements above will help you start your lists. Keep to the arguments during the debate. Remember to respect the views of your opponents. You need to appoint a chairperson who will be in charge of the debate.

13.4 World Trade issues

Free Trade

Free Trade is a relatively new tool in international relations. It promotes economic interdependence between countries and this can directly enhance national security. Free Trade Agreements (FTAs) are legally binding agreements involving two or more states. In recent years FTAs have become popular as they are easier and quicker to negotiate than multilateral agreements. In addition, the commitment of an FTA between two countries has become an important way of cementing a closer relationship between them.

Information

Free Trade Agreements made between two countries are not managed by the World Trade Organization.

Objectives

To investigate a range of the issues involved in World Trade discussions.

Activity

1 Are Free Trade Agreements helpful to the whole world economy or are they aimed at making the strong nations stronger? Discuss.

Poverty and hunger

The United Nations reports that about 25,000 people die every day of hunger or hunger-related causes. This is one person every three and a half seconds. Unfortunately, it is children who die most often. There is a strong connection between hunger and poverty.

Everyone acknowledges that there is plenty of food in the world for everyone. The problem is that hungry people are trapped in severe poverty. They lack the money to buy enough food to nourish themselves. Being malnourished, they become weaker and often sick. This makes them unable to work, which then makes them even poorer and hungrier. This downward spiral often continues until death for them and their families.

Activities

2 Go to the United Nations World Food Programme website (**http://beta.wfp.org/**). Go to the Food Assistance section and find out how WFP breaks the poverty trap.

3 No one should be starving in the 21st century. Discuss in groups. What do you think you can do to help?

A *Poverty and hunger*

Child labour

Some children have to work in appalling and dangerous conditions. In its worst forms, child labour involves children living in confined and dirty conditions, separated from their families or exposed to serious danger and illness. The International Labour Organization (ILO) has estimated that 218 million children between the ages of five and seventeen work in developing countries. Child labour ranges from four-year-olds tied to rug looms to keep them from running away, to seventeen-year-olds helping out on the family farm. Children who work long hours, often in dangerous and unhealthy conditions, are exposed to lasting physical harm.

B *Child labour*

In some cases, a child's work can be helpful to him or her and to the family. Working and earning can be a positive experience in a child's growing up. This depends largely on the age of the child, the conditions in which the child works, and whether work prevents the child from going to school.

Aid programmes

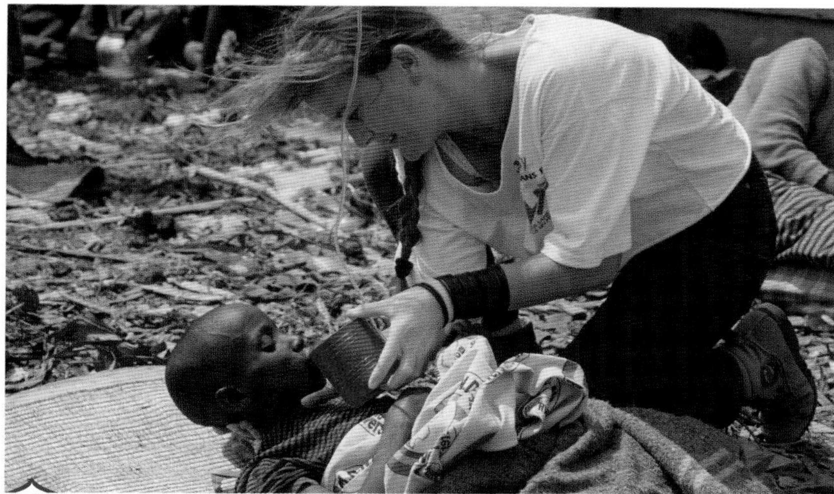

C *Aid workers help during epidemics*

International aid provides a key element of development financing for many of the world's poorest countries. Aid can support a country's education, health, public infrastructure, agricultural and rural development. But only a handful of rich countries meet the UN target of giving 0.7 per cent of their gross national product (GNP) in international assistance. Aid often has political strings attached and it may be used to promote local business interests of the donor, not the real development needs of the recipient.

Inequality and injustice

Billions of people continue to exist on less than a dollar a day, and poverty remains extensive throughout the world, particularly in south Asia and Africa. The achievement of poverty reduction in part depends on the extent of inequality, and inequality is an important issue in its own right given its impact on social stability, and economic growth. There needs to be a global debate on this, especially from the perspective of developing countries. Projects need to take account of the Millennium Development Goals, especially those relating to the eradication of extreme hunger and poverty, achieving universal primary education, promoting gender equality, improvement of health and development of a global partnership with respect to aid, debt and trade.

In the developing world, women face many difficulties. Globalisation has recast gender relations and altered the status and working conditions of women. More women work outside the home in the labour force. This has undermined traditional family systems and it has burdened women with a double load of work, exposed them to harshly exploitative conditions in the paid workplace, and scarcely improved their material wellbeing.

Activity

4 Save the Children says that 'Millions of children are exposed to abuse, violence, exploitation and neglect'. Go to the website (**www.savethechildren.org.uk/**). Find out what Save the Children are doing about child protection issues.

Activities

5 How can governments be made to give the correct amount of international assistance?

6 Go to the UN website (**www.un.org/**). Find out which countries give the correct amount.

Activity

7 The UN holds meetings to discuss aid. The Third High Level Forum on Aid Effectiveness was held in September 2008. It's aim was to:

- review progress in improving aid effectiveness
- broaden the dialogue to newer actors
- chart a course for continuing international action on aid effectiveness.

Go to the UN website (**www.un.org/**) and find out how successful this meeting was.

13.5 The Geobar

Case study

Fair trade practices are now widely accepted in Britain. They have been developed by a firm commitment to a market-based approach that empowers developing country producers and promotes sustainability. It advocates the payment of a fair price in addition to acceptable environmental standards in the production of a wide variety of goods. It focuses in particular on exports from developing countries to developed countries.

Traidcraft Geobar is a fair trade cereal bar. It is made from South African raisins, Pakistani apricots and Chilean honey.

> *"Beekeepers, Juan and Marina Inostraza are members of Apicoop, a Chilean co-operative which supplies honey for Geobar. Through the co-op they have been able to find a stable market and a good price for their product, and thanks to low interest loans, have been able to grow berries on their farm as well. 'You are helping to increase the quality of our lives.' Thanks for buying the product."*

A *Fair trade honey producers Juan and Marina Inostraza*

Honey producers in Chile

Beekeepers of Apicoop are pleased with the difference fair trade benefits have made to their lives. They have access to low-interest loan schemes and the opportunity to share resources. They have gained experience to develop their honey-producing capacity and improve their standard of living. Apicoop began in 1980 and has become the biggest beekeeping co-operative in Chile with more than 40,000 hives. The co-operative has been supplying honey to Traidcraft for over 15 years, and it's this honey that is used in Geobars. However, relying on one product can be risky and so, in October 2007, Apicoop took an important step towards diversifying into blueberry production.

B *Honey made in foothills of Andes in Chile*

Dried fruit producers in South Africa

C *Raisins grown in Northern Cape region of South Africa*

Based on the Lower Orange River, EFA (Eksteenskuil Farmers' Association) is an association of 113 farmers. Members live and farm on 16 'islands' linked by dirt roads and small bridges. Conditions are difficult as farmers often use uneconomical plots and, despite continued attempts to formalise tenure, many do not have title deeds for the land. This means no security for loans, investment and land extension. This situation is slowly improving.

Their annual crops do not give a good return as prices of seeds and fertilizer have risen much more quickly than selling prices. Resources are often bought on credit, which leads to rising debts. There has been a lack of education, expertise and training. Vines are seen as a solution to this problem, and there is a marked economic division between those with vines and those without. But they are expensive to plant and take three years to yield their first crop.

Apricot producers in Pakistan

The Aga Khan Rural Support Programme (AKRSP) is a charitable foundation that works to improve the livelihood of people living in the higher areas of the Karakorum Mountains in the Northern Areas of Pakistan.

The highland environment, where fruit is grown at between 4,500–9,500 feet during long summer days creates fruits with extraordinarily beautiful taste and flavour. The Hunza apricot is known the world over for its bright and tangy flavour. The farmers of the Northern Areas of Pakistan produce a variety of fruits: apricots, apples, cherries, mulberries, peaches, nuts including almonds, walnuts and pine nuts. Due to seasonal gluts in production most of this output is wasted as it rots before it can be consumed or marketed. Communities are extremely poor, living in some of the harshest environmental conditions known, with summer temperatures exceeding 40°C and winter temperatures below 10°C. Farming in these extremely arid conditions is made possible only with forced irrigation.

Traidcraft products say that by buying their product you have helped the organisation to:

- guarantee producers a fair deal
- secure sustainable livelihoods
- provide schooling and health care
- fund community projects like clean water.

D *Apricots grown in Karakorum Mountain region of Pakistan*

About Traidcraft

Traidcraft has been a Fairtrade organisation since 1979. It is the UK's leading fair trade organisation. Its slogan is Fighting Poverty Through Trade. It runs development programmes in some of the poorest countries in the world, and campaigns in the UK and internationally to bring about trade justice.

Activities

1. Find out about Traidcraft. How did it begin? How successful is it now?
2. Find out about one other fair trade organisation. How does it help to promote fair trade in the UK?
3. Arrange a 'fair trade coffee morning'. Serve fairly traded refreshments. Make a donation to an appropriate organisation. Remember to advertise your event. Make a poster.
4. Invite a Traidcraft speaker to your school. Contact Traidcraft by letter or email speakers@traidcraft.co.uk
5. Go to the Traidcraft website (**www.traidcraft.co.uk/**). Download The Banana Game. Play the game.

Chapter summary

What you should know:

From this chapter your knowledge should now cover:

Short course

- ✔ what globalisation is
- ✔ what world trade is and how it works
- ✔ different types of trade agreement
- ✔ the nature of the world's economic system
- ✔ the nature of LEDCs and MEDCs
- ✔ issues surrounding globalisation
- ✔ free trade, fair trade, ethical trade
- ✔ how does debt occur?

Full course

- ✔ key players in the world's economic system
- ✔ the UN, The WTO, The World Bank, The IMF, G8
- ✔ world trade issues
- ✔ free trade, poverty and hunger, child labour
- ✔ aid programmes, inequality and injustice
- ✔ an in-depth study of fair trade

Check your knowledge

You should be able to answer the following questions without looking back over the text. If you cannot answer all of the questions you need to learn the material more thoroughly.

1. What is globalisation?
2. What does WTO stand for?
3. What is meant by the term 'multinational'?
4. Name three multinational companies.
5. What do 'LEDC' and 'MEDC' stand for?
6. Name two facts about life in a LEDC.
7. How does debt occur?
8. Name three MEDCs.
9. What is ethical trade?
10. What does IFAT do?

Further study

- Go to the IFAT website (**www.ifat.org/**).
  - Choose one of the areas of the world – Africa, Asia or South America.
    - Choose a country from the area you have chosen.
    - Find out what sort of product is supplied.
    - Why is fair trade important to these producers?
- Go to the Global Call to Action Against Poverty (GCAP) website (**www.whiteband.org/**). Make Poverty History is the UK organisation.
  - Choose one of the issues of concern for the organisation.
  - Find out what GCAP feels about your chosen topic.
  - Decide what you feel about it and what you can do about it.
  - Look at a forthcoming event. Why is it important that people attend this?
  - Choose a LEDC to study. You will have to use a search engine to find the country's website.
    - Find out about this country – make a list of the capital city, the population, the climate, the main products, its people, its currency.
    - What problems does the country face? How could these problems be resolved?
    - Find out what NGOs are working in the capital city of this country. What do you think they are doing to help? What could you do to help?
- For your chosen area of study you should:
  - Make a report
  - or Prepare a talk
  - or Make a poster for display
  - or Discuss it with someone
  - or Write a letter to your MP
  - or Prepare a PowerPoint presentation
  - or Write a poem
  - or Draw a picture
  - or Write in support of the NGO
  - or Take part in an event or hold an event to support it.

Your teacher may have some other ideas for your work.

Picture stimulus

A *Poverty in Africa*

Twenty per cent of Africa's children will die before the age of five (UNICEF figures).

Go to the actionaid (www.actionaid.org.uk/) website.

- Find out about the problems facing the people of Africa.
- What happens when the price of food increases?
- What can world leaders do to help?
- What are you going to do to improve the lives of millions of children like this one?

14 Sustainable development – facing the challenges

14.1 What is sustainable development?

Sustainable development or sustainability is recognising that the earth's resources are finite, so everyone must use them responsibly. It means that we need to consider what is probable in our future and what is preferable in the future. To achieve what is preferable we need to adapt our resource use to achieve the desired outcome.

Securing the Future – UK government sustainable development strategy

The UK government launched its strategy for sustainable development, Securing The Future, in March 2005. The strategy places greater emphasis on delivery at regional level and the new relationship between government and local authorities. The lead government Department is Defra, but all departments share responsibility for making sustainable development a reality.

The strategy for sustainable development aims to enable all people to satisfy their basic needs and enjoy a better quality of life without compromising the quality of life of future generations. The new strategy has four agreed priorities:

- sustainable consumption and production
- climate change
- natural resource protection, and
- sustainable communities.

Activities

1. Who is the current Secretary of State for the Environment?
2. Go to the Defra website (www.defra.gov.uk/). Choose the sustainable development section. Find out what events are happening.
3. What does the Sustainable Development Commission do?

Agenda 21

Agenda 21 is an international agreement made at the first Earth Summit held in Rio de Janeiro in June 1992. This conference agreed that changes were necessary to tackle environmental, social and economic problems around the world. One hundred and seventy nine countries signed up to this agreement and more than 1,800 local authorities across the world are working on this project.

The 40 chapters in Agenda 21 are divided into the following four sections:

Section 1: Social and Economic Dimensions

This includes combating poverty, population issues, promoting health and promoting sustainable settlement patterns.

Objectives

To understand the meaning of sustainable development and to understand what Local Agenda 21 is about.

Key terms

Sustainable development: means understanding the need to maintain and improve the quality of life now without damaging the planet for future generations.

Information

Defra is the Department for the Environment, Forestry and Rural Affairs.

A *Sustainable forestry*

Key terms

Agenda 21: a comprehensive plan of action to be taken globally, nationally and locally by organisations in every area in which human beings impact on the environment. Its motto is *Think globally, act locally*.

Section 2: Conservation and Management of Resources for Development

This includes atmospheric protection, combating **deforestation**, protecting fragile environments, **biodiversity** and control of pollution.

Section 3: Strengthening the Role of Major Groups

This includes the roles of children and youth, women, Non-governmental Organisations (NGOs), local authorities, business and workers.

Section 4: Means of Implementation

This includes science, technology, education, international institutions and finance.

Key terms

Deforestation: usually refers to the cutting, clearing, and removal of rainforests. It is one of the causes of the greenhouse effect.

Biodiversity: put simply is the variety of life on earth. It embraces all living plant and animal ecosystems on which they depend for life.

What is Local Agenda 21?

Local Agenda 21 is the local version of Agenda 21. The local councils in the UK have prepared their own Local Agenda 21, based on the action and concerns expressed by people in their communities.

The hope is that, through everyone's participation and effort, progress will be made to improve our quality of life.

Local councils were required to prepare a document to meet the challenges of sustainability for their area. Each council outlined the current position and what action would be needed to meet the targets they had set for improvement. They made an action plan to deal with each of the strategic objectives and put plans in place to monitor progress. Local Agenda 21 programmes were the subject of consultation and local councils incorporated the results of consultation into the final policy for the area. The objectives included:

- Air quality and noise management
- Energy conservation
- Biodiversity – the variety of animals and plants
- Green purchasing
- Land use planning
- Sustainable transport
- Waste management.

B *Local Agenda 21 activity*

Activities

4 Write to your local council and find out what its plans and priorities are for sustainable development. How is their success being measured? What are the criteria for and indicators of their success? Are young people consulted on policies? How?

5 What have you learned about the impact of local policies and priorities for sustainable development? How can you use your right to be consulted by the local authority and contribute responsibly to local decision making?

6 In one or more of the following ways present the results of your findings to other pupils and members of the local community:

- Design a poster to explain the local issues and options.
- Write a leaflet to explain the local issues for sustainable development and encouraging other pupils to join the debate.
- Create a website or page on the school website which updates pupils, parents and others on the local issues and school involvement/events.
- Organise a school assembly to explain the local issues and inform other pupils.
- Write a proposal for discussion in class and at the school council.

14.2 The demand for resources

Objectives

To look at how the world uses its resources and to understand the effects this is having on the world's climate and environment.

An increasing global population needs more resources. To cover basic needs, we require uncontaminated food and water supplies, shelter, clothing and good health. Resources are also required to make all the things that we use in our daily lives, from the oil that is used to make plastic, to the wood and metal that is used to make furniture.

There is an increasing demand for goods and services by the people of the world, especially those in MEDCs. This means the world's resources are being used up more quickly. The consumption of resources is spread unequally between people in MEDCs, who use more resources, and LEDCs, who use less.

Countries that use a lot of **fossil fuels** to produce energy to power industry and electricity and heat for homes, also produce a lot of carbon gases, as an unwanted by-product. Carbon Dioxide [CO_2], particularly, is given off when fossil fuels, such as oil and coal, are burnt. This build up of CO2 is believed to contribute to **global warming** through the **greenhouse effect**. This is why CO_2 is called a **greenhouse gas**.

Key terms

Fossil fuels: are fuels that have been formed from the organic remains of prehistoric plants and animals like coal, oil and gas.

Global warming: the increase in average temperatures of the atmosphere, oceans and landmasses of Earth.

Greenhouse effect: the insulating effect of atmospheric greenhouse gases on the earth's temperature.

Greenhouse gas: a gas, such as water vapour, carbon dioxide or methane, which contributes to climate change.

What is climate change?

Many people consider climate change to be the biggest challenge facing the people on the planet. In basic terms, 'climate change' is a change in the weather conditions that prevail in a certain area, and is the result of the increasing temperature of the Earth's surface. This increase in temperature is occurring faster than it would naturally, which raises many questions as to the cause. The science for the whole planet is very complex, but many scientists believe that our actions are a major contributing factor to observable differences in the earth's climate.

A *Industrial site using fossil fuels*

Balancing the world's resources

It is difficult to manage the world's natural resources when there are conflicting demands upon them. Here are some of the issues:

- The environment should be preserved.
- Resources need to be retained for future generations to enjoy.
- Humans need to continue to make and do the things that allow them to live comfortably.
- LEDCs need to develop, through exploiting their resources.
- There should be a better balance between the consumption of those resources between LEDCs and MEDCs.

In order to conserve natural resources for future generations, sustainable management of the natural environment is necessary. Alternative resources might be developed in order to ease the strain on finite resources. However alternative resources can be expensive and take time to develop. Existing resources could be used more efficiently, to prevent finite resources being used up so quickly.

How can we save the environment?

Here are a number of ways in which we can help limit the damage caused by humans to the environment:

- Recycling resources that have already been used is popular and reduces waste. Many people recycle their used cans, bottles and paper.
- Limiting the amount of carbon emission generated through industrial and domestic use of fuels can assist in reducing levels of pollution. This can limit environmental problems such as global warming and **acid rain**.

B *Most people in Britain now use recycling facilities*

Information

Some governments, including the UK, signed the Kyoto Protocol to say they will try to reduce carbon emissions. One hundred and thirty seven developing countries have ratified the protocol but have no obligation beyond monitoring and reporting emissions. The US has not signed the protocol. The Kyoto Protocol is an international agreement setting targets for industrialised countries to cut their greenhouse gas emissions in an attempt to stop global warming.

Resource substitution is another sustainable way in which resources can be managed.

Renewable resources can be used instead of finite resources.

Sustainable resource management can help ensure that resources don't run out. Increasingly, sustainable practices are being encouraged in order to preserve animal and plant life for the benefit of life of future generations.

Key terms

Acid rain: is a result of air pollution caused by invisible gases that can be harmful to our environment.

Activity

If you are committed to changing a few straightforward things in your lifestyle, you really can have an impact. What can you do to make a difference?

14.3 Greenpeace – Renewable Energy

Case study

To study one developed case of sustainable development and its impact on Britain.

Greenpeace believes that Britain could, and should, be a global leader in the field of renewable energy. It believes that we could be reaping huge benefits from harnessing our indigenous energy sources, which use no fuel and will never run out by being at the forefront of the fastest growing new technologies.

Greenpeace believes that the UK is only seizing a small percentage of the new technologies market, and we're being left behind. Germany, Denmark, the US, Italy, Spain, China and India all have more wind capacity than us. Canada, France and Portugal are at about the same level or slightly less but, last year, they all grew faster than the UK.

Greenpeace says that the government has mishandled the development of renewable technologies. They have been indecisive and this has placed obstacles in the way of developments. When heat and transport energy is included, the UK ranks near the bottom of the EU league table for renewable development. Only Belgium, Cyprus and Malta are worse (based on figures in July 2008).

Greenpeace believes that renewable energy can and must form the heart of our energy system.

Wind power

Greenpeace states that wind power is a large-scale, reliable source of power that's already having an impact. It provides enough electricity to supply 1.2 million UK homes every year. However, despite the fact that our wind is stronger and more constant than Germany's, it has built more than ten times our wind farm capacity.

A *Wind power*

Information

Indigenous energy means power and heat derived from sources native to Britain.

Activities

1. Give two reasons why Greenpeace thinks that renewable energy should be used in Britain.
2. Go to the Greenpeace website (**www.greenpeace.org.uk/**). Find out what it is doing to promote improvements in renewable energy development.
3. Do you think renewable energy is the way forward? Give reasons for your answer.

The UK is falling behind other countries because the government has not made the right decisions. For example, wind farms that could provide five times the capacity of the ones we already have are being held up by the planning system. The time taken to get approval is growing and the proportion of successful applications is falling. This policy failure is undermining the future of wind power in the UK. It is also endangering our renewable energy and CO2 targets. We need to speed up the decision process if we are to meet our 2010 renewable energy target. Once approved, a wind farm doesn't take long to build.

Offshore wind farms like the London Array are planned on a scale that will generate the equivalent of the electricity needs for 750,000 homes. A predicted output from one offshore wind farm is about the same as the output from a typical nuclear power station.

Between onshore and offshore wind, the long-term potential for wind power in the UK is enormous. Government figures suggest that more than a quarter of today's electricity consumption could be provided by wind power by 2025. Greenpeace believes that to do this would be both economic and practical.

B *Ocean power*

C *Tidal power*

Ocean power – wave and tidal

Greenpeace believes that as an island nation we should look to the power in the seas. Wave and tidal power is at an innovation stage but it is an opportunity we can't afford to miss. The world's first commercial wave power generator is on Islay, in the Western Isles of Scotland. According to government and industry figures wave and tidal power combined could meet 12.5 per cent of today's electricity demand by 2025.

Greenpeace's position

Greenpeace is lobbying for Britain to use renewable energy sources rather than the nuclear sources currently being used. It believes that support for renewable energy will bring benefits, not just of clean, fuel-free energy, but the jobs and economic growth that come from pioneering new industries and technology.

Activities

4. Find out if Britain is meeting its energy targets.
5. Find out where the UK stands in the EU for renewable energy development. What can be done to improve the position?
6. Do you think wind power and ocean power are good energy generators for an island?
7. Make a poster to explain the importance of wind/wave power.
8. Find out about the London Array and where it is.
9. Find about the wave power generator on the Isle of Islay.

14.4 Understanding global interdependence

> *Before you finish eating breakfast this morning, you've depended on more than half the world.*
>
> *Martin Luther King*

Objectives

To understand what interdependence is and how it affects our lives.

What is interdependence?

Interdependence is about:

- understanding how people, places, economies and environments are interrelated, and that choices and events have consequences on a global scale
- understanding the impact of globalisation and that the choices we make have consequences at different levels, from personal to global
- appreciating the links between the lives of others and your own life
- understanding the influence that diverse cultures and ideas (political, social, religious, economic, legal, technological and scientific) have on each other and appreciating the complexity of interdependence
- understanding how the world is a global community and what it means to be a citizen
- understanding how actions, choices and decisions taken in the UK can impact positively or negatively on the quality of life of people in other countries.

All living things and the processes that sustain them are interdependent. So, global interdependence means that as a world we depend on each other.

Activities

1. List six items you might find in a typical family breakfast. Make a list of the people involved and processes used to produce these items.
2. Do you think Martin Luther King's statement is accurate? What point was he trying to make?
3. Which of the statements best describes interdependence for you? Give a reason for your answer. Discuss in groups.

Issues about global interdependence

Our economic prosperity is created from the raw materials nature provides. We must look after these to ensure that future generations will continue to enjoy the benefits of the earth's resources. We call this sustainability. Today, the forces affecting us are not only natural, but also economic, social, and political.

With the growing **interdependence** in the world comes the need for increased collaboration. We live in a global market place; one in which we are all participants. Globalisation is drawing us closer together and increasing our interdependence. Our fates and prosperities are tied to the global economy.

The economic expansion in China and India has been so powerful that their need for oil, metals, and other basic commodities has spurred growth in the formerly slow economies of Africa and Latin America.

Chinese and Indian demand for **primary commodities** has raised prices for the natural resources that are often the main exports of developing countries. This has contributed to a bigger growth rate for Africa. However, this windfall should be used by these countries to invest in such basics as education and infrastructure to set the stage for more stable, long-term progress.

AQA Examiner's tip

You will need to give your own opinion on issues and the reasons for that opinion in the examination.

Key terms

Interdependence: we are mutually dependent on one another for survival.

Primary commodity: a commodity in its raw or unprocessed state like wood or oil.

One global market – the oil industry

The oil industry is a truly global market place. The price of oil today is determined through the interaction of buyers and sellers in thousands of daily transactions. When it comes to the world oil markets and oil prices, interdependence is not just some vague academic concept to be studied in textbooks. It is real and its impact is reflected each day in world oil prices. Oil prices are the result of complex interactions of many different factors.

Factors determining current prices include:

- global oil demand and supply
- geopolitical risks
- global refining capacity and
- infrastructure bottlenecks.

The challenge for the oil industry is to provide more energy at reasonable costs; in a manner that is both safe and environmentally friendly. Meeting this challenge has less to do with the resources under the ground than with factors on the surface. While talk of oil running out has been with us for decades, the reality is that today the world has more oil reserves than ever before. The great promise of globalisation is to increase world economic activity and to spread prosperity to developing countries. More energy, particularly oil, will be required to fuel these growing economies.

A *Industry in China*

B *The oil industry*

How can these challenges be met?

Although globalisation has meant that countries are increasingly linked, strategies on how best to develop to benefit the welfare of the whole population must meet each country's specific needs. Every country is different and has its own priorities and concerns but international rules and cooperation are essential in order to ensure economic stability in an increasingly globalised world.

Development strategies will include different policies:

- macroeconomic tools such as interest rates and taxation
- trade policies such as tariff rates
- education policy and
- infrastructure investment.

These policies need to address complex challenges such as:

- commodity dependence
- lack of natural resources and
- high levels of debt.

Discussion activity 

How can we use more oil to support economic activity and encourage developing countries and save the planet from climate change? Discuss.

Information

The world economy is complex and fluctuating. All of the elements listed above are interlinked: debt repayment has an impact on how much money a government can spend on infrastructure and education. There is no easy answer to the problems and there is no global agreement to the solution.

Case study

14.5 Global food crisis 2008

Food prices had been rising for a while. This resulted in food riots in Haiti, Cameroon, Indonesia and Egypt. In Haiti, where food prices increased by 50 to 100 per cent, the Prime Minister was forced out of office. The World Food Programme's (WFP) biggest concern is for the people living on less than $1 a day who have nothing to fall back on. It is not so much famine that is the worry, it is widespread misery and malnutrition.

A *People react strongly when they are hungry*

> *The World Bank reports that global food prices rose 83 per cent over the last three years and the Food and Agriculture Organization (FAO) cites a 45 per cent increase in their world food price index during just the past nine months. As of March 2008, average world wheat prices were 130 per cent above their level a year earlier, soy prices were 87 per cent higher, rice had climbed 74 per cent, and maize was up 31 per cent.*
>
> *Institute for Food and Development Policy, May 16, 2008*

Immediate factors for the food crisis

Factors include the following:

- droughts in major wheat-producing countries in 2005–06
- low grain reserves
- high oil prices
- a doubling of per-capita meat consumption in some developing countries
- diversion of 5 per cent of the world's cereals to biofuels.

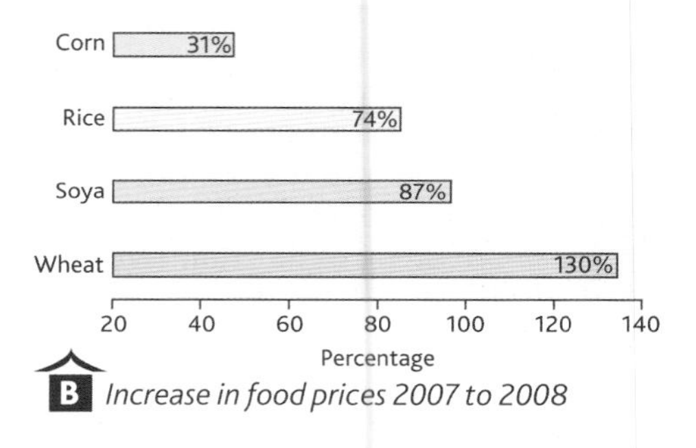

B *Increase in food prices 2007 to 2008*

What are the issues?

The rise in food prices has caused consternation and problems across the world. Some of the arguments used are listed here:

- The US and some European countries have insisted that the impact of biofuels on the food crisis has been small and have attempted to blame demand from rising poorer countries as the cause.
- Overpopulation has been raised as a concern, although there is no evidence that supply has reduced while population growth has slowed.
- A lot of land goes into producing products that could be considered unnecessary or excessive in their production (for example, tobacco, sugar, beef).
- Eighty per cent of the world's production is consumed by the wealthiest 20 per cent of the world suggesting an inequality in resource use due to social, economic and political reasons.
- While many go hungry an equally large number are considered obese.

These factors do not explain why, in an increasingly productive and affluent global food system, next year up to one billion people are likely go hungry.

To understand why people go hungry we need to consider that:

- Much of the best agricuitural land in the world is used to grow other commodities such as cotton, sisal, tea, tobacco, sugar cane, and cocoa, items for which there is a large market.

Information

Biofuels have forced global food prices up by 75 per cent according to a World Bank report. Governments in Washington and across Europe have turned to plant-derived fuels to reduce emissions of greenhouse gases and reduce their dependence on imported oil.. Over a third of US corn is now used to produce ethanol and about half of vegetable oil in the EU goes towards the production of biodiesel.

- Millions of acres of potentially productive farmland is used to pasture cattle, an extremely inefficient use of land, water and energy, but one for which there is a market in wealthy countries.
- More than half the grain grown in the United States (requiring half the water used in the US) is fed to livestock.

The Organisation for Economic Co-operation and Development (OECD) is an international organisation created in 1961. Its headquarters are in Paris, France. It brings together the governments of member countries committed to democracy and the market economy to:

- support sustainable economic growth
- boost employment
- raise living standards
- maintain financial stability
- assist other countries' economic development
- contribute to growth in world trade.

OECD also shares expertise and exchanges views with more than 100 other countries and economies including the least developed countries in Africa.

C *Why are some people starving while others have plenty?*

Activity

1. Go to the OECD website (**www.oecd.org/**). Find out which countries are members of this organisation. The OECD's work on global issues covers seven topics. What are they?

The Organisation of the Petroleum Exporting Countries (OPEC) is an intergovernmental organisation created in 1960. Its headquarters are in Vienna, Austria. OPEC's objective is to co-ordinate and unify petroleum policies among Member Countries, in order:

- to secure fair and stable prices for petroleum producers
- to deliver an efficient, economic and regular supply of petroleum to consuming nations; and
- to produce a fair return on capital to those investing in the industry.

Information

The Organisation for European Economic Co-operation (OEEC) which became the Organisation for Economic Co-operation and Development (OECD) was founded in 1948.

Discussion activity

- When OPEC increases the price of oil, it depresses growth in the oil-importing countries and raises it in the oil-exporting countries. Should OPEC have the power to determine the price of oil and how much is available at any time?
- What effect has the price of fuel had on the price of food?
- Should we be feeding animals grain and keeping them on acres of land to feed a few people when we could use these acres of land to grow grain to feed thousands?
- If you are trying to live on less than $1 each day, does this discussion about oil and prices mean anything to you? How can the world's leaders tackle the issue of poverty?
- Food prices are one of many problems facing the world. Make a list of five more problems. Put the issues raised by the whole class together and you will start to see the size of the problem. Where would you start?

Activity

2. Go to the OPEC website (**www.opec.org/**). Find out which countries are members of this organisation. Go to the OPEC Fund section and find out what this fund is doing.

links

You studied the oil industry on pages 176–177.

What you should know:

From this chapter your knowledge should now cover:

Short course

- ✔ what sustainable development is
- ✔ securing the future – government plans
- ✔ Agenda 21
- ✔ Local Agenda 21
- ✔ the demand for resources
- ✔ what climate change involves
- ✔ balancing the world's resources
- ✔ how we can save the environment
- ✔ what Greenpeace is
- ✔ what Greenpeace does
- ✔ wind and wave power

Full course

- ✔ what interdependence is
- ✔ what global interdependence is
- ✔ the global oil market
- ✔ how the challenges of globalisation can be met
- ✔ issues connected to world food crisis
- ✔ OECD and OPEC
- ✔ what biofuels are

Check your knowledge

You should be able to answer the following questions without looking back over the text. If you cannot answer all of the questions you need to learn the material more thoroughly.

1. What is sustainable development?
2. What is Agenda 21?
3. What is Defra?
4. Name three things local councils included in Local Agenda 21 Programmes.
5. What is an LEDC?
6. Describe fossil fuels.
7. What is a greenhouse gas?
8. What is Greenpeace?
9. What is renewable energy?
10. Where in Britain is the first wave power generator?

Further study

- Go to your local council website.
  - Find out the name of your local Councillors, the leader of the council and the Councillor responsible for the environment.
  - Go to the section dealing with the environment.
  - Find out what your council is doing to protect the local environment.
  - Find out how your local council keeps the streets, parks and schools clean.
  - Is your local council a fair trade council?
- Go to the US Environmental Protection Agency website (**http://epa.gov/climatechange/**).
  - Look at what another country is doing to educate its young people.
  - Choose the 'We can make a difference' section of the homepage.
  - Make a list of the five things you think people should do to make a difference.
  - Make a list of the five things you will commit to doing to do your bit.
- Go to the Friends of the Earth website (**www.foe.co.uk/**).
  - Go to the 'Green your school/group' section.
  - Make a list of the things you can do at school to be more sustainable.
  - Go to the 'Case Studies' section and choose one of the case studies.
  - Find out what this school has done to promote sustainability.
  - Decide what you feel about it and what you can do about it.
- For your chosen area of study you should:
  - Make a report
  - or Prepare a talk
  - or Make a poster for display
  - or Discuss it with someone
  - or Write a letter to your MP
  - or Prepare a PowerPoint presentation
  - or Write a poem
  - or Draw a picture
  - or Write in support of the NGO.

Your teacher may have some other ideas for your work.

Picture stimulus

A *Fuel protest*

- Why are these road haulage users protesting?
- What are the arguments used by the government to support high fuel taxes?
- Why should we be concerned about the amount of petrol and diesel used in Britain?
- Do national protests make the government take notice? Give reasons for your answer.

15 The UK's role in world affairs

15.1 What is the EU?

The EU stands for the European Union. It has 27 members at present. The benefits to being a member of the EU are:

- being able to trade goods without tariffs
- being part of a market of over 300 million people
- having a guaranteed price for farming produce through the Common Agricultural Policy (CAP)
- getting financial support for industries through grants
- support for isolated areas, for example, Scottish Highlands and Islands; Southern Italy
- support for projects such as new roads, bridges.

However problems do exist:

- some countries say they pay too big a share of the EU budget
- free trade has led to competition but at the expense of small local industries
- huge surpluses of food have been created because of the CAP
- money has been wasted on badly thought-out projects
- the EU loses millions each year through fraud.

A *The EU*

Objectives

To understand the United Kingdom's role in the European Union.

Activity

1 Go to the EU website (www.europa.eu/).

a Make a list of the 27 members of the EU.

b Find out about the CAP. Does this policy help Britain? What do you think?

links

You will find details of how the EU makes decisions in the reference section on page 224.

The UK in the European Union

As a member of the European Union, the UK is bound by its legislation and policies. These are based on a series of treaties which set out the EU's powers and how it can use them.

UK government ministers take part in the discussions and decision making, and the final decision is taken collectively by all the Member States.

> *"The European Union is essential to the success of Britain and a Britain fully engaged in Europe is essential to the success of the European Union."*
>
> *Prime Minister Gordon Brown*

Activity

2 Some people believe that Britain should leave the European Union.

- Do you think this would be a good idea? Give reasons for your answer.

Why is the EU important to the British citizen?

Many things in life can be improved when groups of countries work together. As a member of the EU, Britain benefits from the common strength of this group of nations. The EU helps citizens by:

- removing trade barriers to boost growth and create jobs
- making improvements to the environment
- improving standards and rights for consumers
- fighting international crime and illegal immigration
- bringing peace and stability to Europe by working with its neighbours
- giving Europe a more powerful voice in the world.

A global Europe

In the 21st century, Europe will face new and unprecedented challenges, from tackling climate change, to fighting international terrorism and sustaining growth and jobs in the face of changing global economic conditions. The European Union has the opportunity to benefit from globalisation and set a new agenda that emphasises openness, fairness and the importance of cooperation between nations.

The Lisbon Treaty set the framework to ensure that an EU of 27 or more Member States can function effectively. The EU now has a chance to focus on the real issues that matter to people in the Member States – competitiveness, jobs, the environment and security.

Information

The Treaty of Lisbon was signed in December 2007. The government supports the Treaty because it contains sensible changes to current Treaties and will modernise the way the EU works. This will make its delivery more effective.

Activity

3 Three countries are candidates to join the EU. What are they?

British influence on European values

European values are central to the political choices Europeans make. In European social and economic policy, these choices include:

- support for political pluralism and democracy
- endorsement of the mixed economy, and
- a strong commitment to public welfare, social cohesion and wealth redistribution.

This reflects the public opinion in Britain that shows unwavering public support for the National Health Service (NHS) and other features of the welfare state such as free schooling and benefits for the infirm and the elderly.

Information

Pluralism is a word that describes a system that includes individuals from groups differing in basic background experiences and cultures. Pluralism allows for the development of a common tradition while preserving the right of each group to maintain its cultural heritage. It implies mutual respect.

15.2 The UK, the United Nations and the North Atlantic Treaty Organization (NATO)

The United Nations (UN)

A *Flags of the UN*

The United Nations is not a world government and it does not make laws. It does, however, provide the means to help resolve international conflicts and formulate policies on matters affecting all of us. At the UN, all the Member States, large and small, rich and poor, with differing political views and social systems, have a voice and a vote in the decision-making process.

The United Nations has six main sections. Five of them (the General Assembly, the Security Council, the Economic and Social Council, the Trusteeship Council and the Secretariat) are based at UN Headquarters in New York. The sixth, the International Court of Justice, is located at The Hague in the Netherlands.

What does the UN do?

According to its Charter, the UN has four purposes:

- to maintain international peace and security
- to develop friendly relations among nations
- to cooperate in solving international problems and in promoting respect for human rights, and
- to be a centre for harmonising the actions of nations.

In addition the UN is committed to:

- removing poverty and improving the wellbeing of people everywhere, and
- giving humanitarian aid. Disasters can occur anywhere, at any time, whether the cause be flood, drought, earthquake or conflict.

Objectives

To understand the role played by Britain at the United Nations and within NATO.

Activity

1 Go to the UN website (www.un.org/).

- Find out what each section of the UN does.

links

You will find information about how the UN works in the reference section pages 220–221.

Information

The United Nations was established on 24 October 1945 by 51 countries. It is committed to preserving peace through international cooperation and collective security. Today, membership of the UN totals 192 countries.

Activity

2 What is the greatest achievement of the United Nations? Discuss in groups.

Britain's role at the UN

The British government sends representatives to all UN meetings, summits and conventions. The General Assembly meets annually in September. Each Member State can send not more than five representatives and as many advisers as may be required by the delegation.

Information

Britain is a permanent member of the UN Security Council.

Activity

3 Go to the website www.un.org/geninfo/faq/briefingpapers/. You want the paper on how to set up a model UN meeting. Do this as a class activity.

Britain and NATO

The North Atlantic Treaty Organization (NATO) is an alliance of 26 countries from Europe and North America. NATO's aim is to safeguard the freedom and security of its member countries, by political and military means. It now plays an important role in peacekeeping, crisis management and fighting terrorism.

B *Building trust on NATO exercises*

The role of NATO remained largely unchanged until the fall of the Soviet Union and the liberation of Eastern Europe. By the 1990s many people believed that NATO was no longer needed. However, NATO found a new role as new conflicts emerged in the Balkans and parts of the former Soviet Union. NATO has helped to end conflicts in Bosnia and Kosovo. NATO-led forces are now helping to bring stability to Kosovo, Afghanistan, Iraq and Darfur.

Information

Britain was one of the twelve nations that formed NATO 1949.

NATO's functions

Membership of NATO is central to UK defence policy. NATO's stated functions are to:

- help provide security and stability in the Euro-Atlantic area
- provide a transatlantic forum for Member States to consult on issues of common concern
- deter and defend against any threat to the territory of any NATO Member State
- contribute to crisis management and conflict prevention on a case-by-case basis
- promote partnership, cooperation and dialogue with other countries in the Euro-Atlantic area.

Activities

4 Which NATO members are members of the EU?

5 Do you think that NATO is necessary for the security of Britain? Give reasons for your answer.

Information

Members of NATO

There are 26 member countries of NATO, the North Atlantic Treaty Organization. They are:

- Belgium, Bulgaria, Canada, Czech Republic, Denmark, Estonia, France, Germany, Greece, Hungary, Iceland, Italy, Latvia, Lithuania, Luxembourg, Netherlands, Norway, Poland, Portugal, Romania, Slovakia, Slovenia, Spain, Turkey, United Kingdom, and United States. In 2008 Croatia and Albania were officially invited to join NATO. This membership is due to start in 2009.

15.3 The UK and world organisations

A CHOGM in Kampala, Uganda 2007

Objectives

To understand the UK's role in the Commonwealth, the World Bank, the World Trade Organization and the International Monetary Fund.

The UK and the Commonwealth

The Commonwealth is a voluntary association of independent countries, nearly all of which were once British territories. There are 53 members including the United Kingdom, which cooperate in the common interests of their people. The Commonwealth does not have a formal charter or constitution. Its structure is based on unwritten and traditional procedures, but it is guided by a series of agreements on its principles and aims.

The Commonwealth promotes international peace and security, democracy, liberty and equal rights, as well as economic and social development. It opposes all forms of racial discrimination. It represents nearly two billion people – almost a third of the world's population – from a wide range of faiths, races, cultures and traditions.

Head of the Commonwealth

The Queen is Head of the Commonwealth. This is a symbolic and unifying role, which reinforces the links by which the Commonwealth joins people together from around the world. The Queen is also Head of State in the UK and 15 other independent states. The Commonwealth Heads of Government (CHOGM) meet every two years.

The UK and the WTO

The EU is one of the key players in the World Trade Organization (WTO). This is because the EU has a common trade policy. In other words, where trade, including WTO matters, are concerned, the EU acts as one single actor.

Activities

1. Find the names of the Commonwealth countries.
2. Choose one Commonwealth country – find out its capital, its population, its climate, where it is in the world, what its features are, and what its resources are. Prepare a presentation for a group or the class about your chosen country.
3. Find out where and when the next CHOGM will take place. Who will chair this meeting?

Information

The European Commission negotiates on behalf of the EU's 27 Member States. The UK is represented by the EU at the WTO.

The EU is disappointed that the round of the world trade talks that have been happening since 2001 have failed to bring a multilateral trade outcome. The EU sees these as necessary measures to integrate developing countries into the world trading system in a way that will help them combat poverty.

WTO decisions are absolute and every member must abide by its rulings. So, when the US and the European Union are in dispute over bananas or beef, it is the WTO that acts as judge and jury. The WTO polices free trade agreements, settles trade disputes between governments and organises trade negotiations.

links

You will find details about trade agreements in chapter 13 page 159.

The UK and the IMF

Delivering the UK's policy at the World Bank and the International Monetary Fund (IMF) is undertaken by the Department for International Development (DFID) and the Treasury. The top UK representatives at the IMF and World Bank are the Chancellor of the Exchequer and Secretary of State for International Development. They are known as UK governors to the Fund and Bank. The UK is the fourth-largest shareholder in both the World Bank and the IMF, holding 4.3 per cent and 4.8 per cent of votes, respectively.

The Treasury now publishes a Report to Parliament on its dealings with the IMF. The report sets out our approach to IMF issues over the previous year and highlights our key priorities going forward. It includes details of the position the UK has taken in votes.

Information

The US is by far the largest shareholder in the World Bank and the IMF with 16.4 per cent and 16.85 per cent vote shares, respectively.

Activity

4 Find the names of the Chancellor of the Exchequer and the Secretary of State for International Development.

The UK and The World Bank

> *"The Bank remains a forum for all countries to work together on development issues on a daily basis. Money, knowledge and partnership – three essential ingredients for poverty reduction. The UK remains a steadfast supporter of the Bank which remains one of the most effective international development organizations."*
>
> *Department for Trade and Development publication The UK and The World Bank 2006–2007*

During this period the UK:

- was the second largest contributor to the Bank's International Development Association and, in 2007, the largest contributor to World Bank Trust Funds
- helped secure significant improvements in the Bank's implementation of agreed good practice, and
- continued to press the Bank to improve the way it works with other donors.

The Board of Governors is the World Bank's highest governing authority. The bank is governed by its member countries, who are also its shareholders. The Secretary of State for International Development is the UK's Governor. He also represents the UK on the Development Committee, the main ministerial forum for discussing Bank policies.

Information

The UK has withheld money it has pledged to the World Bank in the past. It held back 50 million pounds in September 2006 in a protest about the conditions the bank attaches to its aid. The government said the Bank had a duty to help those in poverty despite the actions of their governments. Oxfam welcomed the move by the UK government, adding that the World Bank's policy on aid was 'disastrous'.

Activities

Go to the world bank website (**www.worldbank.org/**).

5 Choose an item from the 'Focus on' section.

6 Find out what the bank is doing to help.

7 Make a poster to show this work.

15.4 The UK and world trade issues

The UK, as a member of the EU, makes its feelings about world trade issues known at the European Parliament and at the Council of Ministers. There are many trade agreements and practices across the world that cause concerns for national governments and international organisations. Many Non-governmental Organisations (NGOs) and charities work to advise governments on the impact that international trade practices have on developing nations and the workers at home. Britain is a member of the EU, but a close ally of the USA. It is possible to be both even when the US and the EU are disagreeing. You are going to investigate two examples of world trade issues.

Objectives

To investigate international interactions and to understand the UK's role in the world.

Case study

The banana case

Challenge by the United States, joined by Guatemala, Honduras, Mexico and Ecuador, against the European Union.

In September 1997, a World Trade Organization (WTO) panel ruled that the European Union (EU) was giving preferential access to bananas produced by former colonies in the Caribbean. This arrangement had been previously negotiated between the EU and its former African and Caribbean colonies under the Lomé Treaty.

A *Banana production in the Caribbean*

The United States, which does not produce any bananas, brought this case against the EU on behalf of the US-based Chiquita Corporation (formerly known as United Fruit). Chiquita produces bananas in Latin America on huge plantations that are notorious for exploiting cheap farm labour and using environmentally damaging techniques. In the Caribbean, which Europe was favouring, banana producers tend to be small-scale farmers who own and work their own land (an average of three acres), often incurring high production costs. Europe wanted to support small producers in their efforts to work as **cooperatives** and reduce poverty in the region.

This was a very divisive case within the WTO because of its economic, social justice, and environmental dimensions. At one point the United States threatened to impose sanctions of more than $500 million on EU exports. This would have led to job losses in the EU. Potentially, this could have caused a trade war. The issue is not resolved as the EU made an appeal against the WTO ruling in 2008.

Information

Bananas are crucial to the Caribbean economy. Over half the Caribbean population depends on the banana industry to supply them with food, shelter and education. Over 71 ACP states receive help from the EU.

Information

The Lomé treaty is a trade agreement that was made in 1975 between the European Union and the ACP (Africa, the Caribbean and the Pacific) states.

Key terms

Cooperative: an enterprise that is owned by members who are workers or consumers in the organisation. Members share responsibilities, profits and opportunities according to a set of agreed principles.

AQA Examiner's tip

You will only need to show knowledge of one case study in the examination. Make sure you form your own opinion about the issue and can give reasons for it.

Activity

1 The WTO agreed with the US that this agreement was unfair on the Chiquita Corporation. There was no time for the Caribbean farmers to do anything else with the land.
   a Was this decision fair on them? Discuss in groups.
   b Should a country be allowed to make a case to the WTO on behalf of a company?

The EU and China

The European Union and China are two of the biggest traders in the world. China is the single most important challenge for EU trade policy. China is now the EU's second trading partner behind the US and the biggest source of imports. The EU is China's biggest trading partner. In 2006 the European Commission adopted a major policy strategy (Partnership and Competition) on China that pledged the EU to accepting tough Chinese competition while pushing China to trade fairly. The EU was a strong supporter of China's accession to the WTO, arguing that a WTO without China was not truly universal in scope. In 2008 the EU and China launched a new strategic plan for driving trade and economic policy.

B *EU and China make a trade agreement*

Trade in goods

- EU goods exports to China 2007: €71.6 billion
- EU goods imports from China 2007: €230.8 billion.

EU's imports from China are mainly industrial goods: machinery and transport equipment and miscellaneous manufactured articles. EU's exports to China are also concentrated on industrial products: machinery and transport equipment, miscellaneous manufactured goods and chemicals.

Trade in services

- EU services exports to China 2006: €12.4 billion
- EU services imports from China 2006: €11.2 billion

Foreign Direct Investment

- EU inward investment to China 2006: €6 billion
- China inward investment to EU 2006: €2.1 billion

Issues and concerns

There are fundamental questions about human rights issues including arbitrary detention, torture and ill-treatment of prisoners.

The Chinese government:

- continues to suppress dissenting opinion
- maintains political control over the legal system, and
- places severe restrictions on freedom of expression and association.

The WTO raised a number of concerns regarding China's trade policy including:

1. inadequate protection of intellectual property rights
2. the maintenance of industrial policies that may discriminate against foreign companies especially in sectors like automobiles, and
3. barriers to market access in a number of service sectors including construction and banking.

Activity

2 Issues for discussion:

a. Many people believe that the growth of industry in China has created a major problem with global warming and climate change. How can the UK's government be part of trade agreements with China when it agrees with the Kyoto protocol?
b. How can the UN allow China to be a member when it does not have a good human rights record?
c. Breaking intellectual property rights means that a country is copying an article that has been designed by someone else. How can the WTO allow countries that do this to be members? What about the rights of the designer?

15.5 The UK and GM foods

Case study

Genetically modified (GM) commodities

General Information

Genetic modification is a special set of technologies that alter the genetic makeup of organisms such as animals, plants, or bacteria. GM products include medicines and vaccines, foods and food ingredients and feeds. In 2006, the EU estimated that 252 million acres of GM crops were planted in 22 countries by 10.3 million farmers. Ninety seven per cent of the products were grown by the following countries:

Country	USA	Argentina	Brazil	Canada	India	China	Paraguay	South Africa
% grown	53	17	11	6	4	3	2	1

Objectives

To understand how public opinion and concerns can influence national and international policy.

Like all new technologies, GM technologies pose some risks, both known and unknown. Most people agree that poverty is one of the major challenges facing the world in the future. Genetically modifying foods offers a dramatic promise for meeting this challenge.

Background

Corn, cotton and soybeans are the most important field crops in the US, both in terms of volume and cash receipts. They are used in the production of human food, animal feed and processed foods. These three crops are also major US commodity exports.

In the United States, large percentages of these crops are genetically modified. In 2001, 69 per cent of cotton, 68 per cent of soybeans, and 26 per cent of corn grown in the US was genetically engineered.

In Europe, a string of highly publicised food safety crises have heightened public concerns about food and have made consumers wary of GM foods. Reflecting those concerns, the European Union (EU) has required mandatory labelling of GM foods since 1997, and no new GM crops have been approved since 1998. The proposals call for strict labelling of all food and animal feed produced from GM crops.

A *Cotton growing in the USA*

US and EU trade

Looking at goods and services combined, the EU and US are each other's main trading partners and account for the largest bilateral trade relationship in the world. For example, in 2001, the value of US exports of agricultural products to the EU was $6.3 billion. The main products exported were soybeans, tobacco, and animal feed. Similarly, the value of EU exports of agricultural products to the US was $7.9 billion. The main products were wine and beer.

UK's royalty speaks out against GM

In August 2008, the Prince of Wales, who has an organic farm on his Highgrove estate, told the press that relying on huge corporations for the mass production of food would threaten future food supplies. He wanted to see more family-run cooperative farms. He believed that farmers must work with nature and not against it.

Prince Charles's intervention comes at a time when the price of food has been pushed up worldwide by poor harvests, rising fuel prices, market speculation and the diversion of land into biofuel production. Green groups and aid agencies support his view and say that claims about the potential benefits of GM foods have not been proven.

B *Prince Charles at Highgrove*

The UK and food safety

It appears that British opposition to genetically modified crops is on the rise causing concern at research laboratories across the country. The Guradian reported that 'since 2000 almost all of the 54 GM crop trials attempted in Britain have been vandalised to some extent' (29 July 2008). Protesters ripped up crops in one of only two GM trials to be approved in Britain this year. Scientists claim the repeated attacks on their trials are stopping vital research to evaluate whether GM crops can reduce the cost and environmental impact of farming. Friends of the Earth say that genetic engineering is imprecise and unpredictable and that only the companies that have the most to gain say GM food is safe.

Consumer opposition to GM foods in Europe

Several food crises have made consumers in Europe extremely wary of changes to the food supply. The first of these major food crises, 'mad cow disease' (Bovine Spongiform Encephalopathy – [BSE]), started in the UK in the 1990s. In 1996, there was alarm over a similar disease in humans (called Creutzfeldt-Jacob disease, or CJD) and consumption of meat from cows with BSE. These cases have created a climate of mistrust towards GM foods because there is no clear evidence to remove them as a cause.

Consumers in the UK blamed the government for slowness to react and they were concerned about the wholesale destruction of animals and the effects this had on farming. This failure in trust in the regulatory system spread throughout Europe and resulted in tight food safety legislation.

Information

In 2002, the EU set up the European Food Safety Authority. It is responsible for risk assessment and risk communication to the public. It says, 'Food is essential to life. We are committed to ensuring food safety in Europe.'

Controversies surrounding GM foods and crops commonly focus on:

- human and environmental safety
- labelling and consumer choice
- domination of world food production by a few companies
- ethics
- food security
- poverty reduction
- environmental conservation.

Benefits attributed to GM foods include:

- enhanced taste and quality
- increased yields and nutrients
- improved resistance to disease, pests, and herbicides
- conservation of soil, water, and energy
- increased food security for growing populations
- reduced maturation time.

Activities

1. GM foods can only be sold in Britain if they pass safety regulations. Go to the Food Standards Agency website (**www.food.gov.uk/**). Find out what must be on a label.
2. Go to the Defra website (**www.defra.gov.uk/**). Find out what the government says about GM foods. You will find this under 'GM Crops'.
3. Why is such a fuss made about GM crops? Discuss in groups.
4. Do you think that Prince Charles's contribution to the argument will make a difference to what the people of Britain think?
5. Look at the controversies and the benefits. What do you think about the GM food argument? Form your own opinion.

Chapter summary

What you should know:

From this chapter your knowledge should now cover:

Short course

- ✔ what the European Union is
- ✔ the UK and the European Union
- ✔ the EU and the British citizen
- ✔ how the British have influenced EU values
- ✔ the United Nations and what it does
- ✔ Britain's role at the UN
- ✔ Britain and NATO
- ✔ NATO's functions
- ✔ the UK and the WTO
- ✔ the UK and the Commonwealth
- ✔ the UK and the IMF
- ✔ the UK and the World Bank

Full course

- ✔ the UK and world trade issues
- ✔ the banana case – the US versus the EU
- ✔ the EU and China
- ✔ the UK and GM foods
- ✔ US and EU trade
- ✔ the UK and food safety
- ✔ consumer opposition to GM foods in Europe

Check your knowledge

You should be able to answer the following questions without looking back over the text. If you cannot answer all of the questions you need to learn the material more thoroughly.

1. How many Member States does the EU have? Name 10.
2. What does CAP stand for?
3. Name three of the sections of the UN.
4. Name two things that the United Nations does.
5. What does NATO stand for?
6. How many members does NATO have?
7. What is the Commonwealth?
8. Who is the Head of the Commonwealth?
9. What does CHOGM stand for?
10. Which country is the biggest shareholder in the World Bank?

Further study

- Go to the EU Trade website (**http://ec.europa.eu/trade/**).
  - Find out who the current Commissioner for Trade is.
  - Which EU country does he/she represent?
  - Select 'Trade Issues' from the menu and go to the EU and Global Trade.
  - Choose a topic that covers health, poverty, aid, social welfare or sustainability.
  - What is the EU doing about this? Do you think that the EU should be doing more?
  - Decide what you feel about this and what you could do about it.
- Go to the Oxfam website (**www.oxfam.co.uk/education/**).
  Select 'Cool Planet', then 'Food from round the world', then 'bananas'.
  - Make a report giving details about how bananas are grown, harvested, packed and exported. Why do the banana farmers need a fair price for their produce?
  - Go to the 'Take Action' section and see what Oxfam suggests you can do to help.
  - Decide what you feel about it and what you can do about it.
- Go to the Commonwealth website (**www.thecommonwealth.org/**).
  Choose the FAQs key. From the 'Our Work' list, choose one area to study.

  For your chosen subject:
  - What does the Commonwealth hope to achieve? How does it intend to achieve it?
  - Has the Commonwealth set any dates or targets for your topic?
  - Who is involved in this work? Do you think enough is being done?
  - Decide what you feel about it and what you can do about it.
- For your chosen area of study you should:
  - Make a report
  - or Prepare a talk
  - or Make a poster for display
  - or Discuss it with someone
  - or Write a letter to your MP
  - or Prepare a PowerPoint presentation
  - or Write a poem
  - or Draw a picture
  - or Write in support of the NGO.

Your teacher may have some other ideas for your work.

Picture stimulus

A *Protestors destroying GM crops*

- Why do you think this person is in these fields destroying the crops?
- Why do you think the protestor is dressed in this way?
- Do you think the protestor is right to take the law into his own hands in this way?
- What do you think about this?
- What can you do to help change things?

16 Influencing international issues

16.1 International pressure groups and NGOs

These are organisations that are working to influence the international arena, so they will aim to influence the policies of the European Union (EU), the United Nations (UN), the World Trade Organisation (WTO) and the International Monetary Fund (IMF). Many of these groups are located in the UK though they have often spread into global or international organisations. Pressure groups must keep to the law of the country in which they operate.

To ensure that their message is heard, pressure groups organise highly publicised demonstrations, meetings and rallies. These events are attended by group members who display banners and placards. The event will often have a prominent speaker. The press and the media will be invited to attend.

B *International pressure groups and NGOs*

What are their rights?	What are their responsibilities?	What are their methods?
They have the right to criticise. They have the right to hold demonstrations, meetings and rallies. They have the right to protest. They have the right to make their views known by using the media. They have the right to campaign and raise funds.	They have the responsibility to base their criticism on fact. Their meetings and rallies should be peaceful and legal. They should inform the local authorities and the police when they are making a protest. They have a responsibility not to intimidate.	Internet – email and websites. Letters. Leaflets and advertising. Lobbying international organisations. Petitions. Demonstrations. Mass media campaigns (TV, radio and newspapers).

Some examples of international pressure groups

Greenpeace

Greenpeace is a non-profit organisation, with a presence in countries across Europe, the Americas, Asia and the Pacific. As a global organisation, Greenpeace focuses on the most crucial worldwide threats to our planet's biodiversity and environment.

Friends of the Earth

Friends of the Earth is one of the leading environmental pressure groups in the UK and the largest international network of environmental groups in the world. Over the years they have won many battles with governments and industry, achieving bans on Chlorofluorocarbons (CFCs), reducing trade in rainforest timber, and increasing support for cleaner energy technologies.

Objectives

To understand how pressure groups and Non-governmental Organisations (NGOs) deal with international issues.

A *Barack Obama speaking at a rally in April 2008*

links

You studied pressure groups in the UK, how they were organised and what they did in chapter 1.

Activity

1 Go to the World Wide Fund for Nature (WWF) website (www.wwf.org.uk/). Go to the One Planet Future campaign. This is an example of an international internet campaign. Choose one issue that the WWF is campaigning on. What is this about? Make a poster or write a report about this issue. What can you do to help?

Amnesty International

Amnesty International is a worldwide campaigning movement that works to promote internationally recognised human rights. Amnesty International has more than a million members and supporters in over 140 countries and territories. Their work is financed largely by subscriptions and donations from their worldwide membership.

International NGOs

The Union of International Organizations estimates that there are 38,000 international NGOs. International NGOs work on a range of international activities and give support and organise relief to countries during times of **natural disaster**. They also undertake development operations, research, training and good practice development, as well as policy analysis and advocacy. Many international NGOs specialise in the type of help they give. Some of them are faith based. Others focus on issues like health, hunger, humanitarian aid, peace, human rights and trade.

Activities

2 The WWF is a charity. Do you think it could be called a pressure group? Give reasons for your answer.

3 Choose one of the pressure groups listed here and find out what their latest campaign is.

Some examples of international NGOs

ActionAid

ActionAid works with over five million of the world's poorest people in more than 30 countries across Africa, Asia, Latin America and the Caribbean.

Oxfam

Oxfam is an international organisation working together with over 3,000 partners in more than 100 countries to find lasting solutions to poverty, suffering and injustice. It seeks increased worldwide public understanding that economic and social justice are crucial to sustainable development.

The Trade Justice Movement

The Trade Justice Movement is a group of more than 80 organisations campaigning for trade justice. One of its major tasks is working with allies internationally on negotiations with the World Trade Organisation.

Case study

NGOs and the International Campaign to Ban Landmines

NGOs join together to make the case for important issues. A committee of six organisations launched the International Campaign to Ban Landmines (ICBL) in 1992. It now brings together over 1,400 international NGOs working locally, nationally, regionally, and internationally to ban antipersonnel (AP) mines. The ICBL succeeded in pushing through the International Mine Ban Treaty in 1997, and received a Nobel Peace Prize for its work. The ICBL laid the groundwork for future NGO advocacy efforts with its strategy of alliance between NGOs serving as a model for other NGO campaigns.

Go to the website (**www.icbl.org/**). Find out what the problem is, what the solution is and what you can do to help.

Key terms

Natural disaster: a destructive force of nature that causes damage and loss of life. It is caused by hurricane, earthquake, flood, volcanic eruption and other natural forces. It usually leaves countries in emergency situations.

C *NGO helping control HIV/AIDS in Africa*

AQA Examiner's tip

Knowledge of pressure groups and NGOs and what they do will be useful in more than one area of your assessment.

Activity

4 Save the Children says:

'Too many children are still dying because they haven't got enough food or because they can't get treatment for simple illnesses. Millions aren't getting an education and are being exploited and abused. This is not good enough.'

a Go to the Save the Children website (**www.savethechildren.org.uk/**). Find out what it does and where it does it. What can you do to help?

b Save the Children is a charity. Do you think it could be called an NGO? Give reasons for your answer.

c Choose one of the NGOs listed above and find out what their latest campaign is.

16.2 Making a difference – playing your part in the community

A *More people volunteer to help in the community*

Objectives

To investigate ways in which an individual young person can participate in the community.

AQA Examiner's tip

Taking part in community activities and volunteering can be used in a Controlled Assessment.

Key terms

Volunteering: activities such as community service, charity, public service, community action, community involvement, trustee, member and helper. It means giving your time unpaid.

Voluntary organisations: organisations involved in activities in the community. Their management committee and members are volunteers.

Working for your community – volunteering

The problems of the world, or even your community, might seem enormous. You might even feel like there's no point in you trying to do anything. How can one person really make a start with everything that needs to be done?

Remember the story of the Enormous Turnip! **Volunteering** is like this. One single person can make a difference. But, a lot of 'ones' gathered together to work on the same problem can make it better or even make it go away. Every person is important, and every person can do some good. It is the commitment of time and energy for the benefit of society and the community and can take many forms. Lots of the work done in the community is undertaken by **voluntary organisations**.

Information

WRVS volunteers provide services in homes, such as Meals on Wheels, Books on Wheels and Good Neighbours. They also provide services in the community with community transport and at day centres, and they provide assistance to visitors, patients and staff in hospitals and in emergency response.

Activities

1. If you were able to volunteer to help an organisation, which one would you chose? Give reasons for your choice.
2. Choose a charity in your area and find out how volunteers help the charity in its work.

What could you do?

Find out about some voluntary organisations in your local community. Your local council should be able to help. Now that you know you can make a difference, what kind of volunteering could you do? Here are some ideas to help you choose:

Think about what you're interested in

What are you passionate about? What's out there in the world that catches your interest? What do you want to be when you grow up? The answers to these questions will help point you to a volunteer cause or group you'll like being part of. For instance:

- If you've always loved animals, you can volunteer to care for abandoned pets or injured wildlife.
- If you want to grow up to be a doctor or nurse, you can look for a youth volunteer programme with the St John Ambulance.

Think about what you're good at

What skills do you have? What kinds of jobs do you do best? Try to find a volunteer position that will let you make the most of your strengths and talents. For instance:

- If you're a great speaker, you could use your voice and thoughts to educate others about a problem you care about, such as animal cruelty.
- If you're a good cook, or even if you just make pretty good sandwiches, you might be able to help at your local Salvation Army soup kitchen or with the Cyrenians.

Think about time

How much of a commitment are you willing to make? Do you have just a few hours now and then, or are you looking for a bigger project? For example:

- If you have a couple of hours on the weekend, you could visit people in the hospital or at a home for senior citizens.
- If you have a whole summer to spend volunteering, you could join a national campaign to help build parks and trails.

Think about your limitations

We can all do great things, but we also have to follow family rules and routines. Involve a parent in the process, so you can be sure that:

- You have permission to do it.
- The adults in your life feel confident that you'll be safe.
- You have transportation to and from places you need to be.
- Your volunteering isn't getting in the way of schoolwork and other responsibilities at home.

National Volunteer Groups

There are many opportunities available to people who volunteer to help. Some of the volunteer groups will be known to you. You probably know about the Women's Royal Voluntary Service (WRVS) – the ladies who make the refreshments during your visits to hospital. Most opportunities are connected to charities. Many charities like the National Trust would not be able to operate or maintain their premises and land without the volunteers who help the full-time staff.

Information

Did you know that the St John Ambulance offer courses and first aid advice? Go to the website (**www.sja.org/uk/sja**). Find out about event first aid cover.

Activities

3. Find out about the work of charities in your area that help the homeless and disadvantaged.
4. What are you good at? Make a list of your skills. Discuss this with someone in the group who knows you well. Ask if they would add anything to your list.
5. Choose a subject you are passionate about and prepare a presentation to give to the class/group.

16.3 How individuals make a difference

Can an individual make a difference?

> *"If the individual acts, society is changed. Society is a combination of individuals. To change, whether right or wrong, good or bad – the start point, the initiative, must come from the individual. So it is good what you do. It is very important. One person can make a difference."*
>
> *Quote from the Dalai Lama*

Objectives

To understand what we do to increase greenhouse gases and what we can do to reduce them.

Information

The Dalai Lama is the supreme head of Tibetan Buddhism. The name means 'Ocean of Wisdom'. Many of the Tibetan people view him as their spiritual and political leader.

Correcting climate change

It may seem hard to believe that people can actually change the Earth's climate. But many scientists think that the things people do that send greenhouse gases into the air are making our planet warmer. Climate change may be a big problem, but there are many little things that individuals can do that will make a difference.

links

We started looking at climate change in chapter 14 page 172.

How do we add to climate change?

We add to the greenhouse gases in the air when we:

- watch TV
- use the air conditioner
- turn on a light
- use a hairdryer
- ride in a car
- play a video game
- listen to a stereo
- wash or dry clothes
- use a dishwasher
- microwave a meal
- use the computer
- use power tools.

Information

To do these things we need to use electricity. Electricity comes from power plants. Most power plants use coal and oil to make electricity. Burning coal and oil produces greenhouse gases.

A *Girl power! Using electricity adds to greenhouse gases*

How can we make a difference?

You can start by:

Saving electricity – Whenever we use electricity, we help put greenhouse gases into the air. By turning off lights, the television, and the computer when you have finished using them, you can help a lot.

Saving fuel – You can save energy by taking the bus, riding a bike, or walking.

Sharing information – Talk with your family and friends about climate change. Let them know what you've learned.

Planting Trees – Planting trees is fun and a great way to reduce greenhouse gases. Trees absorb carbon dioxide, a greenhouse gas, from the air.

B *U2's Bono planting trees in Japan*

Recycling – Recycle cans, bottles, plastic, cardboard and newspapers. When we recycle, we send less rubbish to the landfill and we help save natural resources, like trees, oil, and elements such as aluminium.

Compost kitchen waste – Put your scraps of vegetables into a compost bin. This will give you material for planting next year and saves on waste collection.

Case study

Earth Hour

C *Brighton Pier took part in 2008*

WWF's Earth Hour is an annual international event created by WWF (formally known as the WorldWide Fund for Nature), held on the last Saturday of March, that asks households and businesses to turn off their lights for one hour to raise awareness of the need to take action on climate change.

On 31 March 2007, 2.2 million people and 2,100 Sydney businesses turned off their lights for one hour - Earth Hour. If the greenhouse reduction achieved in the Sydney CBD during Earth Hour was sustained for a year, it would be equivalent to taking 48,616 cars off the road for a year. Inspired by the collective effort of millions of Australians, many major global cities joined Earth Hour in 2008, turning a symbolic event into a global movement.

Earth Hour 2008 demonstrated that collectively people can make a difference. So what happened?

- 50 million people around the world switched off their lights for one hour
- More than 370 cities, towns and municipalities took part
- Earth Hour was held in more than 35 countries across more than 18 different time zones.

In the UK, more than 30 local authorities and communities took part with buildings like Buckingham Palace and City Hall in London, the Spinnaker Tower in Portsmouth, and Brighton Pier joining in.

WWF's Earth Hour is also about the small changes that everyone is capable of making in their lives and building the Earth Hour ethos into each day's living. Try to imagine what would happen if everyone around the globe switched off their lights for one hour?

Information

Did you know that you can help the environment if you buy recyclable products instead of non-recyclable ones? Look for the recycle mark on the package. Recyclable products are usually made out of things that already have been used. It usually takes less energy to make recycled products than to make new ones. This helps the environment by using less energy.

Activity

- Go to the Earth Hour website **www.earthhour.org/**. Find out what happened at Earth Hour. Was it successful? Did more people and businesses take part? Do you think this a good idea? Give reasons for your answer. Will you take part?
- What is an ecological footprint? Work out your footprint at **www.footprint.wwf.org.uk/home**. You will need to collect some information first.
- The WWF Network is the world's leading environmental organisation founded in 1961, is now active in over 100 countries. More information at **wwf.org.uk**

16.4 Influencing an international issue

Case study

Make Poverty History (MPH)

Information

The Make Poverty History campaign is supported by more than 200 charities, campaigns, trade unions, faith groups, celebrities and ordinary citizens. These range from Oxfam to the Church of England to the Transport and General Workers' Union.

The Make Poverty History campaign believes that the gap between the world's rich and poor has never been wider. Malnutrition, AIDS, conflict and illiteracy are a daily reality for millions. They say that it isn't chance or bad luck that keeps people trapped in bitter, unrelenting poverty, it's man-made factors like an unjust global trade system, a debt burden so great that it limits any chance of recovery and that aid given to poor countries is insufficient and ineffective. MPH is committed to the delivery of the Millennium Development Goals (MDGs).

Objectives

To demonstrate an understanding of how groups campaign on an international issue in order to bring about change.

What are the Millennium Development Goals (MDG)?

In 2000 all 191 UN Member States pledged to meet eight goals by 2015. Make Poverty History (MPH) is calling for pressure to be put on nations to fulfil their promise to achieve the MDGs. The goals are:

1. Eradicate extreme poverty and hunger: Halve the number of people living on less than $1 a day.
2. Achieve universal primary education: Ensure every child has a good, free, basic education.
3. Promote gender equality and empower women: Eliminate gender disparity in primary and secondary education.
4. Reduce child mortality: Reduce by two-thirds the mortality rate of under fives.
5. Improve maternal health: Reduce by three-quarters the number of deaths of women in childbirth.
6. Combat HIV/AIDS, malaria and other diseases: Halt and reverse the spread of HIV/AIDS and malaria.
7. Ensure environmental sustainability: Targets include halving the proportion of people without access to safe drinking water.
8. Build a global partnership for development: Targets include debt relief, fairer trade rules and more aid.

Why choose 2005?

Make Poverty History (MPH) was formed to highlight world poverty and injustice. 2005 was chosen as it provided the unique opportunity of targeting three high-level world leader meetings:

- G8 Summit, Gleneagles, Scotland, July 2005
- UN Summit, New York, September 2005
- World Trade Organization Ministerial Meeting, Hong Kong, December 2005.

Information

The white band was adopted as the common symbol of the global fight to end poverty. In 2005, 8 million people wore the white band in the UK. The great thing about the white band is that it is simple and flexible, and can be used easily by anyone in the world.

A *Images of Make Poverty History and Live 8*

What happened at Gleneagles?

- **AID: G8 promised** to increase aid to US$50bn with half of this going to Africa by 2010.
- **DEBT: G8 promised** significant debt relief for 18 of the world's poorest countries.
- **TRADE: G8 promised** little, except for agreeing to reduce domestic subsidies and eliminate export subsidies in the future.
- **CLIMATE CHANGE: G8 promised** little, but all G8 members agreed for the first time that climate change is happening and urgent action must be taken.

MPH is concerned that no specific targets were set, no concrete actions were agreed and no time limit was given but MPH recognises that G8 2005 marks a turning point in the fight against poverty.

What happened in New York?

The UN Summit brought together world leaders in what was expected to be an official review of progress towards the MDGs. The pre-summit report, stated 'The MDGs can be met by 2015 – but only if all involved break with business as usual and dramatically accelerate and scale-up action now.'

Terrorism and security led the agenda.

Make Poverty History

Official statement on the UN Summit:

'We are sorely disappointed that the UN World Summit has failed to agree anything near the historic development deal that campaigners had hoped for. It has done little more than recognise the limited steps taken by the G8 and demonstrated insufficient commitment to the urgent action needed to achieve the Millennium Development Goals.'

What happened in Hong Kong?

- The WTO meeting failed to deliver the trade justice deal needed to make poverty history.
- The positions taken by the major developed countries in Hong Kong favoured the rich over the interests of the world's poor.
- The developed countries, the EU and the US, tried to use the WTO meeting to push forward their agenda to open the markets in developing countries for the interests of their corporations.
- The Global Call to Action Against Poverty (of which MPH is the UK arm) demanded Europe's trade commissioner Peter Mandelson remove the white band he wore in Hong Kong. The white arm band is the symbol of commitment to this campaign.

B

C *Live 8 concert 2005*

Live 8 concerts were held as follows:

- On 2 July 2005 in London, Paris, Berlin, Rome, Philadelphia, Barrie, Chiba, Johannesburg, Moscow, and the Eden Project.
- On 6 July 2005 in Edinburgh.

The Live 8 concerts aimed to raise awareness about poverty and reached a massive global audience of three billion. Many more people are now aware of the G8 and the ability of rich nations to help or hinder the fight against poverty. It has, however, also raised many questions:

- Live 8 aimed to raise awareness (not money), but do people really understand the issues? Does it matter if people didn't realise what Live 8 was about?
- Through its publicity did the Live 8 concerts succeed in highlighting the global challenges?
- Were these concerts about making poverty history or giving entertainment a place in history?
- Did Live 8 move people to take action or distract them from the protests in Edinburgh and Gleneagles and the outcomes of the G8?

Activities

1 Do you think the Make Poverty History campaign has been successful in:

- **a** raising awareness of the world poverty problem?
- **b** solving the problem of poverty in the world? Discuss in groups.
- **c** Was MPH happy with the outcome of the three meetings of world leaders? Give reasons for your answer.

2 Go to the Make Poverty History website (**www.makepovertyhistory.org/**). Find out what is happening with world poverty now. Make a report and present it to your class.

16.5 Being a global citizen

The global village

The **global village** is mostly used to describe the internet and World Wide Web. Modern communications and the speed with which they operate have made it easy for people to search for online communities and interact with others that share the same interests and concerns. It gives individuals the opportunity to read about, spread, and react to global news very rapidly.

The idea of a global village is criticised because not all people are connected to the internet. The people who lack web access are excluded from global news and participating in online communities. In this case, modern communication technology does not truly promote a global village.

For many people the idea of a global village will bring opportunities for people to:

- interact with different cultures
- challenge their own limited physical and local experiences and beliefs
- acquire the skills and knowledge to participate in the global discourse
- understand global issues concerning the environment, health, religion, culture, education and poverty, and
- learn the truth rather than media or government versions of events.

Global citizenship

Oxfam explains global citizenship as:

> "*gaining the knowledge, skills and understanding of concepts and institutions necessary to become informed, active, responsible citizens by:*
> - *developing skills to evaluate information and different points of view on global issues through the media and other sources*
> - *learning about institutions, declarations and conventions and the role of groups, NGOs and governments in global issues*
> - *developing understanding of how and where key decisions are made*
> - *appreciating that young people's views and concerns matter and are listened to; and how to take responsible action that can influence and affect global issues*
> - *appreciating the global context of local and national issues and decisions at a personal and societal level understanding the roles of language, place, arts, religion in own and others' identity.*"

Activity

3 You have studied all of these requirements during your study of citizenship for this examination. Look at the list carefully. Are you a global citizen? Prepare your own profile and say how you match each requirement.

Objectives

To show understanding of the concept of global citizenship, what it means and how organisations work to deliver fairness.

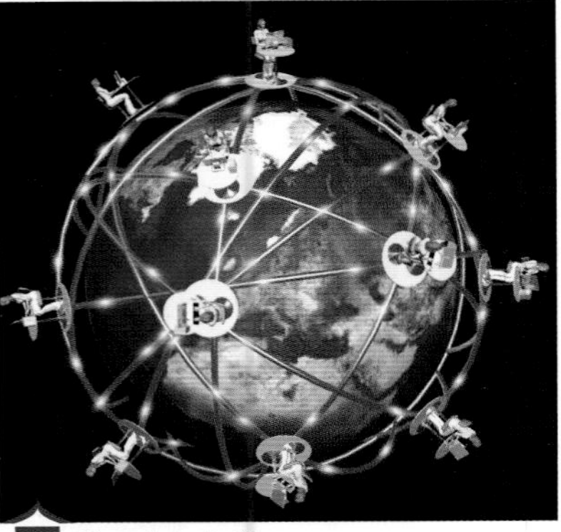

A *The global village*

Activities

1 Do you think there is such a thing as the global village?

2 Are you part of the global village or do you use the internet for other reasons? Discuss in groups.

Key terms

Global village: a term for describing the world where people are considered to live without borders/boundaries.

Information

The global village is a term first recorded by Marshall McLuhan in his 1962 book *The Gutenberg Galaxy*. McLuhan described how electronic mass media collapse space and time barriers in human communication, enabling people to interact and live on a global scale.

Amnesty International and the UN

Case study

B *The Human Rights Council was created by the UN Human Rights Committee and Amnesty International*

The protection of human rights, alongside peace and security, and economic and social development has been one of the three pillars of UN's work since its creation. Since the adoption of the Universal Declaration of Human Rights in 1948, the UN has developed a broad range of international human rights standards. It has established a range of mechanisms to promote and protect these rights and to assist governments in meeting their human rights obligations.

Amnesty International's vision is of a world in which every person enjoys all the human rights enshrined in the Universal Declaration of Human Rights. To make sure the vision happens, Amnesty International has worked for many years at the UN and has contributed to many important developments in human rights protection, including:

- the adoption of the UN Convention against Torture
- the establishment of the High Commissioner for Human Rights; and
- the creation of the Human Rights Council.

Amnesty International works with all sections of the UN system to help achieve its human rights objectives. This includes the Human Rights council, the General Assembly and the Security Council.

How does Amnesty International do this?

Amnesty International:

- makes regular submissions of information and briefings on both country specific and thematic issues to the bodies of the UN.
- campaigns for the universal ratification and effective implementation of international human rights treaties and standards as well as campaigning for new ones.
- is active in lobbying for institutional reform of the UN to achieve a strong and effective UN for the promotion and protection of human rights.

In addition, Amnesty International is actively promoting the reform of UN systems including the reform of the Treaty Bodies and Special Procedures, building the brief of the Human Rights Council, and the creation of a stronger UN agency on women's rights.

Amnesty International's work at the UN is carried out by Amnesty International's membership in more than 35 countries as well as by its representatives to the UN in New York and Geneva.

AQA Examiner's tip

You will be able to use some of this profile in your assessment task.

links

You learned about the sections of the UN on page 184.

Activities

4 Amnesty International is only one of the international groups that work with the UN. Do you think that this is a good way for views to be heard? Can you think of better ways? Give reasons for your answer.

5 The UN holds a conference with NGOs. The 61st Annual Department of Public Information/Non-governmental Organizations (DPI/NGO) Conference was held in Paris in September 2008. Find out what this conference was about. What have been the subjects of the conferences held since this one?

6 What does the DPI of the UN do?

Chapter summary

What you should know:

From this chapter your knowledge should now cover:

Short course

- ✔ international pressure groups and NGOs
- ✔ the rights of pressure groups and NGOs
- ✔ the responsibilities of pressure groups and NGOs
- ✔ the methods pressure groups and NGOs use
- ✔ some international pressure groups and NGOs
- ✔ the Campaign against Landmines
- ✔ participation and volunteering
- ✔ people who volunteer
- ✔ how individuals can make a difference
- ✔ how we can correct climate change
- ✔ Earth Hour campaign

Full course

- ✔ Make Poverty History campaign
- ✔ the Millennium Development Goals
- ✔ how MPH felt about the campaign outcomes
- ✔ what the global village is
- ✔ what is involved in being a global citizen
- ✔ how a pressure group or NGO can influence the UN

Check your knowledge

You should be able to answer the following questions without looking back over the text. If you cannot answer all of the questions you need to learn the material more thoroughly.

1. Name three methods used by pressure groups and NGOs.
2. Give three examples of natural disasters.
3. Describe volunteering.
4. Name two international pressure groups.
5. What does WRVS stand for?
6. Name two international NGOs.
7. Give five ways in which we add greenhouse gases to the air.
8. Name three ways in which we can change the climate.
9. What is Earth Hour?
10. Name three things you can recycle.

Further study

- Go to the Disasters Emergency Committee website (**www.dec.org.uk/**).
  - Choose, 'Other DEC Appeals', then 'DEC past appeals'.
  - Choose three appeals from the long list given. Find out how much money was raised for your three chosen appeals from the British public.
  - Choose a natural disaster:
    * Flood * Hurricane * Earthquake
    * Volcanic eruption * Tsunami
  - Find out what happens when this disaster hits using past details from this site.
  - Decide what you feel about this and what you could do about it.
- Go to the Global Village website (**www.globalvillage2006.org/**).
  - Choose – 'find out about ...', then choose your area, and then choose your topic.
  - Find out about your chosen topic.
  - Make notes about it.
  - Decide what you feel about it and what you can do about it.
- Go to the UNICEF (**www.unicef.org/**) website.
  - Go to the 'UNICEF PEOPLE', then 'Goodwill ambassadors', then 'Find out more'.
  - Choose one of the people from the list of ambassadors.
  - Find out what the person does to help this organisation.
  - Why do you think it is important for UNICEF to use celebrities to promote its work?
  - What do you think about a wealthy celebrity being a volunteer?
- For your chosen area of study you should:
  - Make a report
  - or Prepare a talk
  - or Make a poster for display
  - or Discuss it with someone
  - or Write a letter to your MP
  - or Prepare a power point presentation
  - or Write a poem
  - or Draw a picture
  - or Write in support of the NGO.

Your teacher may have some other ideas for your work.

Picture stimulus

A *Make Poverty History march in Edinburgh*

Look at this picture carefully.

- Do you think that these marchers are exercising their right to peaceful protest correctly? What evidence can you give to support your view?
- Do you think that the issue must be important for so many people to march in support?
- What can you do to help campaigns like this one?

17 Assessment

The best way to use this chapter is to look at the information for each **Unit** before you study that Unit so that you know exactly what is required.

In the introduction to the book you were given a diagram of how these courses fit together; look back to this on page 7.

The short course is made up of Units 1 and 2.

The full course is made up of Units 1, 2, 3 and 4.

You will be familiar with the four different Themes that you have studied throughout the course.

The rest of this chapter gives you guidance on what to expect on the exam papers in Units 1 and 3 and what you are expected to do for the **Controlled Assessment** tasks in Units 2 and 4. These tasks require you to take an active part in a citizenship activity.

Look back to the introduction on page 9 to see the variety of skills and **concepts** that may be involved in your task. You will not use all of these, but the ones you do use you should understand and be able to explain clearly.

Look again at the skills and concepts and try these activities.

Activities

1. Working in pairs, choose three concepts each and explain them to your partner.
2. On your own, choose a different three concepts and write out an explanation of them giving examples.
3. One of you should explain the structure of the short course and the other should explain the structure of the full course.

Objectives

To understand the types of question on exam papers and the expected style of response required for Units 1 and 3.

To learn about the Controlled Assessments and what you have to do for each Task for Units 2 and 4.

Key terms

Unit: different parts of the course which you have to study and learn or tasks you have to participate in and complete.

Controlled Assessment: a citizenship activity which you take part in (coursework).

Concept: a concept is a collection of ideas about a particular thing or attitude.

A *Discussion*

B *Participation*

Unit 1 Short course

The written examination paper

The time allowed for the paper is one hour.

The exam paper consists of two sections:

Section A

This section sets a number of questions which require short answers. The questions will be based on **Theme 1 only**. They will be worth one or two marks each. The questions require factual knowledge and sometimes a relevant example to be quoted. This type of question is found at the end of each chapter so you should be familiar with them. This section will be worth a total of **20 marks**.

Section B

Three questions will be set. You must answer ONE question. The topics for all three questions will be sent out before the exam so that you are able to study the topics in detail. There will be three different questions – one from Theme 2, one from Theme 3 and one from Theme 4. You have to choose **ONE** of them to answer.

Choose the one you know most about.

All the questions set in section B are worth a total of **20 marks**.

Each question will be broken down into three parts:

a a short question worth **2 marks**. Usually the answer will be found in the source.

b a longer question related to the issue in the source and worth **6 marks**. You will be expected to use the source material and your own knowledge to answer this question, perhaps express an opinion or give a different view on the issue.

c a question requiring an extended piece of writing relating to the issue in the source. You will be asked to apply your own knowledge to the situation and perhaps present or argue a case or suggest ways in which action could be taken to bring about a change. This part of the question is worth **12 marks**.

This section is worth a total of **20 marks**.

Allow yourself adequate time for revision and preparation of the topics before the exam.

You will know which topic to work on for Section B.

Information

These are the major topics in each Theme.

Theme 1
Being an active citizen.
Campaigning – types of actions

Pressure groups. Voluntary organizations. Charities. Trade Unions. Power. The Media. Health and Safety.

Theme 2
Government and Parliament. Devolution. How democracy works. Identity and Britishness. Immigration. Racism and discrimination. Community cohesion.

Theme 3
Roles and responsibilities. fairness. Freedom. The criminal justice system. The rule of law. The media and censorship.

Theme 4
The United Nations, the European Union and the Commonwealth. Conflict and cooperation. The global economy and ethical trade. The Global village. Sustainability.

Controlled Assessment task

Advocacy and Representation

This is about taking an active part in a citizenship task.

This unit is worth 60 per cent of the marks for the short course or 30 per cent of the marks for the full course. This is an important piece of work and should take about 20 hours of time to complete, with the supervision of your teacher. You will be allowed to do some research outside of lesson time.

You may be asked to work in a group of your own choice or you may be put into a group chosen by your teacher. Some people may work on their own. However, the written work must be all your own individual work. You will be asked to sign a statement to this effect on the Candidate Record Form which your teacher will give you. This is an official form and it is important that you read it and understand it before you sign it.

The written work is evidence of your participation and contribution to the activity and is provided by completing the Skills Profile. It will be assessed by your teacher and moderated by AQA.

The Skills Profile is a booklet. It guides you through each stage by asking questions. Your responses are written in the spaces provided.

You will be set or you may be given a choice of a topic to explore. As a group you will need to examine different views about the topic. It may be a local issue, an issue within your school/college or it may be to promote a special group, for example, a pressure group or charity or it may be to raise awareness about an international issue, for example, clean water, deforestation, sustainability, or global warming issues such as encouraging local people to recycle more. Within the group you will have to decide on definite aims you want to achieve, negotiate decisions, put together and deliver a presentation and/or a display. You may choose to write letters to someone who has influence or could help you to achieve your aims – remember you could use email to do this. Next you will find out how effective your **advocacy** and action was, before finally evaluating the whole task.

Key terms

Advocacy: the representation or support of a person or an organisation by writing, speaking or taking action on behalf of that person or organisation.

A *How marks are awarded for the Task*

Stage	Marks
1 Inform yourself	10
2 Justify choices and prepare the case	10
3 Advocacy/raise awareness	20
4 Assess the impact	10
5 Reflect and evaluate	10
Total	**60**

Before you begin

Keep notes or lists of things that you discuss, the decisions you make and the roles and responsibilities of all members of the group as you progress through the task.

It is easier to write up each stage in the Skills Profile as you complete it; then it is not such a huge piece of work to do at the end.

Throughout the stages be prepared to take part in discussions. Remember you have to take account of views and opinions that you may not agree with and you will have to accept the decisions of the majority, even if you do not think it is the right decision.

Stage 1 Inform yourself

There are a possible **10 marks** for this section.

Working in a small group, select the topic or issue you are going to advocate or represent. Discuss and decide what your aims really are and make a list of three or four – what change are you trying to bring about – an increase in knowledge and understanding or a change in attitude about the topic or are you gathering support for a particular action to be taken.

Find out different views about the issue you have chosen. Look back to the list of citizenship concepts and skills and identify which ones you are using.

You will need to gather a range of different views and opinions that are for and against your issue. Where might you find the information? Think of as many different ways as possible about how you could find out what you need to know; write them down as you talk about them. From the list of ideas (strategies) negotiate which will be the best ones for the group to work on.

Decide who will carry out the different strategies you have chosen – you are deciding who would be best for each role; give that person the responsibility to complete the work within the time set.

Discuss all the different information that each person has found, sharing all the details – working collaboratively. Make sure you do your part – don't let the group down.

What you need to do:

- as a group decide on the topic area – be able to explain your decision
- set clear aims for what you want to achieve
- describe which citizenship concepts are involved
- list what information you need – facts, statistics
- different views – for and against; gather as many as you can – from newspapers, television, magazines, and talking to a range of people
- how you are going to find the information and views you need – the strategies
- what are the roles and responsibilities of each member of the group
- be able to explain why each person was given their role/responsibility
- set deadlines and complete your part on time
- working in your group, discuss all the information you have discovered
- write up the Skills Profile.

Stage 2 Justify choices and prepare the case

There are a possible **10 marks** for this section.

Be able to give reasons (justify) your choice of issue.

Now you have to decide on the best way to present your case. Discuss the various methods of presentation – a short role play, an informative talk, a formal debate, an informal discussion, a PowerPoint presentation, a display, a leaflet, etc. It all depends on your topic and who your audience is going to be.

Decide on the key points and which contrasting view you are going to put forward – be able to justify your choices.

What you need to do:

- justify choice of issue
- discuss methods of presentation – justify choices
- decide on key points for presentation
- complete all preparations for the presentation
- write up the Skills Profile.

Stage 3 Advocacy and taking action

There are a possible **20 marks** for this section.

This is where you present your case as a group or as an individual. Marks will be awarded for how you participated in the activity, how organised you were, and how well you carried out your roles and responsibilities. Be really well organised, do not leave everything until the last minute. Know what you are doing, when and why.

Gather some evidence about your presentation, notes for a speech, photographs of the event or display, a print out of a PowerPoint presentation, a copy of the leaflet you all worked to produced. Some problems may arise along the way, the group should solve them. You do not have very much to write about in this stage. Your teacher will make the assessment on the action you take.

What you need to do:

- be well organised, do your part, carry out the plans
- identify and solve any problems that occur
- collect evidence – information used – photographs, leaflets, PowerPoint print outs – notes for speech, etc.
- write up the Skills Profile.

ROLE PLAY

talk

presentation

PowerPoint

formal debate

make a leaflet

create a display

A *Ideas*

Stage 4 Assess the impact

There are a possible **10 marks** for this section.

At this stage you have to find out how successful your advocacy has been. You could undertake this as a group, but you will have to write up the results individually.

You need to find out how well you have achieved the aims you set at the beginning – what effect has your advocacy had? This could be done as a survey or short questionnaire distributed to your audience to be completed by them at the end. Then your group analyse the results and individually you draw accurate conclusions so that you can give your own personal opinion on how effective your advocacy was.

As a group discuss what further action could be taken; keep notes for the Skills Profile.

What you need to do:

- collect information from people about the advocacy
- collate results
- draw individual conclusions
- suggest further action that could be taken on the issue
- write up the Skills Profile.

REVIEWS
strategies
plans & aims
skills
role
concepts
responsibilities
contributions
changes
improvements

B *Ideas*

Stage 5 Reflect and evaluate

There are a possible **10 marks** for this section.

This is the last stage of the task where each person looks back on what has been done and reviews the process.

Look back at the aims again and be able to explain how the task has increased your knowledge and understanding of the citizenship concepts involved. You should also be able to explain which citizenship skills you have used during the activity.

Consider how well your presentation went and what changes could have been made to improve it. For example, how well did each member of the group carry out their roles and responsibilities? Was the presentation well organised? Was there enough information? Was the method of presenting the information the right one to use? Why/why not? Did you make any changes? Why? What would you change if you were to do something similar again?

What you need to do:

- explain the citizenship concepts and skills used
- explain how the task has increased your own knowledge and understanding of citizenship
- review own and others' contributions
- assess how well were the plans carried out
- give suggestions for improvement
- write up the skills profile.

C *Advocacy and taking action*

Units 1 and 2 of the short course are the first half of the full course. Unit 3, an exam paper, and Unit 4, a different task to participate in, completes the assessment for the full course. The work you will cover during the full course follows the same Themes as in the short course. The topics are designed to increase your depth of knowledge and further develop citizenship skills, by looking at a variety of issues at different levels and from different perspectives.

Unit 3 Full course

The written examination paper

The time allowed for the paper is one hour.

For this exam paper you will need to have studied all the sections in the book marked full course as well as retaining the knowledge learned in the short course.

The exam paper will be divided into **two** sections:

Section A

There will be **4 questions** based on a short source giving information on an issue or giving a scenario or perhaps some statistics that you then have to answer questions on.

There will be one question from each Theme. You have to answer all four questions.

Each source will have three questions:

a short response for **1 mark**

b and **c** two short questions requiring some of your own knowledge with a short factual response.

Questions **b** and **c** are worth **2 marks each**.

There are **5 marks** for each of the four questions. A total for Section A of **20 marks**.

Section B

In this section you will have a **choice**.

You will be asked to answer **one** of the three questions set. The topics covered by the questions will be sent out before the exam, so you will have an opportunity to research the topic area thoroughly. These topics of the questions will be one from Theme 2, one from Theme 3, and one from Theme 4.

Answer the question you know most about.

All three questions will follow the same style, they will be divided into three parts:

a a short question asking you to explain or identify or describe something clearly for **2 marks**.

b a source will be given and you will be asked to show your knowledge or give views/opinions or make a case about the issue in the source. This is worth **6 marks**.

c will ask what could be done about the issue/topic or how changes could be made. Your response will be in an extended piece of writing, using your own knowledge of the topic area. There are **12 marks** available for this.

This gives a total for Section B of **20 marks**.

Allow yourself adequate time for revision and preparation before the exam.

Unit 4 Full course

Controlled Assessment Task

Taking informed and responsible action

This unit is worth 30 per cent of the marks for the full course. This task is about taking informed and responsible action to bring about some kind of change.

You may work in a group or on your own but the written work must be done individually. The Candidate Record Form must be completed and signed.

This task will take about 20 hours of time, some research and carrying out your plans in taking the responsible action may be done outside of lesson time. The evidence of your participation and contribution to the activity is presented in the Skills Profile.

This task could follow on from the one you participated in in Unit 2, where you could follow up your suggestions for further action. This could be the opportunity to put those ideas into action or you may be set a totally different task on a particular current issue of the time. How you are assessed in this unit is similar to Unit 2; there is a total of **60 marks** available in the following stages. Again it is best to complete the **Skills Profile** as you complete each stage of the task.

A *How marks are awarded for the Task*

Stage 1	Marks
1 Justify choices and select information	10
2 Action plan	10
3 Taking action	20
4 Assess the impact	10
5 Evaluate	10
Total	60

Stage 1 Identify and justify choices and select information

Working in a small group you will be set, or will choose, or will negotiate a specific citizenship issue to base your action on. Be able to justify choices. Discuss and set achievable aims. You will need to be able to explain clearly why the information you research is necessary, identify how you will find this information and how you will use it to make decisions.

Again each group member will have their own roles and responsibilities to carry out, depending on their interests and skills. You may choose to record this in the form of a chart. Complete the Skills Profile.

There are **10 marks** available for this stage.

Activity

Responsible Action.

You have to be involved in doing something positive that could help to bring about a change.

participate get involved
take part volunteer

Stage 2 The action plan

During this stage you will plan the most appropriate course of action you intend to take. As a group you have to look at a range of possible courses of action and negotiate which to pursue. In the Skills Profile you will be asked to justify your chosen actions.

Working collaboratively draft a detailed plan of the action you have decided upon.

Complete this chart in the Skills Profile.

You will need details of the time scale you are working to so that you can all meet the deadlines/targets. Some decisions the group makes may not be the ones you wanted; it is part of being a good citizen to accept the majority vote and then work as best as you can to ensure the plans are carried out successfully. Your own comments will be useful when you finally evaluate the task.

There are **10 marks** available for this stage.

Stage 3 Taking action

This stage is actually carrying out your plans.

Sometimes it may be necessary to change plans as unexpected things do happen – remember these, keep notes if you can and make reference to what changes you had to make when you write up your evaluation in your Skills Profile.

Be well organised, know what you are doing, keep focused on the task, and show how you were able to solve any problems that arose.

You will be awarded marks according to how well you carry out your roles and responsibilities within the group and how effective the action was in achieving your stated aims. Your teacher will assess this.

There are **20 marks** available for this stage.

Stage 4 Assessing the impact

In this stage you are asked to assess the impact your action has had.

This is assessed using the same criteria as for Unit 2, but the task you are assessing the impact of is quite different. The same guidance applies: ensure the conclusions you draw and the comments made are done individually, not as a group.

There are **10 marks** available for this stage.

Stage 5 Evaluate

In this stage you are asked to review what you have done in taking responsible and informed action. You are expected to explain the effects your action has had on the community now and in the future.

You should explain how participation in the task has increased your citizenship knowledge, understanding and skills.

Discuss in detail how your own contribution and that of others achieved the aims you set at the beginning.

This task should have been enjoyable and you should know at the end that you have made a change in some way that will benefit others. You are well on the way to being a well-informed active citizen.

What you should know

From this chapter your knowledge should now cover:

Short course

- ✔ how the course is structured
- ✔ Unit 1 – what you have to learn and what to expect on the exam paper
- ✔ Unit 2 – how to approach the Controlled Assessment Task
- ✔ what the Skills Profile is and how to use it

Full course

- ✔ how the course is structured
- ✔ Unit 3 – what you have to learn and what to expect on the exam paper
- ✔ Unit 4 – how to approach the Controlled Assessment Task
- ✔ what the Skills Profile is and how to use it

Revision

Allow yourself plenty of time for revising your work.

Do not expect to be able to do everything the night before the exam.

Plan out what you need to do. You should know what to expect on the exam papers for Unit 1 and Unit 3, and you will have already prepared a specific topic that you know the questions in Section B will cover. You need to know this well so that you can apply the knowledge to the situation in the source to answer the question.

Make sure you complete the front of the exam paper accurately.

Read each question thoroughly, don't rush and misunderstand the question.

If you have prepared properly you should do well.

GOOD LUCK.

A *Results*

References

Age-related rights

Age 18

- You can get married.
- You can go abroad to act and perform music professionally.
- You can get a credit card.
- You can apply for a mortgage, and own houses and land.
- You can be called for jury service.
- You can change your name.
- You can act as an executor of a person's will.
- You can buy alcohol.
- You can buy tobacco and cigarettes.
- You can bet.
- You can vote.
- You can become a local Councillor.
- You can buy fireworks.

Age 17

- You can apply for a driving licence to drive a car.
- You can get a street trading license.
- You can leave home without your parents' consent.

Age 16

- You can choose your own GP, and can sign a medical consent form.
- You can get married if you have the consent of one parent.
- You can get a full-time job.
- You can join the Army (but won't be able to go on active service until you are 18).
- You can claim social security benefit under certain circumstances.
- You can leave home with your parents' consent, or without it if you are leaving an abusive or neglectful situation.
- You can get a license to drive a moped.
- You can drink wine, beer or cider with a meal in a restaurant.
- You can smoke tobacco (but can't legally buy it until you are 18 years old).
- You can buy a National Lottery ticket.
- You can hold a full 10-year passport.
- The National Society for the Prevention of Cruelty to Children (NSPCC) recommends this as a minimum age for a babysitter.

Age 14

- You are responsible for wearing a seatbelt in a car or bus. You can be given a fine if you don't.
- You can go to a pub (but can't buy or drink alcohol).
- You can have your fingerprints taken if you are held in custody and then be charged with an offence.

Age 13

- You are legally allowed to work up to five hours a day on Saturdays or during the school holidays as long as it does not get in the way of your schoolwork.

Age 12

- Legally you can buy a pet. However some shops can legally have a policy of not selling animals to persons under 16 years of age.

Age 10

- In England, Wales and Northern Ireland, you are criminally responsible at 10 years old. That means that you are legally responsible for your actions. Any criminal behaviour will be dealt with by the courts.
- You will be allowed to hold an account at a bank or building society.

Age 5

- You are of the age to be educated. This would usually be at school but it might be at home.
- You are allowed to drink alcohol in private.

Any age

- You can visit a doctor or adviser to talk about a pregnancy related issue, such as contraception or abortion, and anything that you say should be private and confidential, even if you're below the age of consent. You should check first whether what you say will be confidential with the medical person concerned.
- You can make a complaint if you think you're being discriminated against because of race, colour, ethnic origin, or sexuality.
- You can make an official complaint against the police.
- You can have a five-year passport.
- You can have a bank account if an adult opens one for you.

An overview of the criminal justice system

1. Someone breaks the law

After someone has broken the law, the victim will tell the police what has happened. This is called reporting an offence. The victim will make and sign a statement outlining what happened.

The police then undertake an investigation to find evidence to support the accusation. The person who is being accused will be taken to the police station. This is called making an arrest.

At the police station the arrested person can ask for help from a solicitor to help them with their case.

2. Charges

The police officers who are finding out about the crime will question the arrested person. This can go on for up to 72 hours. After this the police have three options.

- let the person go
- ask a magistrate for 24 hours more questioning time
- **charge** the person.

Charging a person means formally accusing them of a crime. To do this the police must think that there is evidence to link them to the offence.

3. Remand

The charged person appears at a Magistrates' Court. The charge sheet will be read out. This explains what the person is accused of. The solicitor representing the accused may ask for bail. The magistrates decide whether to remand into custody or on bail.

Remanded in custody

Someone who has been charged must stay locked up until they appear in court again.

Remanded on bail

This means they are charged with a crime but can go free until they appear in court again.

Bail conditions mean the accused promises to behave in a certain way, for example, they may be told not go near the crime victim. Money may be asked for as a guarantee that they will attend court.

4. Preparing for court

The accused person and their solicitor write down exactly what they say has happened. The police help other people who may have seen what happened to write down what they saw. These people are called witnesses.

The Crown Prosecution Service (CPS) gets all of the police's information and decides if there is enough evidence to prove the person did the crime. In court, the accused becomes the defendant.

5. The Magistrates' Court

Most defendants now appear in this kind of court. There is no jury in this type of court. A team of magistrates make the decisions. The defendant has to say if they are 'guilty' or 'not guilty'. This is called entering a plea.

If the defendant says that they are guilty then the magistrates make their decision what the punishment will be. This is called 'sentencing'.

If the defendant says they are not guilty then the Crown Prosecution Service tells the court why they think they are guilty. The defendant's legal team will say why they are not guilty. The magistrates will decide and pass a sentence.

6. The Crown Court

More serious crimes like murder are dealt with in this type of court with a judge and a jury making the decisions. The jury is a group of 12 people chosen at random from everyone in the country eligible for jury service.

When the jury has heard the reasons for the defendant being guilty and the reasons for them being innocent they make their decision. At least ten of the people on the jury must agree for them to be able to give their 'verdict'.

7. The sentence

If it is found that the defendant is guilty, the judge decides the punishment. The defendant now becomes a convicted criminal. The judge has to think about the facts of the crime and the kind of person the criminal is when deciding their 'sentence'.

Only the more serious crimes may end in the criminal going to prison; many criminals have to pay fines or do work for their community instead.

A sentence will not be made on a young offender until the Youth Offending Team has prepared a pre-sentence report for the magistrates or the judge.

The stages of a conflict

Conflicts are processes, a cluster of events' taking time to evolve and reshape. They are always complicated – after all, they are part of the complex lives of human beings. But there are distinct stages that many conflicts have in common.

1. Beginnings

A conflict begins to take shape as the differences between the conflicting parties become clearly defined and people begin to take sides openly. The language of 'us and them' starts being widely used, and the idea of a 'cause' to support emerges on both sides. There is no violence at this point.

If a society is strong, a conflict can be dealt with in a constructive and positive way at this stage and a worsening situation can be avoided.

2. Entrenchment

If there are no existing ways of dealing with social tensions and divisions, the conflict grows worse. The two sides express open hostility, so that 'us and them' now becomes 'the enemy'. Each side increases its demands, and its sense of grievance swells. Each side looks for allies from outside the conflict area, for moral and physical support. Acts of violence begin. If violence is not repressed, the opposing sides hit back at one another and a destructive cycle begins.

3. Deadlock

The two sides are openly in conflict. Each side perceives the other as the aggressor. Each blames the other for the conflict. Each side regards itself as having the just cause. Inhibitions and restraints on violence are abandoned. Three possible situations can now be reached:

1. a stalemate with each side matching the other in violence. This continues the spiral of violence, or may halt it at a particular level that both sides maintain
2. a surge of violence on one side. This can make a change: for example, one side's increased power may cause the other side to withdraw; the conflict remains unresolved and is likely to begin again later
3. exhaustion of strength and resources on both sides. This is the position from which the conflict can most readily move to its next stage.

4. Withdrawal

If and when the conflict reaches a stage where both sides are unhappy with the state of things they may enter into ceasefire agreements. These provide a pause, which is often used for resting and regrouping before embarking on the earlier stages again. If both sides decide that ending the conflict is something they want, a compromise may be reached, though it has to be done without loss of face. At this point a third party can be introduced to mediate and negotiate.

5. Resolution

Settlements involve compromise, often with bitter arguments over what the compromises will be. They seldom lead to a solution in which the two sides can collaborate to establish a firm peace. Settlements establish ways in which either side is prepared to end conflict at least for the time being.

Conflict resolution, however, looks at the underlying causes which started the conflict and deals with them, so that the risks of future conflict are removed, or initially reduced. Both sides join together to achieve this outcome.

Complete resolution of a conflict is difficult after such great hostility, but may be reached after the passage of healing time if everyone has this aim.

6. Cooperation

When the agreement has to be put into effect, both sides need to create a new order together, rebuilding homes, restoring jobs and education, establishing enlightened management/government, disarming fighters and allowing refugees to return home. Even more important, the two sides have to face up to the past, share their concerns, and reconcile their differences. This needs sensitivity, courage, and, above all, immense patience.

This was adapted from Understanding Conflict by The Peace Pledge Union

UN Universal Declaration of Human Rights (1948)

Overview of the rights

Article 1

All human beings are born free and equal in dignity and rights. They are endowed with reason and conscience and should act towards one another in a spirit of brotherhood.

Article 2

Everyone is entitled to all the rights and freedoms set forth in this Declaration, without distinction of any kind, such as race, colour, sex, language, religion, political or other opinion, national or social origin, property, birth or other status. Furthermore, no distinction shall be made on the basis of the political, jurisdictional or international status of the country or territory to which a person belongs.

Article 3

Everyone has the right to live, have liberty, and security of person.

Article 4

No one shall be held in slavery or servitude; slavery and the slave trade shall be prohibited in all their forms.

Article 5

No one shall be subjected to torture or to cruel, inhuman, or degrading treatment or punishment.

Article 6

Everyone has the right to recognition everywhere as a person before the law.

Article 7

All are equal before the law and are entitled without any discrimination to equal protection of the law. All are entitled to equal protection against any discrimination in violation of this Declaration and against any incitement to such discrimination.

Article 8

Everyone has the right to an effective remedy by the competent national tribunals for acts violating the fundamental rights granted him by the constitution or by law.

Article 9

No one shall be subjected to arbitrary arrest, detention or exile.

Article 10

Everyone is entitled in full equality to a fair and public hearing by an independent and impartial tribunal, in the determination of his rights and obligations and of any criminal charge against him.

Article 11

1 Everyone charged with a penal offence has the right to be presumed innocent until proved guilty according to law in a public trial at which he has had all the guarantees necessary for his defence.
2 No one shall be held guilty of any penal offence on account of any act or omission which did not constitute a penal offence, under national or international law, at the time when it was committed. Nor shall a heavier penalty be imposed than the one that was applicable at the time the penal offence was committed.

Article 12

No one shall be subjected to arbitrary interference with his privacy, family, home or correspondence, nor to attacks upon his honour and reputation. Everyone has the right to the protection of the law against such interference or attacks.

Article 13

1 Everyone has the right to freedom of movement and residence within the borders of each state.
2 Everyone has the right to leave any country, including his own, and to return to his country.

Article 14

1 Everyone has the right to seek and to enjoy in other countries asylum from persecution.
2 This right may not be invoked in the case of prosecutions genuinely arising from non-political crimes or from acts contrary to the purposes and principles of the United Nations.

Article 15.

1 Everyone has the right to a nationality.
2 No one shall be arbitrarily deprived of his nationality nor denied the right to change his nationality.

Article 16

1 Men and women of full age, without any limitation due to race, nationality or religion, have the right to marry and to found a family. They are entitled to equal rights as to marriage, during marriage and at its dissolution.
2 Marriage shall be entered into only with the free and full consent of the intending spouses.
3 The family is the natural and fundamental group unit of society and is entitled to protection by society and the State.

Article 17

1 Everyone has the right to own property alone as well as in association with others.
2 No one shall be arbitrarily deprived of his property.

Article 18

Everyone has the right to freedom of thought, conscience and religion; this right includes freedom to change his religion or belief, and freedom, either alone or in community with others and in public or private, to manifest his religion or belief in teaching, practice, worship and observance.

Article 19

Everyone has the right to freedom of opinion and expression; this right includes freedom to hold opinions without interference and to seek, receive and impart information and ideas through any media and regardless of frontiers.

Article 20

1 Everyone has the right to freedom of peaceful assembly and association.
2 No one may be compelled to belong to an association.

Article 21

1 Everyone has the right to take part in the government of his country, directly or through freely chosen representatives.
2 Everyone has the right of equal access to public service in his country.
3 The will of the people shall be the basis of the authority of government; this will shall be expressed in periodic and genuine elections which shall be by universal and equal suffrage and shall be held by secret vote or by equivalent free voting procedures.

Article 22

Everyone, as a member of society, has the right to social security and is entitled to realisation, through national effort and international cooperation and in accordance with the organisation and resources of each State, of the economic, social and cultural rights indispensable for his dignity and the free development of his personality.

Article 23

1. Everyone has the right to work, to free choice of employment, to just and favourable conditions of work and to protection against unemployment.
2. Everyone, without any discrimination, has the right to equal pay for equal work.
3. Everyone who works has the right to just and favourable remuneration ensuring for himself and his family an existence worthy of human dignity, and supplemented, if necessary, by other means of social protection.
4. Everyone has the right to form and to join trade unions for the protection of his interests.

Article 24

Everyone has the right to rest and leisure, including reasonable limitation of working hours and periodic holidays with pay.

Article 25

1. Everyone has the right to a standard of living adequate for the health and wellbeing of himself and of his family, including food, clothing, housing and medical care and necessary social services, and the right to security in the event of unemployment, sickness, disability, widowhood, old age or other lack of livelihood in circumstances beyond his control.
2. Motherhood and childhood are entitled to special care and assistance. All children, whether born in or out of wedlock, shall enjoy the same social protection.

Article 26

1. Everyone has the right to education. Education shall be free, at least in the elementary and fundamental stages. Elementary education shall be compulsory. Technical and professional education shall be made generally available and higher education shall be equally accessible to all on the basis of merit.
2. Education shall be directed to the full development of the human personality and to the strengthening of respect for human rights and fundamental freedoms. It shall promote understanding, tolerance and friendship among all nations, racial or religious groups, and shall further the activities of the United Nations for the maintenance of peace.
3. Parents have a prior right to choose the kind of education that shall be given to their children.

Article 27

1. Everyone has the right freely to participate in the cultural life of the community, to enjoy the arts and to share in scientific advancement and its benefits.
2. Everyone has the right to the protection of the moral and material interests resulting from any scientific, literary or artistic production of which he is the author.

Article 28

Everyone is entitled to a social and international order in which the rights and freedoms set forth in this Declaration can be fully realised.

Article 29

1. Everyone has duties to the community in which alone the free and full development of his personality is possible.
2. In the exercise of his rights and freedoms, everyone shall be subject only to such limitations as are determined by law solely for the purpose of securing due recognition and respect for the rights and freedoms of others and of meeting the just requirements of morality, public order and the general welfare in a democratic society.
3. These rights and freedoms may in no case be exercised contrary to the purposes and principles of the United Nations.

Article 30

Nothing in this Declaration may be interpreted as implying for any State, group or person any right to engage in any activity or to perform any act aimed at the destruction of any of the rights and freedoms set forth herein.

Understanding the United Nations

How the UN works

The United Nations was established on 24 October 1945 by 51 countries committed to preserving peace through international cooperation and collective security. Today, nearly every nation in the world belongs to the UN: membership totals 192 countries.

When States become Members of the United Nations, they agree to accept the obligations of the UN Charter, an international treaty that sets out basic principles of international relations.

The United Nations is not a world government and it does not make laws. It does, however, provide the means to help resolve international conflicts and formulate policies on matters affecting all of us. At the UN, all the Member States – large and small, rich and poor, with differing political views and social systems – have a voice and a vote in this process.

The UN and peace

Preserving world peace is a central purpose of the United Nations. Under the Charter, Member States agree to settle disputes by peaceful means and refrain from threatening or using force against other States.

Over the years, the UN has played a major role in helping defuse international crises and in resolving protracted conflicts. It has undertaken complex operations involving peacemaking, peacekeeping and humanitarian assistance. It has worked to prevent conflicts from breaking out. And after a conflict, it has increasingly undertaken action to address the root causes of war and make the foundation for durable peace.

The UN and justice, human rights and international law

Through UN efforts, governments have concluded many multilateral agreements that make the world a safer, healthier place with greater opportunity and justice for all of us. This comprehensive body of international law, including human rights law, is one of the UN's great achievements.

The UN and humanitarian assistance

Humanitarian disasters can occur anywhere, at any time. Whether the cause be flood, drought, earthquake or conflict, a humanitarian disaster means lost lives, displaced populations, communities incapable of sustaining themselves and great suffering.

The UN and development

One of the UN's central mandates is the promotion of higher standards of living, full employment, and conditions of economic and social progress and development. As much as 70 per cent of the work of the UN system is devoted to accomplishing this mandate. Guiding the work is the belief that eradicating poverty and improving the wellbeing of people everywhere are necessary steps in creating conditions for lasting world peace.

The UN has unique strengths in promoting development. Its presence is global and its comprehensive mandate spans social, economic and emergency needs. The UN does not represent any particular national or commercial interest. When major policy decisions are taken, all countries, rich and poor, have a voice.

United Nations Convention on the Rights of the Child

A summary of the articles is given below:

1 Everyone under 18 years of age has all the rights in this convention.

2 The convention applies to everyone whatever their race, religion, abilities, whatever they think or say, and whatever type of family they come from.

3 All organisations concerned with children should work towards what is best for each child.

4 Governments should make these rights available to children.

5 Governments should respect the rights and responsibilities of families to direct and guide their children so that, as they grow, they learn to use their rights properly.

6 All children have the right to life. Governments should ensure that children survive and develop properly.

7 All children have the right to a legally registered name, the right to nationality and the right to know and, as far as possible, to be cared for by their parents.

8 Governments should respect children's rights to a name, a nationality and family ties.

9 Children should not be separated from their parents unless it is for their own good, for example, if a parent is mistreating or neglecting a child. Children whose parents have separated have the right to stay in contact with both parents, unless this might hurt the child.

10 Families who live in different countries should be allowed to move between those countries so that parents and children can stay in contact or get back together as a family.

11 Governments should take steps to stop children being taken out of their own country illegally.

12 Children have the right to say what they think should happen when adults are making decisions that affect them, and to have their opinions taken into account, when those decisions are made.

13 Children have the right to get and to share information as long as the information is not damaging to them or others.

14 Children have the right to think and believe what they want and to practise their religion, as long as they are not stopping other people from enjoying their rights. Parents should guide their children on this matter.

15 Children have the right to meet together and to join groups and organisations, as long as this does not stop other people from enjoying their rights.

16 Children have the right to privacy. The law should protect them from attacks against their way of life, their good name, their families and their homes.

17 Children have the right to reliable information from the mass media. TV, radio and newspapers should provide information that children can understand and should not promote materials that could harm children.
18 Both parents share responsibility for bringing up their children and should always consider what is best for the child. Governments should help parents by providing services to support them, especially if both parents work.
19 Governments should ensure that children are properly cared for and should protect them from violence, abuse and neglect by their parents or anyone else who looks after them.
20 Children who cannot be looked after by their own family must be looked after properly, by people who respect their religion, culture and language.
21 When children are adopted the first concern is what is best for them. The same rules apply whether the children are adopted in the country where they were born or taken to live in another country.
22 Children who come into a country as refugees should have the same rights as children born in that country.
23 Children who have any kind of disability should have special care and support so that they can lead full and independent lives.
24 Children have the right to good quality health care and to clean water, nutritious food and a clean environment so that they will stay healthy. Rich countries should help poorer countries achieve this.
25 Children who are looked after by the local authority rather than their parents should have their situation reviewed regularly.
26 The government should provide extra money for the children of families in need.
27 Children have the right to a standard of living that is good enough to meet their physical and mental needs. The government should help families who cannot afford to provide this.
28 Children have a right to an education. Discipline in schools should respect children's human dignity. Primary education should be free. Wealthy countries should help poorer countries achieve this.
29 Education should develop each child's personality and talents to the full. It should encourage children to respect their parents and their own and other cultures.
30 Children have a right to learn and use the language and customs of their families, whether these are shared by the majority of people in the country or not.
31 All children have the right to relax and play and to join a wide range of activities.
32 The government should protect children from work that is dangerous or might harm their health or education.
33 The government should provide ways of protecting children from dangerous drugs.
34 The government should protect children from sexual abuse.
35 The government should make sure that children are not abducted or sold.
36 Children should be protected from any activities that could harm their development.
37 Children who break the law should not be treated cruelly. They should not be put in prison with adults and should be able to keep in contact with their families.
38 Governments should not allow children under 15 to join the army. Children in war zones should receive special attention.
39 Children who have been neglected or abused should receive special help to restore their self-respect.
40 Children who are accused of breaking the law should receive legal help. Prison sentences for children should only be used for the most serious offences.
41 If the laws of a particular country protect children better than these articles of convention then those laws should stay.
42 The government should make the convention known to all parents and children.

The European Convention on Human Rights and Freedoms (1950)

This covers the following rights and freedoms:

Article 1 Respecting your rights

Article 2 The right to life

Article 3 Freedom from torture or degrading treatment.

Article 4 Freedom from forced labour

Article 5 The right to liberty

Article 6 A fair trial

Article 7 Retrospective penalties

Article 8 Privacy.

Article 9 Freedom of conscience

Article 10 Freedom of expression

Article 11 Freedom of assembly

Article 12 Marriage and family

Article 14 Freedom from discrimination

NB The other articles or protocols refer to an individual's right to representation when rights are violated.

Charter of Fundamental Rights of the European Union

The European Parliament, the Council and the Commission agreed the Charter of fundamental rights of the European Union. It was signed at Nice on the seventh day of December in the year two thousand. This a brief summary of the articles of the charter.

Introduction

The European Union is founded on the indivisible, universal values of human dignity, freedom, equality and solidarity; it is based on the principles of democracy and the rule of law. It places the individual at the heart of its activities, by establishing the citizenship of the Union and by creating an area of freedom, security and justice.

To this end, it was necessary to strengthen the protection of fundamental rights in the light of changes in society, social progress and scientific and technological developments by making those rights more visible in a Charter.

The Union set out the rights, freedoms and principles in this charter.

Chapter I

Dignity

Article 1: Human Dignity

Article 2: Everyone has the right to life.

Article 3: Everyone has the right to respect for his or her physical and mental integrity.

Article 4: No one shall be subjected to torture or to inhuman or degrading treatment or punishment.

Article 5: Prohibition of slavery and forced labour

Chapter II

Freedoms

Article 6: Everyone has the right to liberty and security of person.

Article 7 :Everyone has the right to respect for his or her private and family life, home and communications.

Article 8: Protection of personal data

Article 9: The right to marry and the right to found a family shall be guaranteed in accordance with the national laws governing the exercise of these rights.

Article 10: Freedom of thought, conscience and religion

Article 11: Freedom of expression and information

Article 12: Freedom of assembly and of association

Article 13: Freedom of the arts and sciences

Article 14: Right to education

Article 15: Freedom to choose an occupation and right to engage in work

Article 16 :Freedom to conduct a business

Article 17: Right to property

Article 18 :Right to asylum

Article 19: Protection in the event of removal, expulsion or extradition

Chapter III

Equality

Article 20: Equality before the law

Article 21: Non-discrimination

Article 22: Cultural, religious and linguistic diversity

Article 23: Equality between men and women

Article 24: The rights of the child

Article 25: The rights of the elderly

Article 26: Integration of persons with disabilities

Chapter IV

Solidarity

Article 27: Workers' right to information and consultation within the undertaking

Article 28: Right of collective bargaining and action

Article 29: Right of access to placement services

Article 30: Protection in the event of unjustified dismissal

Article 31: Fair and just working conditions

Article 32: Prohibition of child labour and protection of young people at work

Article 33: Family and professional life

Article 34: Social security and social assistance

Article 35: Health care

Article 36: Access to services of general economic interest

Article 37: Environmental protection

Article 38: Consumer protection

Chapter V

Citizens' rights

Article 39: Right to vote and to stand as a candidate at elections to the European Parliament

Article 40: Right to vote and to stand as a candidate at municipal elections

Article 41: Right to good administration

Article 42: Right of access to documents

Article 43: Ombudsman

Article 44: Right to petition

Article 45: Freedom of movement and of residence

Article 46: Diplomatic and consular protection

Chapter VI

Justice

Article 47: Right to an effective remedy and to a fair trial

Article 48: Presumption of innocence and right of defence

Article 49: Principles of legality and proportionality of criminal offences and penalties

Article 50: Right not to be tried or punished twice in criminal proceedings for the same criminal offence

The process of decision making in the European Union

Decision making at European Union level involves various European institutions, in particular:

- the European Commission
- the European Parliament (EP)
- the Council of the European Union.

In general, it is the European Commission that proposes new legislation, but it is the council and parliament that pass the laws. In some cases, the council can act alone. Other institutions also have roles to play.

The main forms of EU law are directives and regulations. The rules and procedures for EU decision making are laid down in the treaties. Every proposal for a new European law is based on a specific treaty article, referred to as the 'legal basis' of the proposal. This determines which legislative procedure must be followed. There are, in general, three main procedures which, depending on the case, govern decision making on the legislative front:

1. codecision
2. assent
3. consultation.

1. Codecision

This is the procedure now used for most EU law-making. In the codecision procedure, parliament does not merely give its opinion: it shares legislative power equally with the council. If council and parliament cannot agree on a piece of proposed legislation, it is put before a conciliation committee, composed of equal numbers of council and parliament representatives. Once this committee has reached an agreement, the text is sent once again to parliament and the council so that they can finally adopt it as law. Conciliation is becoming increasingly rare. Most laws passed in codecision are, in fact, adopted either at the first or second reading as a result of good cooperation between the three institutions. It is based on the principle of parity and means that neither institution (European parliament or council) may adopt legislation without the other's assent.

The areas covered by the codecision procedure are:

- non-discrimination on the basis of nationality
- the right to move and reside
- the free movement of workers
- social security for migrant workers
- the right of establishment
- transport
- the internal market
- employment
- customs cooperation
- the fight against social exclusion
- equal opportunities and equal treatment
- implementing decisions regarding the European Social Fund
- education
- vocational training
- culture
- health
- consumer protection
- trans-European networks
- implementing decisions regarding the European Regional Development Fund
- research
- the environment
- transparency
- preventing and combating fraud
- statistics
- setting up a data protection advisory body.

2. Assent

The assent procedure means that the council has to obtain the European parliament's assent before certain very important decisions are taken.

The procedure is the same as in the case of consultation, except that parliament cannot amend a proposal: it must either accept or reject it. Acceptance ('assent') requires an absolute majority of the vote cast.

The assent procedure is mostly used for agreements with other countries, including the agreements allowing new countries to join the EU.

3. Consultation

The consultation procedure is used in areas such as agriculture, taxation and competition. Based on a proposal from the Commission, the council consults parliament, the European Economic and Social Committee and the Committee of the Regions.

Parliament can:

- approve the Commission proposal
- reject it
- or ask for amendments.

If parliament asks for amendments, the Commission will consider all the changes parliament suggests. If it accepts any of these suggestions it will send the council an amended proposal.

The council examines the amended proposal and either adopts it or amends it further. In this procedure, as in all others, if the council amends a Commission proposal it must do so unanimously.

Law-making in the European Union is usually now the result of interaction between the 'institutional triangle' (parliament, council and Commission).

How the EU works

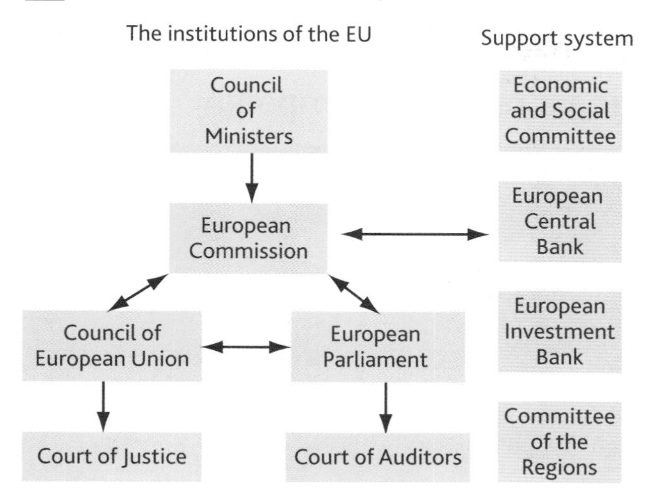

The Institutions of the EU

The Council of Ministers – The Council is composed of the ministerial representatives of the Member States. It is the supreme legislative authority in the Union.

European Commission – This is based in Brussels. The Commission consists of 27Commissioners, one from each country. They appointed for a five-year term by Member States' governments. There is an EU civil service of approximately 14,000 officials.

European Council – The Heads of State or Government meet, at least twice a year, as the European Council to provide the Union with overall direction and to reach decisions on the key issues.

European Parliament – This has been directly elected since 1979. The European Parliament is composed of 626 Euro-MPs who sit in political, not national, groups. Elections to the Parliament are held every 5 years.

The European Court of Justice – The European Court of Justice consists of 15 judges and 9 Advocates-General. It is based in Luxembourg. Its judgements are binding.

The institutions are supported by:

The Economic and Social Committee – It covers areas such as agriculture and fisheries, industry and commerce, financial and monetary questions, social and cultural affairs, transport and communications, trade and development policy, nuclear questions and research, regional development, environment and consumer affairs.

The Committee of the Regions – The Committee of the Regions is an advisory body composed of representatives of Europe's regional and local authorities. It has to be consulted before EU decisions are taken on matters such as regional policy, the environment, education and transport – all of which concern local and regional government.

The European Investment Bank – The European Investment Bank, based in Luxembourg, provides loans and guarantees to help the EU's less developed regions and to help make businesses more competitive.

The European Central Bank – The European Central Bank, based in Frankfurt, is responsible.

Appendix

Drink driving campaign – Investigating a national campaign

The Christmas drink drive campaign is launched annually by the Department of Transport. It aims to remind drivers, and young men in particular, how getting behind the wheel after a few drinks can affect their lives. In an effort to eliminate drinking and driving at Christmas, the government and police join forces to urge people who are going out to parties or celebrations to leave their car keys at home. Every year across the UK more than half a million drivers are stopped and breathalysed. More people are stopped in December than any other month, in a bid to stop deaths and injuries caused by drink-driving.

A *Anti-drink-driving advert 2008*

Safety campaigners, health professionals and police want a reduction in the permitted blood alcohol limit from 80mg per 100ml to at least 50mg. This would bring the UK in line with 23 other European states. They say that this reduction, combined with random breath-testing would save dozens more lives. The UK does not use random breath testing.

Research by driving organisations has shown that more of the general public feel that having a drink and getting behind the wheel of a car is unacceptable behavior. A Royal Automobile Club (RAC) survey showed widespread support for a lowered alcohol limit. Many people believe that raising the price of alcohol or raising the tax on alcohol is the most effective way of cutting consumption.

The content of these campaigns has changed over the years. The scary images of the 1980s have been replaced by more sophisticated messages emphasising the risk to livelihood and reputation.

Activity

- Discuss in groups. Do you think an annual drink campaign will help the campaign to curb binge drinking?
- Go to your local police website and find out what your area does about drink driving.
- Make a poster highlighting a drink driving campaign.

Terrorism

Terrorism and the law

In August 2008, Hammaad Munshi became the youngest Briton to be found guilty of terrorist offences, at the age of 18. He was arrested when police investigated an extremist cell. He was described as the computer expert and he was found guilty of distributing detailed instructions on how to make napalm, explosives, detonators and grenades online. In the London court a jury of 11 people convicted the three defendants of eight offences under the Terrorism Act between November 2005 and 20 June 2006.

B *London bombing, July 7th 2005*

Following the terrorist attacks of 7 July 2005 in London, the government took steps to make everyone in Britain aware of the threat of terrorism in our country. One way of tackling this threat was to introduce new, stronger laws against terrorism.

Terrorism Act 2006

The Terrorism Act contains a comprehensive package of measures designed to ensure that the police, intelligence agencies and courts have all the tools they require to tackle terrorism and bring perpetrators to justice. The Act received Royal Assent on 30 March 2006.

The Terrorism Act specifically aims to make it more difficult for extremists to abuse the freedoms we cherish, in order to encourage others to commit terrorist acts. The Act creates a number of new offences:

- Acts Preparatory to Terrorism
- Encouragement to Terrorism
- Dissemination of Terrorist Publications
- Terrorist training offences.

The Act also makes amendments to existing legislation, including:

- introducing warrants to enable the police to search any property owned or controlled by a terrorist suspect
- extending terrorism stop and search powers to cover bays and estuaries
- extending police powers to detain suspects after arrest for up to 28 days (though periods of more than two days must be approved by a judicial authority)
- improved search powers at ports
- increased flexibility of the proscription regime, including the power to proscribe groups that glorify terrorism.

The anti-terrorism law was criticised by the House of Lords as restricting freedom of speech. Many people believe that restrictive laws challenge the freedoms we value so much.

Activity

- Discuss the following statement as a class or in small groups:

  'Terrorism laws must strike a delicate balance between providing effective tools to investigate and prevent terrorism, while ensuring that our civil liberties are not unnecessarily infringed.'
- Some people think that the media should stop reporting on atrocities so that terrorists would not have free publicity for their acts. They stress such exposure gives terrorists the publicity they crave. Others do not agree. They maintain that in democratic countries freedom of speech comes first. What do you think? Discuss in pairs or small groups.
- Go to the Home Office website (**www.homeofficegov.co.uk**) and look at the statistics on terrorism. Why do you think there were so many arrests? Why do you think there were so few convictions?

Case study – Theme 3

The criminal justice system

Brent Martin was kicked to death near his home in Sunderland in August 2007. Brent had learning difficulties. Brent thought his killers were his friends. He told them that he loved them as they rained down kicks and punches on his body, but Brent's three killers didn't stop. The attack began when Brent's assailants bet each other £5 that they could knock him down with one punch. The brutal and prolonged attack continued across three estates before the 23-year-old was left slumped up against a car in a pool of blood. He died in hospital three days later.

Three men aged 21, 17 and 16, were found guilty of his murder and sentenced to 22 years, 18 years and 15 years respectively at Newcastle Crown Court in February 2008. Sentencing them, Judge John Milford QC said the three had attacked Brent for sport, describing the murder as pure sadism.

At the Court of Appeal in June 2008, the case was considered by Mr Justice Goldring – sitting with Lord Phillips and Mr Justice Plender. They said that the youths had taken advantage of Martin for many years before his death, but they accepted the arguments that the sentencing judge had wrongly categorised Martin's murder as 'sadistic', concluding that the case did not fulfil the strict legal criteria for that.

Britain's top judge, the Lord Chief Justice, Lord Phillips, described the attack as a 'pack of hounds on a fox'. The judge said Brent had been the victim of 'gratuitous gang violence directed at a vulnerable person', but he reduced one term from 15 to 13 years, another from 22 to 19 years, and the last from 18 to 15 years.

Activity

- A cabinet office review says '*the public feels "cut-off" from our justice system*' and has labelled the British justice system 'distant, unaccountable and unanswerable'.
- Discuss this case with reference to the rights of the victim and the rights of the accused.
- *'We're all a little tired of hearing about the human rights and civil liberties of people who break the law. For years we have been listening to that – who is speaking up for the rights of law-abiding decent people?'*

  Discuss this opinion in small groups.
- This case is one of the cases highlighted in a petition that was handed to Downing Street on 11 June 2008. The petition was organised by the father of a man who was knifed in Sunderland when he asked a group of youths to be quiet. He thinks the sentence of life should mean that the offender stays in jail for the rest of his life. What do you think of this suggestion? Discuss in groups. What do you think?

Nike

Nike is one of the largest, most popular, and most profitable shoe and clothing companies in the world. But the reality for many workers overseas making Nike shoes and clothing is less than acceptable. Workers are paid wages that are insufficient to meet their basic needs, they are not allowed to organise independent unions, and they often face health and safety hazards.

C *Nike factory in Asia*

A brief history

During the 1970s most Nike shoes were made in South Korea and Taiwan. Workers became organised and wages began to rise so Nike moved to Indonesia, China, and Vietnam. In these countries labour laws are poorly enforced and cheap labour is abundant. Also in China and Vietnam, the law prohibits workers from forming independent trade unions. These three countries continue to be the major places where Nike shoes are made.

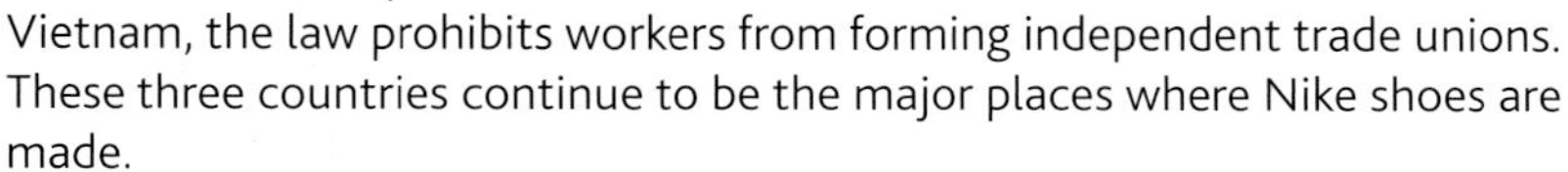

Nike does not own any of the factories where its shoes are produced. It contracts the work to factory owners. This allows Nike to say it is 'in the business of "marketing" shoes, not making them'. However, Nike dictates the terms to the contractor: it determines the design, the materials, and the price it will pay.

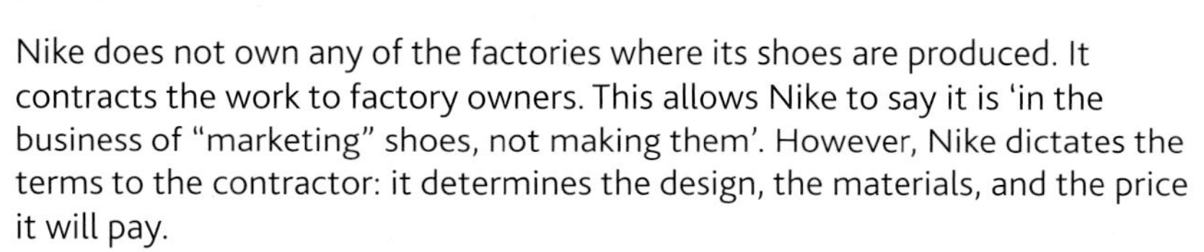

Nike is not the only clothing producer that uses overseas labour. However, Nike is the biggest shoe company in the world and puts itself forward as an industry leader. Its Code of Conduct says: 'in the area of human rights... in the communities in which we do business, we seek to do not only what is required, but what is expected of a leader.'

Where are we now?

Nike has raised Indonesian wages and improved health conditions. However, Nike still has a long way to go to meet the requirements of workers in Western society, that is:

- for companies to pay a living wage
- to allow independent monitoring in all factories, and
- to ensure that workers have the right to organise into independent unions.

There have been improvements in health and safety measures in Vietnam However, significant health and safety issues still remain. Workers in some sections of the plant still face overexposure to hazardous chemicals and to heat and noise levels. The same investigator has been invited by the company to look at health and safety issues in any of Nike's shoe factories. Plans are underway to allow the same investigator to look at health and safety issues in several factories in Indonesia and China, but there are still major issues relating to workers' rights and pay.

Activity

- Workers in Asia are expected to work in unhealthy conditions for long hours and low pay so we can buy cheaper clothes. This is not acceptable.
- Discuss in groups. What is your opinion?
- You have learned about ethical trade. Is this ethical? Is it fair? Discuss in groups. Write a short report or make a poster about this issue.

Glossary

A

Acid rain: is a result of air pollution caused by invisible gases that can be harmful to our environment.

Acquittal: a verdict of not guilty.

Advocacy: to represent or support a person or an organisation by writing or speaking or taking action on behalf of that person or organisation.

Advocate: someone who supports or represents another person or a cause which they believe in.

Agenda 21: a comprehensive plan of action to be taken globally, nationally and locally by organisations in every area in which human beings impact on the environment. Its motto is *Think globally, act locally*.

Anarchy: a state of lawlessness and disorder where there is no government and no laws.

Anti-Social Behaviour Order (ASBO): a statutory order. A breach of this order can lead to imprisonment.

Arab: a person whose first language is Arabic.

Arab League: formed in 1945 for the purpose of securing Arab unity. Today, the League has 22 members.

Arbitration: the hearing and determination of a dispute by an impartial referee agreed to by both parties.

Asylum Seeker: a foreigner who wishes to live in Britain because they have been abused in their own country.

Authority: the right to influence, control or direct the actions of other people.

B

Bill: draft of a law.

Biodiversity: the variety of life on earth. It embraces all living plants and animals ecosystems on which they depend.

C

Campaigning: actions or events organised by an individual or a group of people to achieve an aim.

Censorship: is the control of information and ideas circulated within a society.

Charities: local, national or international organisations to help others in need, for example, Children In Need.

Charter: a document that bestows certain rights on the people or country it covers.

Child Safety Orders: only apply to children under 10 years of age. Under a Child Safety Order a social worker or officer from the youth offending team (YOT) supervises the child.

Civil liberties: freedoms that protect the individual by setting limits for government interference in the lives of its citizens.

Collective bargaining: an agreement negotiated by a union on behalf of its members about an issue, for example, salaries.

Commission: a special group set up to consider some matter of importance.

Common law: the law based on decisions made by judges over the years.

Communism: State controls the economy, media, police, ownership of property and businesses.

Community: the people living in an area, or place, or the people who work in a particular place, for example, the school community.

Community cohesion: enabling people within an area to have shared values and understanding and a sense of belonging, by providing good facilities and the same opportunities for all.

A community group: a group of people who meet together to follow a shared interest (for example, a craft group, a sports team) or to influence a decision or campaign for a change.

Concept: a concept is a collection of ideas about a particular thing or attitude.

Conflict: a dispute: a disagreement or argument about something important.

Constitutional monarchy: a democracy where a monarch is the head of State but the government is responsible for running the country.

Controlled Assessment: a citizenship activity which you take part in (coursework).

Convention: name given to an international agreement.

Conviction: the verdict that results when a court of law finds a defendant guilty of a crime.

Cooperative: an enterprise that is owned by members who are workers or consumers in the organisation. Members share responsibilities, profits and opportunities according to a set of agreed principles.

Criminal responsibility: when a young person is held responsible for his/her own behaviour and can be found guilty in a court.

D

Declaration: a formal statement, generally in writing that makes a position very clear.

Deforestation: usually refers to the cutting, clearing, and removal of rainforests. It is one of the causes of the greenhouse effect.

Democracy: a system of government of the people of a country, by those people electing representatives to make laws and decisions.

Democratic process: the actual process of electing the people's representatives.

Deterrence: the theory justifies a punishment in order to discourage the offender and other people from committing the particular offence or other offences.

Devolution: this is the transfer of some powers from the government to the Welsh Assembly, the Northern Ireland Assembly and the Scottish Parliament.

Dictatorship: ruled by one leader.

Discrimination: treating someone unfairly because they are different in some way because of their gender, sexuality, age, religion, age, disability, or ethnicity.

Disenfranchisement: removing a person's right to vote.

Disposable income: money we have left to spend when all direct taxes have been taken from earnings.

The right to due process: (more fully due process of law) is the principle that the government must respect all of a person's legal rights.

E

The economy: this term describes the financial and production levels of a country or region in relation to the manufacture and use of food, products and services.

Electorate: the people eligible to vote in an area.

Entitlement: a right given to an individual by law.

Equal opportunities: treating everyone with the same rights, giving the same chances to all.

Extremism: a term used to describe the actions of individuals or groups outside the political centre of a society.

F

Fairness: achieving the right balance of interests without regard to one's own feelings and without showing favour to one person against another.

Flying pickets: pickets transported from one region to another.

Fossil fuels: are fuels that have been formed from the organic remains of prehistoric plants and animals like coal, oil and gas.

Freedom: ability to do something without restraint.

Freedom of assembly: used in the context of the right to protest.

Freedom of association: the individual right to join with other individuals to collectively pursue and defend common interests.

Freedom of the press: allows the press to publish thoughts, beliefs or opinions without interference from the government.

G

General election: an election where the country elects a new government.

Globalisation: the process by which the world has become interconnected as a result of increased trade and cultural exchange.

Global village: a term for describing the world where people are considered to live without borders/boundaries.

Global warming: the increase in average temperatures of the atmosphere, oceans and landmasses of Earth.

GM (genetically modified): means that the genes in a seed or food have been altered to produce something that does not occur naturally, for example, this might make the crops bigger or resistant to disease.

Greenhouse effect: the insulating effect of atmospheric greenhouse gases on the earth's temperature.

Greenhouse gas: a gas, such as water vapour, carbon dioxide or methane, which contributes to climate change.

H

Host nation: the country the migrants live in.

Human: means having the nature or attributes of a human being.

I

Identity: how a person describes themselves as an individual.

Immigrant: a person born in a foreign country who wishes to live and work in Britain for a short time or permanently.

Immigration: the process of people moving into this country to live and work.

Inclusion: being included – not left out.

Indigenous: a citizen naturally belonging to that country.

Inflation: a measure of the amount of increase in prices; a comparison of annual and quarterly costs.

Insider group: this is a pressure group that the government recognises and consults when forming policies associated with their cause or interest.

Interdependence: we are mutually dependent on one another for survival.

Intifada: the Palestinian uprising (meaning 'shaking off' in Arabic) which began in 1987 against Israeli military occupation and continued until the peace process began in 1993. A second intifada began in 2000.

Israeli: a citizen of the state of Israel. This includes Jews and Palestinians (sometimes known as Israeli Arabs), 18 per cent of Israeli citizens are Palestinians who can vote but are not asked to serve in the army and are denied access to many benefits in housing, employment and social security.

J

Jew: someone whose mother is Jewish or who has converted to the religion of Judaism.

Justice: a term used to refer to fairness though this is usually related to the administration of law within a society.

K

Knesset: the parliament of Israel.

L

Labelling: a theory where terms or labels applied to a person or group may influence their behaviour.

Legal: means founded upon law or accepted rules.

Liberty: a non-governmental organisation protecting civil liberties and promoting human rights.

Lobbying: person or group of people meeting and trying to persuade a politician to take up their cause.

M

Manifesto: a list of policies that a political party would introduce if elected.

Mass media: a term used to denote a section of the media designed to reach a very large audience.

Mediation: an intervention conducted by some impartial party for the purpose of bringing about a settlement to a dispute.

The media: referring to the mass media – television or radio broadcasts or printed media as in newspapers and magazines or mass communication via the internet.

Migration: the movement of people between different countries.

A miscarriage of justice: when a person is convicted or punished for a crime that he or she did not commit.

Multiculturalism: a mixture of different races, with many cultures and much ethnic diversity within a country/region/city/town/locality.

Multinational: a large corporation or company with offices and/or factories in several countries.

N

Natural disaster: a destructive force of nature that causes damage and loss of life. It is caused by hurricane, earthquake, flood, volcanic eruption and other natural forces. It usually leaves countries in emergency situations.

Negotiation: the process of achieving agreement through discussion.

O

Occupied Territories: the West bank, Gaza strip and East Jerusalem, which were taken over by Israeli military occupation in the Six Day war of 1967.

Oligarchy: rule by a small group of people.

Ombudsman: a person in a government agency to whom people can go to make complaints.

Opinion poll: a survey of public opinion using a sample of the total adult population to show how people think.

P

Palestine Liberation Organization (PLO): an umbrella organisation founded in 1964 to represent the different Palestinian resistance groups. The largest, Fatah, was led by Yasser Arafat.

Palestinian: someone whose family originates from what was Palestine before 1947. Most Palestinians are Muslim, a large number are Christian.

Participation: taking part – the act of sharing something in common with others.

Pickets: people who stand outside a place of work trying to persuade workers not to enter.

Pluralism: different beliefs/faiths/cultures existing within a society.

Political Literacy: knowledge of politics and how democracy works.

Politics: is the means by which groups make decisions.

Prejudice: when a person forms a bias opinion or belief that is not based on personal experience.

Pressure group: a group of people who take action to try to influence the government (local or national) about a specific issue.

Primary commodity: a commodity in its raw or unprocessed state like wood or oil.

Propaganda: specially created information that aims to make people think a certain way.

Proportional representation: a system of electing people that reflects the wishes of the voters.

Public opinion: the belief held by the majority of adults – the popular view.

R

Racism: a dislike or hostility towards a particular race, or believing one race is better than another.

Rapporteur: appointed by a body like the United Nations to investigate an issue or a situation and report back to that body.

Rehabilitation: the theory that the sentence is intended to reform the offender's behaviour.

Referendum: a vote on a single issue.

Reparation: aims to make some compensation to society, the victim and/or the victim's relatives.

Responsibilities: a responsibility is something that we are expected to do – a duty. Responsibilities may be legal or moral.

Retribution: the theory that the offender deserves punishment.

Rights: a right is something that we are entitled to by law, sometimes also referred to as an entitlement or a freedom.

S

Scab and Blackleg: a worker who will not take part in a strike – continues working when others are on strike. (Terms used frequently during the strike.)

Secretary General: the chief administrator of the United Nations.

Settlers: someone who moves to new land to settle. Almost 300,000 Jews have settled in the occupied territories of Palestine since 1967.

Specification: the document which contains all the details about the short and full course.

Spin: a way of presenting information in an attempt to control the public's response.

Social exclusion: being unable to access the things in life that most of society takes for granted, such as decent housing, adequate information and support, and the ability to exercise basic rights.

Social system: the parent system that includes social structures like family, law, religion, class, and economy.

Society: the term given to a large social group having a distinctive cultural and economic organisation.

Statute law: the law made by parliament.

Stereotypes: a generalised view about a type of person or group of people.

Suffrage: the right to vote.

Supranational: means beyond the borders or scope of any one nation especially through organisations that encompass more than one nation.

Sustainability: a system where natural resources are used and replaced so that they are not depleted.

Sustainable development: means understanding the need to maintain and improve the quality of life now without damaging the planet for future generations.

T

Target group: a target group is the organisation that the action is aimed at.

Trade Union: a trade union is a group of workers in the same trade or profession who join together to protect their rights and pursue common interests.

Tolerance: acceptance of people or things as they are, even though you may not like or agree with them.

Totalitarianism: the State rules every aspect of life, the economy, media, values in society.

Turnout: this is a percentage figure. It means the number of people who actually cast a vote as a percentage of all those on the electoral register.

U

Unit: different parts of the course which you have to study and learn or tasks you have to participate in and complete.

United Nations: an international organisation that aims to facilitate cooperation throughout the world.

V

A voluntary group: a group of people who work without pay to provide a service for others, for example, St John's Ambulance.

Voluntary organisations: organisations involved in activities in the community. Their management committee and members are volunteers.

Volunteering: activities such as community service, charity, public service, community action, community involvement, trustee, member and helper. It means giving your time unpaid.

Voter apathy: a significant number of the electorate deciding not to vote.

W

Wellbeing: a positive state of mind, brought about by the simultaneous satisfaction of personal, organisational, and collective needs of individuals and communities.

Y

The youth justice system: the section of the criminal justice system that deals with young offenders.

Z

Zionist: a person who believes that Jews have the right to a nation state. Most of the political parties in Israel are Zionist.

Index

Acknowledgements

Photo Acknowledgements

Alamy; topdog images 0.01, Troy GB Images 1T.2.D, Graham Lawrence 3.6.E, BennettPhoto 4.2.E, eye35.com 4.4.J, Enigma 6.3.B, Ian Shaw 7.2.A, 7.6.D, Jim West 7.3.B, imagebroker 8T.1.A, vario images GmbH & co.kg 9.6.D, Bubbles Photolibrary 10.2.B, Norman Price 10.4.C James Andrew 10.4.E, Janine Wiedel Photolibrary 10.5.I, 17.1.A, Sally & Richard Greenhill 10.5.J, Robin Beckham 10.5.K, Gianni Muratore 10.6.L, Israel Images 12.1.I, Michael Ventura 12.5.M, Howard Harrison 13.2.C, Lenscap 13.2.E, Jack Sullivan 13.3.H, Mike Hayward/ Photoshropshire.com 14.1.A, Lou Linwei 14.5.G, Jenny Matthews 14.7.L, David Taylor 17.1.B, Howard Barlow 17.7.F, Photoshot Holdings Ltd 14.1.B, Corbis; 15.7.H, Sion Touhig 1T.1.A, Reuters 8.7.O, 12.5.O, 12.7.W, 15.8.J, David Turnley 8.7.P, 13.8.R, Patrick Robert/ Sygma 12.2.E, 12.1.F, Lynsey Addario 12.7.V, Sygma/ Liz Gilbert 13.3.I, Peter Turnley 13.5.K, 13.6.M, 14.7.I, Sygma/ Sophie Elbelz 13.6.L, Sygma/ Pizzoli 15.3.D, Actionaid/ Gideon Mendel, 16.1.B, epa/ Salvatore di Nolfi 16.8.O, epa/ Peter Macdiarmid 18.1.C, Steve Raymer 18.3.E, Getty; 11.4.E, Hulton Archive 2.6.N, AFP 4.7.P, 8.1.F, 8.3.I, 8.4.L, 8.5.M, 11.7.Kii, 12.1.G, David Levenson 6.2.A, Christian Lagereek 6.5.C, AFP/ Tomohiro Ohsumi 12T.1.B, AFP/ Gianluigi Guercia 12.7.S, AFP/ Alessandro Abbonizio 12.7.U, AFP/ Saul McSween 16.1.A, PA; 2.3.D, 4.1.A, 16.6.K, 16.9.P, Empics 1T.1.B, 1.3.F, 3.6.D, 11.4.F, 12.5.N, 15.6.G, 15.7.I, AP/PA Photos 1.2.E, 11.2.C, 11.4.G, 11.7.Ki, 12T.1.A, 12.5.P, 12.7.T, 13.1.A, 15.4.E, 16.5.H, The Canadian Press 14.4.F, Scott Barbour 16.6.J, Rex Features; 1.7.I, 4.1.C, 4.3.G, 4.3.H, 8.1.E, 11.5.H, Stephen Lock 4.1.B, Huw John 4.4.I, Jane Mingay 7.5.C, Image Source 9.7.H, 10.4.F, Rory Gilder 9.8.I, Masatoshi Okauchi 11.1.B, Stephen Butler 14.8.M, Brian Rasic 16.6.L, Andy Paradise 16.6.M, iStockphoto; 2.4.F, 2.9.P, 4.1.F, 9.7.F, 9.7.G, 10.1.A, Families Need Fathers 11.6.I, 10.4.D, 10.4.G, 10.7.M, 12T.2.C, 12T.2.D, 13.4.J, 14.5.F, 14.7.K, 15.5.E, 16.5.I, Fotolia;12.3.J, Gino Santa Maria 4.7.N, Elena Abramova 6.2.B, 8T.2.C, 12.6.R, 15.2.C, Courtesy Amnesty International; 1.4.G, Courtesy Greenpeace UK; 1.6.H, 141.4.D, Davison/ Greenpeace 14.4.E, Marcus Lyons; 1.8.J, The Photolibrary Wales; 2.2.C, 2.6.I, USDAW (trade union) logo, 2.6.J, GMB (trade union) logo, 2.6.K, UNISON (trade union) logo, 2.6.L, FBU (trade union) logo, 2.6.M, COMMUNITY (trade union), 3.3.B, Moodboard RE/ Photolibrary, Courtesy of Which? Magazine; 3.4.C, Courtesy of Cadbury plc; 3.7.F; Courtesy of Nissan Motor Manufacturing (UK) Ltd 3.8.G, Photolibrary; 4.4.K, Courtesy UK Youth Parliament 4.9.Q, 4.9.R, 4.9.S; Photofusion Picture Library 7.7.E; Courtesy www.liberty-human-rights.org.uk; 8.3.H, 9.4.C; Courtesy UNICEF UK; 8.6.N; Mirrorpix; 11.7.J; Courtesy Shell International Limited; 13.2.B,Courtesy The Coca-Cola Company; 13.2.D,Courtesy McDonald's Corporation; 13.2.F; traidcraft/ Richard Else; 13.7.N; Courtesy St John Ambulance;16.3.D; Photofusion; 16.3.F; John Walmsley; 17.4.D; Advertising Archive; 18.1.B,(c) Parliamentary copyright. Photography by Terry Moore 16.3.E

Text Permissions

The authors and publishers would like to thank the following for permission to reproduce material:

Chapter 1, 4th double-page spread The article 'Climate Actions in Gatwick, Essex and Legoland' by Jamie, is used with kind permission of www.greenpeace.org.uk

Chapter 1, last double-page spread Information about the Fairtrade Foundation is used with kind permission of the Fairtrade Foundation

Chapter 2, 4th double-page spread Information about the Employment Relations Act 2004 is used with kind permission of the Department for Business, Enterprise & Regulatory Reform (BERR)

Chapter 2, 6th double-page spread the Housing Strategy diagram is reproduced with kind permission of Sevenoaks Council.

Chapter 3, 1st double-page spread The Employment Contracts information box is used with kind permission from Lawrite HR

Chapter 3, 3rd double-page spread The quote about Which? magazine and photograph of the magazine cover is used with kind permission from Which?

Chapter 3, 4th double-page spread Information about the Cadbury Cocoa Partnership is used with kind permission from Cadbury Plc

Chapter 4, 6th double-page spread Photographs and information about the UK Youth Parliament are given with kind permission by the UK Youth Parliament

Chapter 5, 2nd double-page spread Permission to reproduce the article about lowering the voting age is given with kind permission from the UK Youth Parliament

Chapter 6, 1st double page spread Permission to reproduce article by Rageh Omaar form Sunday 6th April 2008 from NI Syndication

Chapter 6, 4th double-page spread The quote about the Race, Cohesion and Faiths Directorate is used with kind permission of www.communities.gov.uk and is under crown copyright

Chapter 7, 3rd double-page spread The information about measures used to control immigration is used with kind permission from the UK Border Agency

Chapter 8, 5th double-page spread The quote about education, which was taken from the Unicef leaflet 'Children's Rights and Responsibilities', is used with kind permission from Unicef

Chapter 10, 5th double-page spread The quote about youth crime is used with kind permission from the Home Office website, www.homeoffice.gov.uk

Chapter 11, 3rd double-page spread The figures used in the table of opinion polls of national newspapers during the 2005 General Election are used with kind permission of www.historylearningsite.co.uk

Chapter 13, 5th double-page spread Information about Traidcraft and the quotation from the Geobar box is used with kind permission from Traidcraft

Chapter 15, 1st double page spread, Quote by Gordon Brown, reproduced under terms of the click licence use form Foreign and Commonwealth Office website www.fco.gov.uk/en/fco-in-action/institutions/britain-in-the-european-union/

Chapter 15, 3rd double-page spread Quote about the UK and the World Bank is used with kind permission from the Department for Trade and Development